淮南师范学院学术专著出版基金资助

自然关联性与性格优势：
内在机制与实践启示

左春荣　著

NATURE RELATEDNESS

AND

CHARACTER STRENGTHS:

UNDERLYING MECHANISM AND

PRACTICAL IMPLICATIONS

WUHAN UNIVERSITY PRESS
武汉大学出版社

图书在版编目(CIP)数据

自然关联性与性格优势：内在机制与实践启示：英文／左春荣著．
武汉：武汉大学出版社，2025.7(2025.9 重印)．－－ ISBN 978-7-307-
25144-1

Ⅰ. B848.6

中国国家版本馆 CIP 数据核字第 2025WH8465 号

责任编辑:吴月婵　　　责任校对:鄢春梅　　　版式设计:马　佳

出版发行：**武汉大学出版社**　　（430072　武昌　珞珈山）

（电子邮箱：cbs22@whu.edu.cn　网址：www.wdp.com.cn）

印刷:湖北云景数字印刷有限公司

开本:720×1000　1/16　印张:20.25　字数:327 千字　插页:1

版次:2025 年 7 月第 1 版　　2025 年 9 月第 2 次印刷

ISBN 978-7-307-25144-1　　定价:99.00 元

Preface

Character Strengths, as positive traits in an individual's thinking, emotions, and behavior, have been widely recognized as key factors in promoting mental health and well-being. In-depth research on Character Strengths not only provides a theoretical framework for understanding the formation mechanisms of individual psychological well-being but also offers scientific evidence for clinical interventions and positive education practices. Although substantial research has been conducted on the role and intervention training of Character Strengths, the exploration of its underlying mechanisms remains insufficient. In recent years, Nature Relatedness, as an important research area in environmental psychology, has gradually attracted broad attention in academia. Studies have shown that both Nature Relatedness and Character Strengths possess relatively stable traits similar to personality and can be enhanced through intervention. Nature Relatedness may significantly affect certain Character Strengths, but how to promote Character Strengths remains unclear. This book aims at exploring the relationship between Nature Relatedness, Trait Mindfulness, and Character Strengths, and analyzing their mechanisms in depth, filling the gap in this research field.

This book focuses on university student populations in China and Malaysia, conducting a preliminary exploration of the underlying influence mechanism of Nature Relatedness on Character Strengths. The attention given by the governments of China and Malaysia, as well as domestic positive psychology associations, to Character Strengths and mental health provides a solid foundation for the promotion of relevant policies and educational practices. In light of this policy, the research objectives include: revising and validating the Chinese version of the Three-dimensional Nature Relatedness Scale, exploring the differences between Chinese and Malaysian university students in terms of Nature Relatedness, Trait Mindfulness, and Character Strengths, analyzing the influence of Nature Relatedness on Character Strengths among university students, and further revealing the mediating role of Trait Mindfulness in the relationship between Nature Relatedness and Character Strengths.

Chapter 1 provides an overview of the overall research framework, introducing the research background, problem statement, research objectives and questions, hypotheses, conceptual framework, key term definitions, and the limitations, laying the foundation for the subsequent content. Chapter 2 reviews the literature relevant to this study, focusing on the definitions and connotations of Character Strengths, Nature Relatedness, and Trait Mindfulness, the development and application of relevant measurement instruments, and the empirical research status of these three areas both domestically and internationally. By reviewing existing research, the foundation and gaps of the study are clarified, providing the theoretical basis for this research. Chapter 3 introduces the research methods used in this study, including research design, sampling procedures, research process, selection and pilot testing of measurement tools, data collection and analysis methods, and ethical considerations. Each step is explained in detail to ensure the scientific and reliable nature of the research. Chapter 4 presents the research results, first revising and validating the Chinese version of the Three-dimensional Nature Relatedness Scale, assessing its validity and reliability using translation and back translation, comprehensibility evaluation, item analysis, exploratory and confirmatory factor analysis, and other methods. Then, descriptive statistics and difference analysis are used to explore the differences between Chinese and Malaysian university students in Nature Relatedness, Trait

Mindfulness, and Character Strengths. A mediation model is built by structural equation modeling, and the model is tested to confirm the mediating role of Trait Mindfulness between Nature Relatedness and Character Strengths. Chapter 5 analyzes the strengths and weaknesses of the research results through the SWOT framework and discusses their practical implications, limitations, and future research prospects.

Through a systematic exploration of the underlying mechanisms of Nature Relatedness and Character Strengths, this book not only provides a solid theoretical foundation for research on their relationship but also establishes a scientific basis for cross-cultural comparative studies by developing a standardized Chinese version of Nature Relatedness Scale. These pioneering findings provide important empirical evidence for designing Nature-Based Mindfulness Intervention systems, especially for constructing integrated nature education intervention programs across different age stages, laying the theoretical foundation and practical guidance for this field and advancing the research into a new development phase.

LIST OF ABBREVIATIONS

M	Mean
SD	Standard Deviation
NR	Nature Relatedness
NRS	Nature Relatedness Scale
NRS-C	Chinese Version of Nature Relatedness Scale
MF	Mindfulness
TMF	Trait Mindfulness
CS	Character Strengths
SPSS	Statistical Package for the Social Sciences
AMOS	Analysis of Moment Structures
APA	American Psychological Association
H0	Null Hypothesis
H1	Alternative Hypothesis
SWOT Analysis	Strengths, Weaknesses, Opportunities, and Threats Analysis

TABLE OF CONTENTS

CHAPTER 1   INTRODUCTION ································· 1

  1.1   Overview ··· 1

  1.2   Research Background ······························· 2

  1.3   Problem Statement ······························· 15

  1.4   Research Objectives ······························ 19

  1.5   Research Questions ······························· 20

  1.6   Research Hypotheses ······························ 21

  1.7   Conceptual Framework ···························· 23

  1.8   Definition of Terminology ························ 23

  1.9   Limitations ·· 30

  1.10 Conclusion ·· 31

CHAPTER 2   LITERATURE REVIEW ················· 33

  2.1   Introduction ······································· 33

  2.2   Previous Research on the Definition-Related Studies ·········· 33

  2.3   Previous Research on the Research Instruments ·········· 42

  2.4   Previous Research on Character Strengths, Nature Relatedness
         and Trait Mindfulness ····························· 54

  2.5   Previous Research on the Relationship Between Nature Relatedness
         and Character Strengths ·························· 81

  2.6   The Influence of Nature Relatedness on Character Strengths:
         The Mediating Effect of Trait Mindfulness ·········· 84

2.7   Theoretical Framework   ·· 89

2.8   Conclusion   ··· 92

CHAPTER 3   METHODOLOGY   ································ 93

3.1   Introduction   ··· 93

3.2   Research Design   ·· 94

3.3   Sampling Procedure   ······································ 96

3.4   Research Procedure   ·· 110

3.5   Research Instruments   ······································ 112

3.6   Pilot Study   ··· 122

3.7   Data Collection   ··· 125

3.8   Data Analysis   ··· 127

3.9   Ethical Considerations and Ethical Code   ···················· 130

3.10 Conclusion   ··· 133

CHAPTER 4   RESULTS OF THE STUDY ···················· 134

4.1   Introduction   ··· 134

4.2   Revision of the Chinese Version of the Three-dimensional Nature
      Relatedness Scale (Answering RQ1)   ······················ 136

4.3   Descriptive Statistics and Differential Analysis
      (Answering RQ2a, RQ2b)   ······························· 160

4.4   Analysis of the Influence of Nature Relatedness on Character Strengths
      Among Chinese and Malaysian University Students (Answering RQ3a,
      RQ3b)   ·· 181

4.5   Analysis of the Mediating Effect of Trait Mindfulness on the Role
      of Nature Relatedness on Character Strengths Among Chinese and
      Malaysian University Students (Answering RQ4a, RQ4b)   ········ 190

4.6   Conclusion   ·· 199

CHAPTER 5   DISCUSSION AND CONCLUSIONS ························ 202

5.1   Introduction ··· 202

5.2   Revision of Chinese Version of Nature Relatedness Scale ·············· 204

5.3   Differences in Nature Relatedness, Trait Mindfulness, and Character
       Strengths Among Chinese and Malaysian University Students Across
       Different Demographic Variables, and Comparative Analysis ··········· 210

5.4   Correlation and Predictive Effect Between Nature Relatedness and
       Character Strengths Among Chinese and Malaysian University
       Students ··· 222

5.5   Correlation and Mediating Effect of Trait Mindfulness on the
       Relationship Between Nature Relatedness and Character Strengths
       Among Chinese and Malaysian University Students ·················· 224

5.6   Implications of Research Findings ································· 229

5.7   Limitations ·· 230

5.8   Suggestions for Future Research ··································· 232

5.9   Conclusion ··· 235

APPENDICES ·· 237

Appendix A   Example of Comments on Translation and Back-translation
              of the Nature Relatedness Scale ·························· 237

Appendix B   The Approval Letter From the Original Scale Developer for
              the Chinese Version of the Nature Relatedness Scale ······· 238

Appendix C   Participant Information Sheet and Consent Form
              (Chinese Version) ······································ 239

Appendix D   Participant Information Sheet and Consent Form
              (English Version) ······································ 243

Appendix E   Example of Data Collection Permission Letters From A, B,
              and C Universities (Chinese Version) ····················· 247

Appendix F   Example of Data Collection Permission Letters From A, B,

and C Universities (English Version) ·················· 248

Appendix G   Documents Submitted to the Human Research Ethics

Committee for Approval ······························· 251

Appendix H   Approval Letter from Human Research Ethics Committee ······ 256

Appendix I   Questionnaire (Chinese Version) ······················ 258

Appendix J   Questionnaire (English Version) ······················ 265

Appendix K   Examples of Campus Natural Elements for Nature-Based

Mindfulness Intervention ·························· 271

BIBLIOGRAPHY ·· 276

AFTERWORD ·· 312

CHAPTER 1　INTRODUCTION

1.1　Overview

Character Strengths refer to positive personality traits that manifest in an individual's thoughts, emotions, and behaviors, benefiting both the individual and others. Within the realm of positive psychology, Character Strengths are closely intertwined with indicators of psychological well-being, including happiness, the flow experience, self-actualization, subjective well-being, and life satisfaction (Park et al., 2004; Peterson & Seligman, 2006). Moreover, Character Strengths play a significant role in various aspects of individuals' lives. They contribute to personal growth and academic performance (Park et al., 2004), career development, and job performance (Harzer & Ruch, 2015), as well as social interactions and interpersonal relationships (Littman-Ovadia & Steger, 2010). Therefore, the exploration and cultivation of Character Strengths hold immense significance and value. By discovering and nurturing these strengths, individuals can effectively tap into their full potential.

In addition to studying the role of Character Strengths, researchers also investigate the development patterns and intervention strategies of Character Strengths. In terms of the developmental research of Character Strengths, some researchers have found that Character Strengths can be enhanced and developed through education and training during childhood and adolescence, as well as continued stable development and application during adulthood (Park &

Peterson, 2006). As university students are in a transitional period between adolescence and adulthood, the development of their Character Strengths is crucial for their growth and development. In terms of intervention research on Character Strengths, some studies have shown that individual Character Strengths can be developed and cultivated through various training and intervention methods, including: positive psychology intervention (Proyer, et al., 2015), social support (Lavy et al., 2014), education and training based on Character Strengths (Lavy et al., 2014).

To provide more precise and evidence-based guidance for Character Strengths education and training, researchers need to delve deeper into the factors influencing Character Strengths and gain a better understanding of the mechanisms through which Character Strengths impact individuals. Therefore, the main focus of this research is to explore the influence of Nature Relatedness on the Character Strengths of university students, and to reveal the mechanism of Character Strengths through constructing a mediation model. The aim of this research is to provide a basis for the cultivation of Character Strengths among university students.

1.2 Research Background

1.2.1 The International Positive Psychology Association and the Governments of China and Malaysia Place Significant Importance on the Character Strengths of University Students

Since its establishment in 2007, the International Positive Psychology Association (IPPA) has been dedicated to promoting the focus on Character Strengths globally within the field of positive psychology. Increasingly, countries worldwide recognize the importance of training and developing Character

Strengths.

The Chinese government has shown great attention to the cultivation of Character Strengths in university students. Since the first China International Conference on Positive Psychology was held at Tsinghua University in 2010, positive psychology has officially become a part of psychology in China, attracting significant attention to topics like Character Strengths and happiness. In 2014, Tsinghua University Positive Psychology Research Center was established, becoming the first research center in China dedicated to positive psychology. In October 2017, Chinese President Xi Jinping emphasized the need to strengthen the development of the social psychological service system and foster a societal mindset characterized by self-esteem, confidence, rationality, peace, and positivity (Xi, 2017). In 2018, the Ministry of Education of the People's Republic of China issued the "Guidelines for Psychological Health Education for University Students", emphasizing the need to standardize the development of psychological health education and counseling services and cultivate students' self-esteem, confidence, rationality, peace, and positive attitudes (Ministry of Education of the People's Republic of China, 2018).

The Malaysian government also places great emphasis on cultivating Character Strengths in university students, which can be seen through the functions of the Ministry of Higher Education Malaysia, the Malaysian Psychological Association (PSIMA), and the Malaysian Positive Psychology Association (MPPA). The Ministry of Education Malaysia proposed the initiative of fostering positive school attributes in the *Malaysia Education Blueprint 2013-2025* (Ministry of Education Malaysia, 2013). The Malaysian Ministry of Higher Education also promotes the cultivation of positive psychology in university students. PSIMA collaborates with the Malaysian government to encourage cooperation, coordination, and partnerships among psychology departments in Malaysian universities, which will contribute to the development of positive psychology in Malaysian students. MPPA aims to contribute to the creation of a mentally healthier society and the growth of individuals and organizations by maximizing their strengths, potential, and well-being (Malaysian Psychological Association, 2024).

In summary, Character Strengths among university students has become an important topic of concern for both the Chinese and Malaysian governments, reflecting the growing societal demand for psychological research that enhances mental well-being. In China, the government's initiatives, such as the inclusion of psychological education in the university curriculum, and the establishment of institutions like the Tsinghua University Positive Psychology Research Center, underline the importance of cultivating Character Strengths for university students. Similarly, Malaysia's commitment is evident through the *Malaysia Education Blueprint 2013-2025* and the active collaboration of associations like PSIMA and MPPA to promote positive psychology in higher education. However, while both countries emphasize the development of Character Strengths, research on the relationship between Character Strengths and other psychological variables, such as well-being, resilience, and academic performance, primarily focuses on the effects of these strengths. Little attention has been given to the underlying factors that promote changes in Character Strengths. In particular, the mechanisms that drive the development and enhancement of Character Strengths in university students remain less explored, with existing studies primarily investigating the outcomes of possessing strong character traits rather than the processes that facilitate their growth (Yang, 2022).

1.2.2 Western Psychologists Have Shown Significant Interest in the Research of Character Strengths, But There is a Lack of Studies Investigating the Mechanisms Through Which Character Strengths Influence Individuals

A large number of positive psychologists are paying attention to the field of

Character Strengths, which presents a rapidly and robustly growing research prospect. At the theoretical research level, many studies have shown that Character Strengths can positively predict individuals' emotions, attitudes and behaviors (Peterson et al., 2007), and have beneficial associations with many outcomes in the organizational domain (Weber et al., 2016), such as promoting employees' work performance and work engagement (Littman-Ovadia & Lavy, 2016) and so on. At the practical research level, Character Strengths interventions are widely applied in fields such as education, psychological counseling, medical health and corporate management (Bressoud et al., 2018; Duan & Bu, 2017; Littman-Ovadia et al., 2013; Boe, 2016). Therefore, Character Strengths are an important resource for individuals, conducive to achieving their psychological well-being and a good life. Thus, research on Character Strengths has important significance at both theoretical and practical levels.

Currently, research on the Character Strengths of university students in academia can be categorized into the following areas: definition and classification of Character Strengths, measurement tools for Character Strengths, relationships between Character Strengths and other variables, cultivation and development of Character Strengths and educational applications of Character Strengths. Definition and classification of Character Strengths: research aims to define and classify Character Strengths, including identifying the dimensions and classification methods of Character Strengths (Peterson & Seligman, 2006). Measurement tools for Character Strengths: research focuses on the development and improvement of measurement tools for Character Strengths, including questionnaires and interviews (Peterson & Seligman, 2006; Park et al., 2004). Relationships between Character Strengths and other variables: research examines the relationships between Character Strengths and other variables such as life satisfaction, health, interpersonal relationships and academic performance (Proyer et al, 2013; Seligman et al., 2005). Cultivation and development of Character Strengths: research explores methods and strategies to discover, inspire, and cultivate students' Character Strengths (Sheldon & King, 2001; Waters, 2011). Educational applications of Character Strengths: research investigates the application of Character Strengths in education, including curriculum design, teaching methods, evaluation and feedback (Seligman et al., 2009; Niemiec & Wedding, 2014).

In summary, in Western research, the focus on Character Strengths in relation to other variables primarily centers around the impact of Character Strengths, while there is relatively little emphasis on factors that promote changes in Character Strengths. There is a lack of research on the influencing factors of Character Strengths.

1. 2. 3　A Comparative Study of Character Strengths, Nature Connectedness, and Mindfulness in Chinese and Malaysian University Students

1.2.3.1　Comparative Research on Character Strengths in Chinese and Malaysian University Students

Researchers have conducted comparative studies on Character Strengths in Chinese and Malaysian university students, revealing the following similarities and differences:

1. Measurement Methods

In the measurement of Character Strengths among Chinese university students, Duan et al. (2012) developed the Chinese Virtues Questionnaire (CVQ-96) and Three-dimensional Inventory of Character Strengths (TICS) specifically adapted for the Chinese cultural context, by refining the VIA-IS (Values in Action Inventory of Strengths) developed by Peterson and Seligman (2006). Pimthong (2015) surveyed Character Strengths among Malaysian undergraduate students, using a selection of 15 items adapted from the VIA-IS (Peterson & Seligman, 2006). Yong et al. (2022) studied personality traits of Malaysian university students using the Big Five Personality Traits and other relevant assessment tools, but not specific measures of Character Strengths.

2. Levels and Characteristics of Character Strengths

Studies on Character Strengths among Chinese university students revealed that the most common Character Strengths are authenticity, kindness, compassion, fairness, creativity, insight, bravery, and social intelligence, with humility being less frequently reported (Zhang, 2009). Other research identified the top five Character Strengths as kindness, fairness, gratitude, teamwork, and integrity, while the bottom five were self-regulation, love of learning, insight, creativity, and social intelligence (Li, 2016). In contrast, the study on personality traits among Malaysian university students (Yong et al., 2022) did not specify the specific characteristics of Character Strengths, but primarily focused on the impact of the Big Five Personality Traits.

3. Related Research

Regarding related research on Character Strengths among Chinese university students, the focus has mainly been on exploring the association between Character Strengths and Subjective Well-being (Li, 2015; Zhou & Liu, 2011), as well as the relationships between Character Strengths and mindfulness, psychological well-being, health behaviors, parenting styles, psychological harmony, among other factors (Yang, 2022; Duan et al., 2012). In contrast, research on Malaysian university students indirectly involves the association between personality traits and other variables, such as internet ethics (Karim et al., 2009), social anxiety (Abdollahi et al., 2022), values (Mustapha & Hyland, 2017), entrepreneurial potential (Rofa, 2022), smartphone addiction (Adawiyah, 2023), among others.

4. Intervention Studies

In conclusion, past research has focused more on Character Strengths in Chinese university students, while direct studies on Character Strengths in Malaysian university students are scarce. There is a lack of comparative research on Character Strengths between Chinese and Malaysian university students, and a deficiency in studying the influencing factors of Character Strengths in both populations.

1.2.3.2 Comparative Research on Nature Relatedness in Chinese and Malaysian University Students

Comparative studies on Nature Relatedness in Chinese and Malaysian university students reveal the following similarities and differences:

1. Measurement Methods

Li (2016) modified the Connectedness to Nature Scale (Mayer & Frantz, 2004) to create a Chinese version and validated its reliability and effectiveness in measuring connectedness to nature among Chinese university students. Jing (2018) adapted the Nature Relatedness Scale by Nisbet et al. (2009) and the New Environmental Paradigm Scale (NEPS) by Dunlap et al. (2000) to survey Chinese-Malaysian university students, but the study did not include students from other Malaysian ethnicities, which is a limitation.

2. Related Research

Researchers have explored the associations between Nature Relatedness and various aspects of university students' lives, including their happiness, self-esteem, depressive emotions, life satisfaction, pro-environmental behavior, body appreciation, and sense of life meaning. For instance, C. Y. Wang and C. Z. Wang (2018) identified a correlation between Nature Relatedness and self-esteem and depressive emotions. Gan et al. (2023) demonstrated that mindfulness influences college students' life satisfaction, with some mediating roles. Chen and Huang (2022) studied the impact of awe on pro-environmental behavior among university students, with Nature Relatedness acting as a mediator and environmental values serving as a moderator. Wang et al. (2020) explored the relationship between Nature Relatedness and the experience of life meaning among university students, with nature appreciation acting as a mediator. Li (2016) conducted a study on Chinese university students and found that mindfulness played a mediating role between Nature Relatedness and happiness. Research on nature connectedness among Malaysian university students is scarce, with only Sahak (2018) investigating students from Johor, Malaysia, and examining spirituality as a mediating factor between nature contact, connectedness, and student well-being.

3. Functions and Intervention Research on Nature Relatedness

Some researchers have focused on how interventions affect Nature Relatedness among Chinese university students. Yang et al. (2017) reviewed the concept and measurement of Nature Relatedness and further examined its functions and intervention measures. Passmore et al. (2022) conducted a study called "Nature Noticing Intervention (NNI): An Extended Replication of a Happiness Intervention," involving a two-week nature intervention experiment with 173 Chinese undergraduate students. The results showed that the increase in participants' happiness and reduction in distress were entirely attributed to their attention to the natural environment encountered in their daily lives. This study further supported the effectiveness of the Nature Noticing Intervention as a happiness intervention. Additionally, Li et al. (2018) also reviewed the functions and promotion of Nature Relatedness. In Malaysia, Roslan et al. (2022) conducted an experiment with 160 Muslim university students from the Malaysian Agricultural Science Foundation, revealing that these students benefitted greatly from yoga meditation and nature experiences, while spending time outdoors was an effective way to enhance their spiritual and ecological self-value.

In summary, previous research has focused more on Nature Relatedness in Chinese university students, while direct studies on Nature Relatedness in Malaysian university students are limited. There is a lack of comparative research on Nature Relatedness between Chinese and Malaysian university students, and a dearth of research on how Nature Relatedness may influence Character Strengths in both populations.

1.2.3.3 Comparative Research on Mindfulness in Chinese and Malaysian University Students

Comparative studies on mindfulness in Chinese and Malaysian university students reveal the following similarities and differences:

1. Measurement Methods

Deng (2009) revised the Five Facet Mindfulness Questionnaire (FFMQ) developed by Baer et al. (2008) to create a Chinese version suitable for measuring Trait Mindfulness among Chinese university students. In Malaysia, Ahmadi et al. (2014) conducted a mindfulness study with 273 freshmen using the Mindful Attention Awareness Scale. Ahmadi (2016) studied mindfulness levels among Malaysian university students, with a particular focus on students from Universiti Malaysia Perlis. Similarly, they used the Mindful Attention Awareness Scale (Brown & Ryan, 2003).

2. Related Research

Research on the relationship between mindfulness and subjective well-being is relatively extensive. Liu et al. (2015) found that mindfulness among university students influenced subjective well-being, with emotion regulation and psychological resilience mediating this relationship. Liu and Tang (2019) explored the relationship between mindfulness levels and subjective well-being in university students, while Ding (2012) and Yang (2014) studied the impact of mindfulness practice and training on mindfulness levels and subjective well-being. Research also indicated that mindfulness training had a positive effect on university students' life satisfaction, with nature connectedness acting as a mediator (Gan, 2023; Li, 2016). The relationship between mindfulness and anxiety/aggression behavior in university students is mediated by psychological resilience (Yu et al., 2022). Duan (2016) investigated the impact of individual mindfulness on psychological well-being, with individual strengths playing a mediating role. Yang (2022) studied the influence of mindfulness on Character Strengths, while Xu (2020) explored the relationships between mindfulness levels, coping efficacy, perceived stress, and intervention research. Chen (2018) focused on the association between mindfulness and life satisfaction in university students, finding that nature connectedness played a mediating role. In Malaysia, Ramli et al. (2018) examined the relationship between academic stress, self-regulation, and mindfulness in Malaysian undergraduate students. The results indicated that mindfulness mediated the relationship between academic stress and self-regulation (Ramli et al., 2018). Jayaraja et al. (2017) studied the predictive effects of mindfulness and procrastination on the psychological well-being of Malaysian university students. The study found significant correlations between mindfulness, procrastination, and psychological well-being. Ramli et al. (2018) selected 384 undergraduate students from Klang Valley, Malaysia, and investigated the influences of academic stress, self-regulation, and mindfulness. The study confirmed that mindfulness played a mediating role between academic stress and self-regulation. Rosenstreich and Margalit (2015) chose students as participants and explored the relationship between loneliness, mindfulness, and academic performance, while also studying the moderating role of mindfulness in this relationship. Tan et al.

(2021) tested the hypothesized positive correlation between mindfulness and life meaning among undergraduate students from Malaysia, Indonesia, and Australia, as well as the potential mechanisms underlying this relationship.

3. Mindfulness Training and Intervention Research

Mindfulness training and intervention among Chinese university students have received considerable attention. Researchers have explored the impact of mindfulness on students' psychological health, subjective well-being, and psychological resilience. Many studies have focused on mindfulness interventions to improve individuals' mental and physical health, promote psychological well-being, and alleviate negative emotions such as anxiety and depression. For example, Shen et al. (2022) found that mindfulness training could enhance students' attentional bias and reduce smartphone dependence. Lu et al. (2023) demonstrated the intervention effect of mindfulness training on social anxiety among university students. Jia (2019), Chen (2018), Li (2016), and Cheng (2024) applied mindfulness training to address issues such as academic stress, depressive emotions, and sleep disorders among university students. These studies provide important theoretical and practical support for the application of mindfulness among university students. In mindfulness intervention research among Malaysian university students, most studies have focused on medical students from Malaysia. Medical students in Malaysia face significant stress (Ramli et al., 2018). To help medical students cope more effectively with stress, Keng et al. (2015) explored the effects of a brief mindfulness-based intervention on psychological symptoms and well-being in Malaysian medical students. The results showed that mindfulness played a statistically significant mediating role in psychological symptoms and well-being. The research also examined whether changes in mindfulness would affect psychological symptoms and well-being, and validated whether changes in mindfulness mediated the effects of Mindful-Gym (a mindfulness training program) on psychological symptoms and well-being. Phang et al. (2016) also selected a sample of medical students from various ethnicities in Malaysia to validate the factorial validity and psychometric properties of the Mindful Attention Awareness Scale (MAAS). They explored the effectiveness of a brief group mindfulness cognitive therapy aimed at reducing stress in Malaysian medical students, confirming the applicability of mindfulness intervention in Malaysia.

In conclusion, while there has been relatively more research on Nature Relatedness among Chinese and Malaysian university students, there is a lack of comparative research on mindfulness in these two populations. Furthermore, there is a dearth of studies examining the role of mindfulness in the relationship between Nature Relatedness and Character Strengths among university students in both China and Malaysia.

1.2.4 Research on the Correlation Between Nature Relatedness and Character Strengths Has Emerged, But There is a Lack of Studies Investigating the Relationships and Mechanisms Between Nature Relatedness, Trait Mindfulness, and Character Strengths in Both China and Malaysia

In recent years, Nature Relatedness has become one of the hot topics in environmental psychology research. Based on a synthesis of previous research, some Chinese researchers have found a close correlation between nature connectedness and certain individuals' Character Strengths, such as fairness, kindness, vitality, creativity, teamwork and self-regulation (Yang et al., 2017). Nature Relatedness intervention (NRI) has also become a positive psychological intervention strategy (Duan & Bu, 2018). All of these studies provide a new perspective for cultivating Character Strengths.

In Malaysia, Jin (2018) discussed the influence of Nature Relatedness on

Pro-Environmental Behaviors among Malaysian Chinese university students. In University of Technology Malaysia, the implementation of a green campus has already shown a positive impact in reducing climate change on their campus through the promotion of cycling, paper-saving, energy-saving, and water-saving initiatives (Najad et al., 2018). Mohamad Muslim (2017), using the case of Peninsular Malaysians, examined the differences in nature-related experiences during childhood between urban and rural areas. The study found that individuals who grew up in rural areas had more nature-related experiences compared to those who grew up in urban areas, providing a basis for environmental education.

From previous research, it can be seen that although Nature Relatedness has potential value for the cultivation and development of Character Strengths, the current research on the influence of Nature Relatedness on Character Strengths is still not sufficient, and there is a lack of systematic research. This indicates that further in-depth study is needed on the influence of Nature Relatedness on Character Strengths, as well as exploration of its specific mechanisms and effectiveness, in order to better apply it to the cultivation and development of Character Strengths in university students. At the same time, studying the influence of Nature Relatedness on Character Strengths can also help further improve the theory and practice of character strength cultivation, and promote the comprehensive growth and development of university students.

Chinese researchers suggest that Nature Relatedness positively predicts levels of Mindfulness, indicating that increasing contact and connection with nature can enhance an individual's Trait Mindfulness (Li, 2016). Yang (2022) found that Trait Mindfulness has a positive and beneficial impact on Character Strengths among university students. In Malaysian research, there is a focus on the association between mental health and Mindfulness in eating among undergraduate students (Talib et al., 2021), but there is a lack of research on the relationship among Nature Relatedness, Trait Mindfulness, and Character

14

Strengths.

Therefore, this study aims at investigating the influence of Nature Relatedness on Character Strengths among university students in China and Malaysia, and exploring potential mechanisms, specifically examining the mediating effect of Trait Mindfulness on the relationship between Nature Relatedness and Character Strengths. This study is grounded in the theory and practice of Character Strengths and holds significant value for both theoretical understanding and practical applications.

1.3   Problem Statement

Through the review of previous studies on Nature Relatedness and Character Strengths, it is found that there are deficiencies and gaps in the following four aspects:

1.3.1   Lack of the Three-dimensional Nature Relatedness Scale in Chinese Version

Mayer and Frantz's (2004) Connectedness to Nature Scale was revised by Li (2016) in Chinese version, which has good validity and reliability. However, the Scale is a one-dimensional structure to measure the emotional connection between individuals and nature. Although Connectedness to Nature Scale is widely used, its single dimension and controversial concept also limit its application (Yang et al., 2017). In this study, it cannot fully reflect the connection between individuals and nature.

Nisbet et al. (2009) have compiled the Three-dimensional Nature Relatedness Scale, according to the Nature Relatedness definition of Three-dimensional, which has good validity and reliability, can measure the Nature Relatedness more comprehensively. However, there is currently no standardized Chinese version of the Three-dimensional Nature Relatedness Scale. Therefore, it is of great practical significance to revise the Three-dimensional Nature Relatedness Scale in Chinese, as it will provide a standardized measurement tool for assessing Nature Relatedness in the Chinese population.

1.3.2   Lack of Comparative Research on Nature Relatedness, Trait Mindfulness and Character Strengths Among Chinese and Malaysian University Students

On the one hand, there has been a lack of research on Nature Relatedness, Trait Mindfulness, and Character Strengths among Malaysian university students. Previous studies on these topics have predominantly focused on samples from countries or regions such as the United States, Canada, Australia, and Europe, with a scarcity of samples from regions such as Asia, Africa, and South America (Henrich et al., 2010). Consequently, there has been limited research on Nature Relatedness, Trait Mindfulness, and Character Strengths specifically among Malaysian university students. Therefore, conducting a study on Nature Relatedness, Trait Mindfulness, and Character Strengths among Malaysian university students would serve as a valuable and complementary addition to the existing research, especially within the Asian sample context.

On the other hand, there has been a lack of comparative research on Nature Relatedness, Trait Mindfulness, and Character Strengths between Chinese and Malaysian university students. Some researchers have highlighted that different Asian countries possess unique cultural values (Oyserman et al., 2002). People from diverse cultures have distinct cognitive perceptions and experiences concerning the relationship between humans and nature. While both China and Malaysia belong to collectivist cultures, they differ in terms of natural environment, history and tradition, religious beliefs, dietary habits, and other aspects, leading to certain cultural variations between the two countries. Therefore, conducting an investigation on Chinese and Malaysian university students and comparing their Nature Relatedness, Trait Mindfulness, and Character Strengths would hold significant research value (Yang et al., 2017). Therefore, studying the Nature Relatedness, Trait Mindfulness, and Character Strengths of Chinese and Malaysian university students serves as a complementary contribution to the field of comparative research.

1.3.3 Lack of the Study on the Relationship Between Nature Relatedness and Overall Character Strengths Among Chinese and Malaysian University Students, and the Causal Relationship is Not Clear

Most researchers focus on the positive effects of Character Strengths (such as happiness, job satisfaction), but few studies have focused on the factors that promote the change of Character Strengths (Yang, 2022). Nature Relatedness is a hot topic in the study of environmental psychology, previous researchers studies the concept, measuring, function, intervention, and about the Nature Relatedness to alleviate psychological symptoms, promoting happiness, improve cognitive function, promote the behavior control. However, there are few studies on the direct influence of Nature Relatedness on Character Strengths. Several studies have found that Nature Relatedness can improve some Character Strengths of individuals (Yang et al., 2017; Li et al., 2018; Merino et al., 2020), not overall, but some studies have found that natural bonds can enhance certain personality strengths, such as cooperative (Zelenski et al., 2015), creativity (Atchley et al., 2012), appreciation of beauty (Frumkin, 2001), love (Weinstein et al., 2009), social intelligence (Wakefield et al., 2007), self-regulation (Taylor et al., 2002), zest (Ryan et al., 2010), love of learning (Benfield, 2015). From these studies, it can be speculated that Nature Relatedness may have a promoting effect on improving the overall Character Strengths. However, the existing studies are scattered and single-dimensional studies, and no researchers have verified the overall effect of natural connection on the Character Strengths, which is a research gap. Therefore, this study fills the gap by comprehensively verifying the effect of Nature Relatedness on Character Strengths from an overall perspective.

There have been few direct studies on Nature Relatedness and overall Character Strengths. Merino et al. (2020) first explored the relationship between Nature Relatedness and Character Strengths, and they found an empirical correlation between Character Strengths and Nature Relatedness, and the correlation between individual Character Strengths and Nature Relatedness indicated significant differences in aesthetic ability, with the highest correlation with Nature Relatedness, followed by love of learning, curiosity and zest. The researchers only used a decision tree to demonstrate the correlation between the two variables, but the causal relationship has not been effectively validated.

1.3.4   Lack of Study on the Mechanism of the Influence of Nature Relatedness on Character Strengths Among Chinese and Malaysian University Students, Trait Mindfulness May Have a Mediating Effect

While the governments and universities in China and Malaysia have implemented various initiatives to promote positive psychology and emphasize Character Strengths among university students, most efforts focus primarily on the positive outcomes of these strengths. There remains a lack of systematic research on how to foster the development and enhancement of Character Strengths, particularly concerning the underlying factors and mechanisms that influence their growth. Addressing this gap is essential for providing effective interventions through government or university policies and educational systems. In recent years, the relationship between Nature Relatedness, mindfulness, and Character Strengths has gained increasing attention from researchers. For example, empirical evidence suggests that Trait Mindfulness has a positive influence on the development of Character Strengths (Yang, 2022). Furthermore, several studies have indicated a positive relationship between Nature Relatedness and Mindfulness levels (Li, 2016). Research has also shown that exposure to nature contributes to an enhancement in individual mindfulness levels (Kaplan, 2001; Brymer et al., 2010; Howell et al., 2011). Additionally, based on Wen et al.'s (2004) definition of mediating effects, it was reasonable to hypothesize that Trait Mindfulness may serve as a mediator in the relationship between Nature Relatedness and Character Strengths. However, the mediating effect of mindfulness on the relationship between Nature Relatedness and Character Strengths had not been extensively explored, thus highlighting a research gap in the literature.

This research aimed to investigate the research gaps in the four aspects mentioned above. First, the Chinese version of the Nature Relatedness Scale will be revised. Subsequently, three scales were used to assess the Nature Relatedness, Trait Mindfulness and Character Strengths of Chinese and Malaysian university students, then analyzed their characteristics and differences. Furthermore, the influence of Nature Relatedness on overall Character Strengths among university students were analyzed. Finally, the mediating effect of Trait Mindfulness on the relationship between Nature Relatedness and Character Strengths among university students were explored and examined.

1.4 Research Objectives

1a: To revise the Three-dimensional Nature Relatedness Scale in Chinese version.

2a: To analyze the differences in Nature Relatedness, Trait Mindfulness and Character Strengths among Chinese and Malaysian university students in different demographic variables.

2b: To analyze the differences in Nature Relatedness, Trait Mindfulness and Character Strengths among Chinese and Malaysian university students.

3a: To examine the relationship between Nature Relatedness and Character Strengths among Chinese and Malaysian university students.

3b: To determine the causal relationship between Nature Relatedness and overall Character Strengths among Chinese and Malaysian university students.

4a: To examine the relationships between Nature Relatedness and Trait Mindfulness, Trait Mindfulness and Character Strengths among Chinese and Malaysian university students.

4b: To examine the mediating effect of Trait Mindfulness on the relationship between Nature Relatedness and Character Strengths among Chinese and Malaysian university students.

1.5   Research Questions

RQ1: Does the Three-dimensional Nature Relatedness Scale have high validity and reliability?

RQ2a: Are there differences in Nature Relatedness, Trait Mindfulness and Character Strengths among Chinese and Malaysian university students in different demographic variables?

RQ2b: Are there differences in Nature Relatedness, Trait Mindfulness and Character Strengths among Chinese and Malaysian university students?

RQ3a: Is there a significant correlation between Nature Relatedness and Character Strengths among Chinese and Malaysian university students?

RQ3b: Does Nature Relatedness predict Character Strengths positively among Chinese and Malaysian university students?

RQ4a: Is there a significant correlation between Nature Relatedness and Trait Mindfulness, Trait Mindfulness and Character Strengths among Chinese and Malaysian university students?

RQ4b: Does Trait Mindfulness have a mediating effect on the relationship between Nature Relatedness and Character Strengths among Chinese and

Malaysian university students?

1.6 Research Hypotheses

H1a: The Chinese Three-dimensional Nature Relatedness Scale have high validity and reliability.

H2a: There are differences in Nature Relatedness, Trait Mindfulness and Character Strengths among Chinese and Malaysian university students in different demographic variables.

H2b: There are differences in Nature Relatedness, Trait Mindfulness and Character Strengths among Chinese and Malaysian university students.

H3a: There is a significant correlation between Nature Relatedness and Character Strengths among Chinese and Malaysian university students.

H3b: Nature Relatedness predicts Character Strengths positively among Chinese and Malaysian university students.

H4a: There is a significant correlation between Nature Relatedness and Trait Mindfulness, Trait Mindfulness and Character Strengths among Chinese and Malaysian university students.

H4b: Trait Mindfulness have a mediating effect on the relationship between Nature Relatedness and Character Strengths among Chinese and Malaysian university students.

The relationships between research problems and research objectives, research questions and research hypotheses are illustrated in Table 1.1.

21

Table 1.1   The Relationships Between Research Problems and Research Objectives, Research Questions and Research Hypotheses

Problem Statement	Research Objectives	Research Questions	Research Hypotheses
1. Lack of the Three-dimensional Nature Relatedness Scale in Chinese version.	1a: To revise the Three-dimensional Nature Relatedness Scale in Chinese version.	RQ1: Does the Three-dimensional Nature Relatedness Scale have high validity and reliability?	H1a: The Chinese Three-dimensional Nature Relatedness Scale have high validity and reliability.
2. Lack of the comparative research on Nature Relatedness, Trait Mindfulness and Character Strengths among Chinese and Malaysian university students.	2a: To analyze the differences in Nature Relatedness, Trait Mindfulness and Character Strengths among Chinese and Malaysian university students in different demographic variables. 2b: To analyze the differences in Nature Relatedness, Trait Mindfulness and Character Strengths among Chinese and Malaysian university students.	RQ2a: Are there differences in Nature Relatedness, Trait Mindfulness and Character Strengths among Chinese and Malaysian university students in different demographic variables? RQ2b: Are there differences in Nature Relatedness, Trait Mindfulness and Character Strengths among Chinese and Malaysian university students?	H2a: There are differences in Nature Relatedness, Trait Mindfulness and Character Strengths among Chinese and Malaysian university students in different demographic variables. H2b: There are differences in Nature Relatedness, Trait Mindfulness and Character Strengths among Chinese and Malaysian university students.
3. Lack of the study on the relationship between Nature Relatedness and overall Character Strengths among Chinese and Malaysian university students, and the causal relationship is not clear.	3a: To examine the relationship between Nature Relatedness and Character Strengths among Chinese and Malaysian university students. 3b: To determine the causal relationship between Nature Relatedness and overall Character Strengths among Chinese and Malaysian university students.	RQ3a: Is there a significant correlation between Nature Relatedness and Character Strengths among Chinese and Malaysian university students? RQ3b: Does Nature Relatedness predict Character Strengths positively among Chinese and Malaysian university students?	H3a: There is a significant correlation between Nature Relatedness and Character Strengths among Chinese and Malaysian university students. H3b: Nature Relatedness predicts Character Strengths positively among Chinese and Malaysian university students.
4. Lack of study on the mechanism of the influence of Nature Relatedness on Character Strengths among Chinese and Malaysian university students, Trait Mindfulness may have a mediating effect.	4a: To examine the relationships between Nature Relatedness and Trait Mindfulness, Trait Mindfulness and Character Strengths among Chinese and Malaysian university students. 4b: To examine the mediating effect of Trait Mindfulness on the relationship between Nature Relatedness and Character Strengths among Chinese and Malaysian university students.	RQ4a: Is there a significant correlation between Nature Relatedness and Trait Mindfulness, Trait Mindfulness and Character Strengths among Chinese and Malaysian university students? RQ4b: Does Trait Mindfulness have a mediating effect on the relationship between Nature Relatedness and Character Strengths among Chinese and Malaysian university students?	H4a: There is a significant correlation between Nature Relatedness and Trait Mindfulness, Trait Mindfulness and Character Strengths among Chinese and Malaysian university students. H4b: Trait Mindfulness have a mediating effect on the relationship between Nature Relatedness and Character Strengths among Chinese and Malaysian university students.

1.7   Conceptual Framework

This study incorporates three variables: an independent variable, a dependent variable, and a mediating variable. A graphical representation depicting the interrelationship among these three variables can be observed in Figure 1.1.

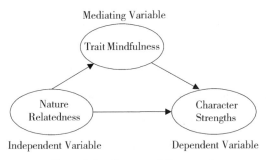

Figure 1.1   Conceptual Framework

In this research, the independent variable is Nature Relatedness, which consists of three factors: NR-self, NR-perspective, NR-experience (Nisbet et al., 2009). The dependent variable is Character Strengths, which consists of three factors: caring, inquisitiveness, self-control (Duan & Bu, 2017). The mediating variable is Trait Mindfulness, which consists of five factors: observing, describing, acting with awareness, non-judging, non-reactivity (Baer et al., 2006).

1.8   Definition of Terminology

1.8.1   Definition of Character Strengths

1.8.1.1   Conceptual Definition

Personality reflects an individual's attitude towards the real world, and is a relatively stable psychological characteristic of individual behavior model (Peng, 2010). At present, the research on personality and character has been relatively mature in the field of psychology. Different from the traditional personality psychology, positive psychologists pay more attention to the research on character quality from positive perspective, focusing on the character quality that is beneficial to the individual's physical and mental health and behavior, which is the character strength.

Character Strengths are defined as a series of positive character qualities reflected in an individual's cognition, emotion and behavior, which are beneficial to oneself and others, and are an important way for an individual to lead a better life (Peterson & Seligman, 2006). Peterson and Seligman (2006) invited more than 50 outstanding young psychologists from all over the world. They extracted six core virtues that are common to all mankind from the philosophical, religious and cultural systems that have the most extensive influence on human society. A further 24 Character Strengths are proposed below six virtues: justice including cooperation, fairness and leadership; courage including courage, honesty, enthusiasm and perseverance; temperance including forgiveness, humility, prudence and self-regulation; kindness including the ability to love and be loved, kindness and sociability; wisdom including creativity, curiosity, criticality, eagerness to learn and insight; self-transcendence including gratitude, appreciation of beauty and excellence, spirituality, humor and hope.

1.8.1.2 Operational Definition

In this research, Character Strengths are defined as a set of positive traits manifested in an individual's thoughts, emotions, and behaviors, which contribute to well-being and benefit of both the individual and others. These strengths are distinct, measurable, and independent of one another. Character Strengths are categorized into three dimensions: caring, inquisitiveness, and self-control. Caring refers to the ability to demonstrate empathy and compassion for others. It includes acts of kindness, concern for the well-being of others, and the willingness to offer help to those in need. Operationally, caring can be measured through behaviors such as helping others, offering emotional support, and showing genuine concern for others' needs. Inquisitiveness refers to the desire and ability to explore, learn, and understand new things. This dimension involves a deep curiosity about the world, intellectual engagement, and a preference for seeking out new information. Operationally, inquisitiveness can be assessed by behaviors such as asking questions, exploring unfamiliar topics, and actively seeking knowledge and new experiences. Self-control involves the ability to regulate one's emotions, thoughts, and behaviors in the face of temptations and impulses. It includes the capacity to delay gratification, resist unhealthy behaviors, and maintain focus on long-term goals. Operationally, self-control can be measured through self-reported behaviors such as managing stress, controlling impulses, or maintaining discipline in task completion. The Three-dimensional Inventory of Character Strengths is used to assess these traits, where higher scores reflect greater levels of Character Strengths. This scale is particularly suitable for assessing the Character Strengths of Chinese and Malaysian university students, providing a reliable and efficient measurement of their strengths.

1.8.2   Definition of Nature Relatedness

1.8.2.1   Conceptual Definition

Overall, Nature Relatedness, alternatively refers to as Nature Relatedness, Connectedness to Nature, Nature Connectedness, Connectivity with Nature, and other terms, represents the essence of the connection between humans and the natural world. Academically, researchers hold varying perspectives on the concept of Nature Relatedness, reflecting diverse interpretations of this fundamental relationship. Specific references are as follows：

　　Some researchers emphasized the emotional relationship between individuals and nature. They studied the Nature Relatedness from the perspective of emotion to explain the relationship between human and nature. The earliest environmental psychologist defined Nature Relatedness as the emotional attachment to nature, including individual's love for nature and sense of freedom, intimacy and identity in the natural environment. Kals et al. (1999) were the first to discuss the concept of Nature Relatedness and introduced the concept of Emotional Affinity Toward Nature. They defined Nature Relatedness as the emotional affinity of individuals toward nature, characterized by a sense of love and closeness to it. This involves feeling an emotional affinity for nature, a tendency to integrate with it, and an emphasis on emotional connection. Mayer and Frantz (2004) also proposed the concept of Nature Relatedness, emphasizing its emotional basis. They described it as the degree to which individuals feel emotionally and experientially connected with nature, as well as a sense of belonging to it. Schultz (2002) approached the human-nature relationship from a cognitive perspective. He argued that connection with nature refers to individuals' understanding of the relationship between humans and nature and their awareness of its importance. They believed that Nature Relatedness involves the inclusion of nature in the self, referring to the extent to which nature is integrated into an individual's self-cognitive representation.

　　Nisbet et al. (2009) approached Nature Relatedness from multiple dimensions. They redefined the conceptby proposing that Nature Relatedness is a multi-dimensional psychological construct encompassing cognitive, emotional, and behavioral experiences. These dimensions include knowledge about nature, worldviews related to nature, familiarity with nature, comfort in natural settings, and a desire for connection with nature. This redefinition provides a more comprehensive explanation of the conceptual essence of connecting with nature.

1.8.2.2 Operational Definition

In this research, Nature Relatedness refers to the intimate relationship between individuals and nature, where individuals emotionally bond with nature, cognitively integrate it into their sense of self, experience its appeal through direct interaction, and are willing to coexist with it. The three dimensions of Nature Relatedness are NR-self, NR-perspective, and NR-experience. NR-self refers to an individual's sense of self-identity with nature. Specifically, it reflects the extent to which an individual sees himself as a part of the natural world. A high NR-self means that an individual feels closely connected to nature and considers the natural environment an important part of their self-concept. Operational definition: this is assessed by measuring the individual's engagement with nature-related activities and their sense of being a part of the natural system. NR-perspective refers to an individual's perspective or attitude toward nature, often expressed in terms of the value, significance, and role of nature in their life. It reflects how an individual cognitively understands the relationship between nature and human life from a broader perspective. Operational definition: This is assessed by measuring the individual's awareness of the importance of nature conservation, their sense of responsibility, and the long-term impact of nature. NR-experience focuses on an individual's direct experiences or contact with nature. It refers to the frequency and quality of interactions with the natural environment, as well as the emotional and psychological impact these experiences have on individuals. Operational definition: this is assessed by evaluating the frequency and depth of the individual's interactions with nature in daily life.

The Nature Relatedness Scale can be used to comprehensively measure the level of individual Nature Relatedness. Higher scores on the scale indicate a higher level of Nature Relatedness, reflecting a greater degree of recognition of nature, increased awareness of the impact of human behavior on nature, stronger attraction to nature, and a greater willingness to engage with nature. This scale is effective for assessing the Nature Relatedness of Chinese and Malaysian university students.

1.8.3   Definition of Trait Mindfulness

1.8.3.1   Conceptual Definition

Mindfulness first originated from Buddhism, and then was widely concerned by Western psychology. At present, the popular Mindfulness-Based Stress Reduction (MBSR) and Mindfulness-Based Cognitive Therapy (MBSCT) have been widely used in medical and counseling fields (Yang, 2022). Mindfulness was first defined as awareness and nonjudgmental acceptance of present experiences (Brown & Ryan, 2003; Kabat-Zinn, 2003).

With the continuous deepening of Mindfulness research, different researchers had different definitions of the concept of Mindfulness. For example, Brown and Ryan (2003) regarded Mindfulness as a state of consciousness. Tusaie and Edds (2009) believed that Mindfulness was a meta-cognitive ability, while Germer (2005) considered it a psychological process of self-regulation of attention.

After much discussion, researchers have developed an operational definition of Mindfulness, suggesting that Mindfulness consists of two components. The first is "attentional self-control". Specifically, it mainly refers to the ability of individuals to take an active way to detect internal and external stimulation, and when interference objects appear, they can voluntarily focus on the correct object, similar to an "active avoidance mechanism" (Bishop et al., 2004; Lau et al., 2006). The second is "maintains a specific attitude to the experience of the moment", which specifically requires individuals to be open to the feelings and experiences of the moment, not to shut them out, and to maintain a curiosity to accept the real feelings, emotions or experiences of the moment (Keng et al., 2011). This two-dimensional operational definition of Mindfulness, which clearly describes the core components of mindfulness, has been affirmed by many researchers (Keng et al., 2011).

Gärtner (2013) proposed that Mindfulness is a psychological state and a personality trait. Within the realm of personality traits, mindfulness refers to a balanced characteristic that individuals possess. In general, at present, researchers mainly define mindfulness from two levels of state mindfulness and Trait Mindfulness. Trait Mindfulness is distinct from state mindfulness, which describes the non-judgmental present-focused awareness experienced in any given moment (Medvedev et al., 2017).

1.8.3.2 Operational Definition

Trait Mindfulness is defined as an individual's tendency to maintain awareness of the present moment in a non-reactive and non-judgmental way. Unlike State Mindfulness, which is the awareness experienced at any given moment, Trait Mindfulness is a stable characteristic. It consists of five components: observing, describing, acting with awareness, non-judging, and non-reactivity. Accurate and reliable measurement of mindfulness ensures that research findings effectively capture changes in mindfulness.

Observing refers to the ability to notice or be aware of internal and external experiences, such as thoughts, emotions, sensations, and environmental stimuli, in the present moment. This is measured by the degree to which an individual can notice and pay attention to sensory experiences, bodily sensations, emotions, and thoughts. Describing involves the ability to put one's internal experiences into words. It reflects the capacity to verbally express thoughts, emotions, and sensations in a detailed and accurate way. This is assessed by evaluating an individual's ability to describe their feelings, thoughts, and experiences with clarity. Acting with awareness refers to the ability to be fully present and engaged in the moment without being distracted by thoughts or automatic habits. It involves mindful attention to actions and behaviors. This is assessed by measuring the degree to which an individual performs tasks consciously, rather than mindlessly or habitually. Non-judging involves observing experiences without evaluating them as good or bad. It refers to an attitude of acceptance and impartiality toward one's thoughts, emotions, and sensations. It is assessed by evaluating an individual's tendency to avoid labeling or judging their experiences. Non-reactivity refers to the ability to allow thoughts and emotions to come and go without reacting to them or being carried away by them. It involves maintaining equanimity and not automatically acting on or being overwhelmed by emotional reactions. This is measured by evaluating the extent to which an individual can remain calm and undisturbed by their internal experiences, such as emotions or urges. The Five Facet Mindfulness Questionnaire (FFMQ) is used to measure Trait Mindfulness, with higher scores indicating greater mindfulness. This scale is applicable for assessing Trait Mindfulness in Chinese and Malaysian university students.

1.9   Limitations

One of the limitations of this research is that the participants were limited to university students in China and Malaysia. Research has indicated that the development of Nature Relatedness may have critical periods, such as the lasting effects of Nature-Related Interventions on children under the age of 11 (Lieflander et al., 2013). Future research could track the development of Nature Relatedness over time and expand the scope to include other age groups or regions, potentially providing a more comprehensive understanding of how Nature Relatedness develops in a wider range of individuals.

Another limitation is that in the case of Chinese university students, the corresponding Chinese revised versions of the questionnaires were used, while Malaysian university students directly used the original English version of the scales without translation into Malay and without a revised version for the Malaysian university student sample. Therefore, there still exist limitations in cross-cultural studies involving the use of these scales. Recognizing the potential impact of language differences or unadapted measures provides a clearer understanding of the challenges involved in cross-cultural research and emphasizes the need for future studies to standardize or culturally adapt assessment tools.

The third limitation is related to the generalizability of the results. The data were collected from a sample of five universities in China and one university in Malaysia, which may not represent students from other universities. Additionally, the tests and methods used in this study were specific to the purposes of the current research and may not necessarily apply to other populations of primary and secondary school students. Recognizing the limitations of the sample representativeness and the specific methods used helps to better understand the results and their applicability. Future research could increase the sample size and diversity to improve the generalizability of the findings.

1.10   Conclusion

Character Strengths are a significant area of study within the field of positive psychology. They encompass a range of positive qualities that manifest in an individual's cognition, emotion, and behavior, contributing to personal well-being and benefiting others. Understanding Character Strengths is crucial for individuals to lead fulfilling lives. Existing research has predominantly focused on the positive outcomes associated with Character Strengths, yet there remains a limited exploration of the factors influencing their development.

This study aims to investigate the influential role of Nature Relatedness in promoting Character Strengths among university students from China and

31

Malaysia. By examining the relationship between these two important constructs in positive psychology, this research expands upon previous studies on Nature Relatedness and Character Strengths. Additionally, the study explores the mediating effect of Trait Mindfulness on the association between Nature Relatedness and Character Strengths in Chinese and Malaysian university students. This investigation provides a theoretical foundation for future research on the practical implementation of Mindfulness-Based Nature Relatedness Intervention, aiming to cultivate Character Strengths among Chinese and Malaysian university students.

CHAPTER 2   LITERATURE REVIEW

2.1   Introduction

This chapter discusses the theories and existing research relevant to the variables used in this study. It covers the definitions, measurement instruments, and previous research on the three variables: Character Strengths, Nature Relatedness, and Trait Mindfulness. Additionally, through previous studies on the interrelationships among these variables, it reveals their mutual associations, potential impact relationships, and underlying mechanisms. The theoretical framework regarding these three variables and their interconnections is also presented and analyzed. Finally, a brief summary of this chapter is provided.

2.2   Previous Research on the Definition-Related Studies

Upon reviewing the literature, it is found that previous related studies on Character Strengths, Nature Relatedness, and the definition of Nature Relatedness have explored various concepts and frameworks, as well as the content they encompass. Analyzing these studies helps to gain a deeper understanding of how these constructs are measured and interpreted across different populations. Overall, these research provide a comprehensive perspective for this study and lay a solid theoretical foundation.

2.2.1   Previous Research on the Definition of Character Strengths

Everyone has unique personality traits, which reflect their attitude toward the world and are relatively stable individual psychological characteristics in their behavioral model (Peng, 2010). Research on personality and character in the field of psychology has become mature, such as the widely recognized theoretical models of the Big Five Personality Traits Model and the Eysenck Personality Questionnaire. Positive psychologists emphasize studying character traits from a positive and constructive perspective, focusing on beneficial traits for individual physical and mental health and behavior, referred to as Character Strengths, as opposed to traditional personality psychology.

Character Strengths, an important way for individuals to lead a good life, are defined as a series of positive character traits reflected in individuals' cognition, emotion and behavior that are beneficial to both oneself and others (Peterson & Seligman, 2006). So, what kind of character traits can be considered Character Strengths? Morally speaking, it is obvious that only those excellent qualities (that have significant value, are in line with ethical norms, do not harm others, and are of importance at all times and recognized by various cultural systems) can become Character Strengths. Seligman and Peterson (2005) have identified the following 12 selection criteria after studying the cultural traditions, religions and philosophies of the East and West: they are generally present in various cultures; they contribute to individuals' self-fulfillment and promote life satisfaction and personal happiness; they have ethical value in themselves; they do not harm others; their opposite is a negative and undesirable trait; they are similar to personality traits and are reflected in individuals' thinking, emotions, and behavior patterns; they can be measured; they are independent and do not overlap; they usually serve as concrete role models; they can be possessed by individuals or more people; some Character Strengths are not obvious in individuals; and they are moral goals advocated and nurtured by society.

2.2.2 Previous Research on the Definition of Nature Relatedness

2.2.2.1 Nature

In this research, the term "nature" refers to the natural environment and the various natural elements encountered by individuals in their everyday lives. The natural environment encompasses both untouched natural landscapes, such as forests, as well as human-made environments that incorporate natural elements, like urban parks. Natural elements include the diverse components of the natural environment, such as plants, animals, rivers, sand, and air (Mcsweeney et al., 2014; Chen, 2018). Nature Relatedness is divided into objective Nature Relatedness and subjective Nature Relatedness.

The objective Nature Relatedness is influenced by the specific environment and reflects the current state of interaction with nature (Chen, 2018). Some evidence supports the claim that spending time in nature provides a range of positive physical, psychological and social health benefits (Ohtsuka et al., 1998; Cimprich & Ronis, 2001; Wu & Lanier, 2003; Loeffler, 2004; Wichrowski et al., 2005; Boniface et al., 2012; Berman et al., 2008; Park et al., 2010; Van Den Berg & Custers, 2011). These health-promoting properties are purportedly linked to humans' adaptive connection to nature. During the course of evolution, outdoor environments provided humans with food, security and a place of restoration, which resulted in positive physiological and psychological benefits (Ulrich, 1983; Wilson, 1993; Kellert & Wilson, 1995; Lorh & Pearson-Mims, 2000). The counterpart of objective Nature Relatedness is subjective Nature Relatedness (Chen, 2018). On the one hand, subjective Nature Relatedness encompasses individuals' subjective perception of their personal connection with nature, which can vary in terms of cognition, emotion, and behavior. Everyday observations reveal individuals who possess a heightened

35

awareness of their natural surroundings, actively engage in field trips, or enjoy indoor gardening. On the one hand, there are those who demonstrate little interest in such activities. The Nature Relatedness discussed in this research pertains to the perceived relationship individuals have with nature, thus falling within the realm of subjective Nature Relatedness.

2.2.2.2   Nature Relatedness

Different researchers named Nature Relatedness differently based on different research focuses. According to previous studies, it was found that more than 13 kinds of terms were used. The purpose of this research is to discuss the relationship between Nature Relatedness and Character Strengths, which belonged to personality. In this research, the conclusions of Nisbet et al. (2009) are adopted, and the term Nature Relatedness is uniformly used as the independent variable. Nature Relatedness was considered to have personality-like characteristics, with relatively stable, situational properties and three-dimensional structure.

Psychologists have come up with a series of terms for the connection between humans and nature, in chronological order, there are: Emotional Affinity toward Nature(EAN, Kals et al., 1999), Inclusion of Nature in the Self (INS, Schultz, 2001), Environmental Identity (EID, Clayton & Opotow, 2003), Connectedness to Nature (CN, Mayer & Frantz, 2004), Implicit Connections with Nature (ICN, Schultz et al., 2004), Connectivity with Nature (CWN, Dutcher et al., 2007), Nature Relatedness (NR, Nisbet et al., 2009), Commitment to Nature (Davis et al., 2009), Love and Care for Nature (LCN, Perkins, 2010), Disposition to Connect with Nature (DCN, Brugger et al., 2011), Dispositional Empathy with Nature (DEN, Tam, 2013b), Emotional Connection to Nature (ECN, Silvas & Daniel, 2013), Ecological Identity (ECI, Walton & Jones 2018). Connectedness to Nature and Nature Relatedness are cited more frequently. Different researchers have made different interpretations of the concept of Natural Relatedness, which can be divided into three types: emotional type, cognitive type and multidimensional relationship type.

1. Nature Relatedness of Emotional Type

From an emotional perspective, researchers focus on the emotional bond between individuals and nature, shedding light on the human-nature relationship. Kals et al. (1999) introduced the concept of Emotional Affinity toward Nature (EAN). They defined EAN as an emotional attachment to nature, encompassing feelings of love, freedom, intimacy, and identity experienced in natural environments. Kals et al. (1999) emphasized the emotional connection with nature, considering Emotional Affinity toward Nature as individuals' emotional inclination to love, connect with, feel affinity for, and integrate with nature. Mayer and Frantz (2004) further developed the notion of Connectedness to Nature (CN) within an emotional framework. They proposed that Connectedness to Nature reflects the extent to which individuals feel emotionally and experientially connected to and belong to nature.

Perkins (2010) introduced Love and Care for Nature (LCN) to capture the nature-related relationship. LCN entails a deep love and care for nature, including a profound recognition of its intrinsic value and a personal responsibility to protect the environment from harm. It represents human acknowledgment of nature's worth and a sense of responsibility towards its preservation. Davis et al. (2009) put forth the concept of Commitment to Nature (CTN), which signifies an individual's psychological attachment to nature and a long-term value orientation. CTN reflects people's reliance on and dedication to nature. Tam (2013a) proposed Dispositional Empathy with Nature (DEN), considering it as a distinct inclination for individuals to understand and share the emotional experiences of nature. DEN highlights a special tendency to empathize with nature.

2. Nature Relatedness of Cognitive Type

Schultz (2001) adopted a cognitive perspective to comprehend the relationship between individuals and nature. He posited that this relationship entailed individuals' cognitive understanding of their connection with nature and their perception of its significance. In accordance with this, the Inclusion of Nature in the Self (INS) represents the degree to which individuals incorporate nature into their self-concept. Schultz et al. (2004) introduced the concept of Implicit Connections with Nature (ICN), which pertains to the implicit cognitive associations individuals hold with nature. They classified ICN as a form of implicit cognition.

Expanding on these ideas, Dutcher et al. (2007) proposed the concept of Connectivity with Nature (CWN). CWN encompasses the perceived affinity between humans and the natural environment, reflecting the extent to which individuals incorporate nature into their own identity. It also reflects the extent to which individuals perceive themselves as integral members of the natural world. Brügger et al. (2011) introduced the notion of Disposition to Connect with Nature (DCN). DCN refers to an individual's attitude towards nature, encompassing behaviors related to nature and evaluations thereof.

3. Nature Relatedness of Multidimensional Relationship Type

Clayton and Opotow (2003) proposed Enviornmental Identity (EID), which refers to the degree that the natural environment plays an important role in self-definition. Environmental Identity includes the emotional connection and identification with nature, the approval of environmental protection policies, and the degree of mutual influence between people and nature. It includes people's interaction with natural elements, awareness of the importance of nature, and positive emotions towards nature. This sense of connection to the natural environment influences perception and performance, and the belief that the environment is important becomes a part of the self-concept, and that Environmental Identity is a "diverse and evolving topic".

Nisbet et al. (2009) understood Nature Relatedness from multiple dimensions. They redefined Nature Relatedness and believed that Nature Relatedness was a multi-dimensional psychological structure with cognitive, emotional and behavioral experiences. It is the level of relatedness between an individual and nature in these three dimensions, including the understanding of nature, the world view related to nature, the degree of familiarity with nature, the degree of comfort and the degree of desire for nature. This concept fully illustrated the conceptual connotation of being connected to nature.

To sum up, the concept of Nature Relatedness can be summarized as the above three types and more than 13 concepts, which are used by researchers to construct the correlation between human and nature from different research perspectives. Tam (2013b) specifically compared and analyzed multiple concepts of Nature Relatedness, and found that they have strong convergent validity, which can be used as markers of common underlying structures, and suggested that future research can use these concepts in the same framework, or select them based on the purpose of the research. According to statistical findings, connectedness to nature proposed by Mayer and Frantz (2004), and Nature Relatedness proposed by Nisbet et al. (2009) were accepted and used more frequently by many scholars.

In this research, the purpose is to explore the relationship between Nature Relatedness and Character Strengths, and verify whether the intervention of Nature Relatedness can enhance individual Character Strengths. Therefore, the concept and connotation are selected in line with the purpose of this research. As stated by Nisbet, Zelenski, and Murphy (2009), Nature Relatedness is a relatively stable structure similar to personality traits, which can be seen as a character-like structure describing the differences in the relationship between humans and nature, but with strong situational characteristics. The purpose of this research is to discuss the relationship between Nature Relatedness and Character Strengths, and Character Strengths belong to personality. Therefore, this research adopts the research conclusion, and uses the name of "Nature Relatedness" as the independent variable. It is believed that Nature Relatedness is relatively stable, with contextual nature and contains three-dimensional structure (Yang, 2017). In this research, Nature Relatedness is defined as the deep connection between humans and nature, where individuals emotionally bond with the natural world, cognitively incorporate nature into their sense of self, engage with nature through physical experiences, and embrace the idea of coexisting with nature. This concept encompasses a three-dimensional structure, which includes cognitive, emotional, and behavioral components.

2.2.3 Previous Research on the Definition of Trait Mindfulness

Mindfulness, first originated from Buddhism, has been widely studied in Western psychology (Lopez, 2012). Currently, popular Mindfulness-Based Stress Reduction (MBSR) and Mindfulness-Based Cognitive Therapy (MBCT) have extensive applications in the fields of medicine and counseling. Mindfulness was initially defined as non-judgmental awareness of present experiences (Brown & Ryan, 2003; Kabat-Zinn, 1990). With the deepening of mindfulness research, different scholars have defined mindfulness differently. Overall, researchers mainly define mindfulness from two levels: State Mindfulness and Trait Mindfulness.

Defined from a state of mindfulness perspective, Mindfulness includes self-awareness and non-judgmental awareness of present experiences, including internal bodily sensations, emotions and thoughts, as well as external stimuli such as visual and auditory sensations (Segal et al., 2002). In this state, individuals can focus on continuously emerging stimuli and accept them without judgment (Baer, 2003). Kabat-Zinn (2003) defined mindfulness as paying attention in a particular way: on purpose, in the present moment, and non-judging. Langer (1989) also proposed that Mindfulness is an individual's spontaneous way of processing information, allowing them to be highly concentrated, alert, and non-judgmentally accept their experiences and sensations in the present moment.

From the perspective of Trait Mindfulness, the researchers believed that mindfulness is a trait that everyone possesses, and is a strengthened attention and perception tendency that individuals have towards their current experiences and life feelings (Park et al., 2013). Individuals with high Trait Mindfulness are more aware of internal and external stimuli in daily life, and also have a higher level of self-acceptance. They do not easily make automatic behavioral responses in daily life, and are constantly aware of their current feelings in order to make conscious behavioral responses (Brown & Ryan, 2003). This trait or ability may differ between individuals, and after continuous mindfulness training, this tendency will become more stable, hence referred to as Trait Mindfulness (Cahn & Polich, 2006; Wang & Huang, 2011).

So far, many researchers have pointed out that although there is a clear difference in concept between State Mindfulness and Trait Mindfulness, individuals with higher levels of Trait Mindfulness are generally more likely to maintain a mindful state of awareness. Therefore, the two are inseparable and need to be combined to understand mindfulness (Yang, 2022; Baer, 2003; Germer, 2005; Shapiro & Carlson, 2009). Overall, it is evident that "being aware of the present moment," "acceptance," and "non-judgment" are the core elements of mindfulness.

The above definitions indicate that the descriptive definitions of "non-judgmental acceptance" and "awareness" are still difficult to understand, and therefore operational definitions of mindfulness need to be studied. After much discussion, Bishop, Lau and Shapiro (2004) developed an operational definition of mindfulness, consisting of two components. The first is "self-regulation of attention" which refers to an individual's ability to actively attend to internal and external stimuli, and to redirect attention when distractions arise. The second is "orientation to experience" which requires an open attitude towards present moment experiences, accepting them without judgment and maintaining curiosity. This dual-component operational definition of mindfulness provides a clearer description of the core elements of mindfulness, and has been affirmed by many researchers (Bishop et al. 2004).

Therefore, based on the above discussions, this research adopt the operational definition to define mindfulness: Mindfulness refers to an individual's continuous awareness of internal and external stimuli, and the ability to use mindfulness to gently bring attention back to the present moment when distracting stimuli arise, and to maintain a curious, open, and accepting attitude toward present experiences (Bishop et al., 2004; Yang, 2022).

2.3 Previous Research on the Research Instruments

2.3.1 Previous Research on Instruments for Assessing Character Strengths

2.3.1.1 Values in Action Inventory of Strengths (VIA-IS)

Psychologists, led by Seligman and Peterson (2004), have spent over five years identifying six core virtues that are widely recognized across cultures: Wisdom, Courage, Humanity, Justice, Temperance and Transcendence. They have selected 24 representative Character Strengths from numerous positive human qualities, categorizing them under these core virtues. This ongoing effort has resulted in the creation of the Values in Action Inventory of Strengths (VIA-IS), which provides a consistent language for discussing positive qualities and virtues, as well as a comprehensive framework for understanding Character Strengths. Peterson and Seligman suggested that cultivating and practicing these Character Strengths can lead to the development of these core virtues, ultimately bringing happiness, health, and meaning to life. See Table 2.1 for details.

Table 2.1　　　　**Values in Action Inventory of Strengths(VIA-IS)**

Name	Classification	First Dimension	Second Dimension
Values in Action Inventory of Strengths, VIA-IS (Peterson & Seligman, 2006)	6 Virtues, 24 Character Strengths, 240 Items	Wisdom(5)	1. Creativity; 2. Curiosity; 3. Judgment; 4. Love of Learning; 5. Perspective
		Courage(4)	6. Bravery; 7. Perseverance; 8. Honesty; 9. Zest
		Humanity(3)	10. Love; 11. Kindness; 12. Social Intelligence
		Justice(3)	13. Teamwork; 14. Fairness; 15. Leadership
		Temperance(4)	16. Forgiveness; 17. Humility; 18. Prudence; 19. Self-Regulation
		Transcendence(5)	20. Appreciation of Beauty and Excellence; 21. Gratitude; 22. Hope; 23. Humor; 24. Spirituality

After Peterson and Seligman (2004) proposed the Values in Action Inventory of Strengths (VIA-IS) , corresponding self-report measures were subsequently developed, including a youth version (VIA-Youth) for ages 11-17 and an adult version (VIA-IS) for those of age 18 and older. The questionnaires contain 240 items, with each character strength measured by 10 items. The VIA-IS and VIA-Youth have been shown to have good validity and reliability. Recently, the VIA Character Institute in the United States has revised the VIA-IS and VIA-Youth based on feedbacks from research on Character Strengths, maintaining the original structure but streamlining the 240 items and adding three versions: a shortened 120-item version of the VIA-IS, a condensed 72-item version of the VIA-IS, and a 96-item version of the VIA-Youth.

2.3.1.2   The Chinese Virtues Questionnaire (CVQ)

With the continuous development of Character Strengths research, scholars from various countries are adapting and modifying the classification structures of Character Strengths to fit different cultural contexts. A study of 837 Chinese university students found cultural adaptability issues with the six virtue structures of the VIA-IS questionnaire, and further modification was needed for the dimensional structure of the six virtues. Subsequently, Chinese scholars, such as Duan et al. (2012), built upon the original VIA classification system and considered the cultural similarities and differences between China and the Western world. They reorganized the 24 Character Strengths into three virtues: humanity, vitality, and willpower, creating a classification structure that aligns with Chinese cultural background. Specific details can be seen in Table 2.2.

Table 2.2   **Chinese Virtues Questionnaire (CVQ)**

Name	Classification	First Dimension	Second Dimension (Contrast with the VIA-IS)
Chinese Virtues Questionnaire (CVQ) (Duan et al., 2012)	3 Virtues, 24 Character Strengths, 96 Items	Relationship(8)	11. Kindness; 13. Teamwork; 14. Fairness; 10. Love; 8. Authenticity(Honesty); 15. Leadership; 16. Forgiveness; 21. Gratitude
		Vitality(10)	23. Humor; 2. Curiosity; 9. Zest; 1. Creativity; 5. Perspective; 22. Hope; 12. Social (Social Intelligence); 20. Beauty (Appreciation of Beauty and Excellence); 6. Bravery; 24. Belief(Spirituality)
		Conscientiousness (6)	3. Judgment; 18. Prudence; 19. Regulation (Self-Regulation); 7. Perseverance; 4. Learning (Love of Learning); 17. Modesty(Humility)

Based on this, Duan et al. (2012) used a combined qualitative and quantitative analysis method to screen and reduce the original 240 items of the VIA-IS, and ultimately developed a Chinese Virtues Questionnaire that measures Chinese Character Strengths and virtues, which has been shown to have good validity and reliability. The questionnaire contains a total of 96 items, with 4 items for each character strength, and is suitable for the Chinese sociocultural system. CVQ is a self-report questionnaire scored using the 5-point Likert scale, with 1 indicating "not like me at all" and 5 indicating "very much like me," and there are no reverse-scored items. Respondents rate each item on a scale of 1-5 based on their actual situation. The average score of the items included for each strength or character trait is the score for that strength or trait, with higher scores indicating a more prominent character strength or trait (Duan et al., 2012).

2.3.1.3 Three-dimensional Inventory of Character Strengths (TICS)

For clinical applications or individuals with significant mental health issues, the existing Virtues in Action Inventory of Strengths (VIA-IS) and the Chinese Virtues Questionnaire (CVQ) may be too lengthy. It is imperative to develop a brief Character Strengths questionnaire for use in cross-cultural (Eastern and Western) and cross-population (medical and community) research and practice. Based on the 96-item Chinese Virtues Questionnaire (CVQ) developed by Duan et al. (2012), and using the criteria for developing brief scales proposed by Marsh et al. (2005), Duan and Bu (2017) constructed a Three-dimensional Inventory of Character Strengths (TICS) to measure Character Strengths in the areas of Caring, Inquisitiveness and Self-control.

The Chinese version of TICS employs a 5-point Likert scale scoring system, where a score of 1 represents "not like me at all" and a score of 5 represents "very much like me." The scale does not include any reverse-scored items, and respondents are required to rate each item based on their personal circumstances using the 1-5 scale. TICS has been utilized with various populations, including university students, adults, community residents, and patients, and it meets the standards of psychometric measurement. Both the total scale and sub-scales can be scored by calculating total or average scores. A higher score indicates more prominent Character Strengths in an individual (Duan & Bu, 2017). Refer to Table 2.3 for specific details.

Table 2.3   **Three-dimensional Inventory of Character Strengths(TICS)**

Name	Classification	First Dimension	Second Dimension
Three-dimensional Inventory of Character Strengths, TICS (Duan & Bu, 2017)	3 Virtues, 24 Character Strengths, 15 Items	Caring(8)	11. Kindness; 13. Teamwork; 14. Fairness; 10. Love; 8. Honesty; 15. Leadership; 16. Forgiveness; 21. Gratitude
		Inquisitiveness (10)	23. Humor; 2. Curiosity; 9. Zest; 1. Creativity; 5. Perspective; 22. Hope; 12. Social Intelligence; 20. Appreciation of Beauty and Excellence; 6. Bravery; 24. Spirituality
		Self-control(6)	3. Judgment; 18. Prudence; 19. Self-Regulation; 7. Perseverance; 4. Love of Learning; 17. Humility

2. 3. 2   Previous Research on Instruments for Assessing Nature Relatedness

Under different conceptual frameworks, researchers have developed different tools. To measure the Nature Relatedness, which can also be classified into three types: emotional, cognitive and multidimensional relationship type.

2.3.2.1   The Measurement of Emotional Nature Relatedness

Kals et al. (1999) were the first to discuss the concept of Nature Relatedness and developed a single-dimensional scale, Emotional Affinity toward Nature Scale (EATNS), to measure love of nature, sense of freedom, sense of security, sense of oneness with nature. Measuring an individual's love for nature, it consists of 16 items with a 7-point scoring.

Mayer and Frantz (2004) also developed a single-dimensional scale: Connectedness to Nature Scale (CNS), which contained 14 items and is 5-point scoring. This scale measures an individual's emotional and experiential connection to nature. There are adults' version and children's version (Frantzet al., 2013). The adults' version of CNS has been adopted and used by scholars in many countries (Hinds & Sparks, 2008; Korpela et al., 2008; Howell et al., 2011), and there has been a standardized Chinese version (Li, 2016). Perkins (2010) created the single-dimension Love and Care for Nature Scale (LCNS) to measure an individual's love and care for nature, consisting of 15 items with a 7-point scoring system. Davis and Green (2009) developed a two-dimensional scale, the Commitment to Nature Scale (CONS), to measure an individual's dependence and commitment to nature. It includes 11 items and 9-point scoring. Tam (2013a) developed a single-dimensional scale, the Dispositional Empathy with Nature Scale (DENS).

2.3.2.2   The Measurement of Cognitive Nature Relatedness

In accordance with the definition of Inclusion of Nature in the Self, the researchers compile a corresponding single-dimensional scale with only one question and 7-point scoring. The overlapping degree of two circles represents the strength of connection, one circle represents the self and the other represents the nature. A self-schema that measures the extent to which nature is included in the self-concept (Schultz et al., 2004).

It is worth noting that, different from other self-reporting scales, the researchers develop the Implicit Association Test (IAT), Implicit cognitive tests were used to examine the degree of implicit connection between human and nature (Schultz et al., 2004). Measuring attitudes with a strong affective component without relying on self-reports. The subjects operate on a computer and the responses to the task are measured and interpreted in terms of associative dominance. The researchers developed a single-dimensional scale as follow. Connectivity with Nature Scale (CWNS) measures the extent to which individuals incorporate nature into their selves and the extent to which people see themselves as members of nature. It consists of four items and 5-point scoring, and a graphical multiple choice question is added (Dutcher et al., 2007). Brügger et al. (2011) proposed the development of a single dimensional scale: Disposition to Connect with Nature Scale (DCN), which evaluated 50 behaviors, 5-point scoring, and answered yes or no (Brügger et al., 2011).

2.3.2.3   The Measurement of Multidimensional Relationship Nature Relatedness

The researchers develop a three-dimensional scale: Environmental Identity Scale (EID), which includes people's interaction with natural elements, awareness of the importance of nature, and positive emotions towards nature. A total of 28 items with 5-point scoring (Clayton & Opotow, 2003).

Nisbet et al. (2009) developed a three-dimensional scale from three dimensions of emotion, cognition and experience: Nature Relatedness Scale (NRS), a total of 21 items with 5-point scoring, comprehensively measured the association between individuals and nature. In 2013, a short version of Nature Relatedness Scale (NRS-6) was revised. The revised scale included two dimensions of emotion and cognition, six items and five ratings, which can measure Nature Relatedness more simply and efficiently. Silvas and Daniel (2013) developed the Emotional Connection to Nature Scale (ECNS), which included three dimensions of cognition, emotion and relationship commitment, evaluated 20 two-level emotional words, and 5-point scoring, used to assess the attitude and willingness to protect nature. In summary, researchers have developed different measurement tools based on various concepts of Nature Relatedness, as clearly shown in Table 2.4.

Table 2.4   **Comparison of the Definition and Measurement of Nature Relatedness**

The type of Nature Relatedness	Serial number	Noun	Concept	The name of the measuring tool	Number of items and scoring	Dimensions of measurement	Method of measurement	Author and year
Nature Relatedness of Emotional Type	1	Emotional Affinity toward Nature, EAN	The emotional relationship between humans and nature. It is the emotional tendency of loving nature and feeling integrated with nature, including the love of nature, identity with nature.	Emotional Affinity toward Nature Scale, EANS	16 items, 7-point scoring	Single dimension	Self-report	Kals et al., 1999
	2	Connectedness to Nature, CN	People are emotionally and empirically connected to nature, and feel the extent to belonging to nature.	Connectedness to Nature Scale, CNS	14 items, 5-point scoring	Single dimension	Self-report	Mayer & Frantz, 2004
	3	Love and Care for Nature, LCN	Deep love and care for nature, including a clear understanding of the intrinsic value of nature and a personal responsibility to protect the environment from harm.	Love and Care for Nature Scale, LCNS	15 items, 7-point scoring	Single dimension	Self-report	Perkins, 2010
	4	Commitment to Nature, CTN	Individual psychological attachment to nature and long-term value orientation, including dependence on nature and commitment relationship.	Commitment to Nature Scale, CONS	11 items, 9-point scoring	Two dimensions	Self-report	Davis et al., 2009

Continued

The type of Nature Relatedness	Serial number	Noun	Concept	The name of the measuring tool	Number of items and scoring	Dimensions of measurement	Method of measurement	Author and year
	5	Dispositional Empathy with Nature, DEN	A trait tendency for people to understand and share emotional experiences with nature.	Dispositional Empathy with Nature Scale, DENS	14 items, 5-point scoring	Single dimension	Self-report	Tam, 2013a
	6	Inclusion of Nature in the Self	The degree of integration of nature and self-concept, that is, the extent to which nature is included in the self-concept of self-schema.	Inclusion of Nature in the Self Scale, INSS	1 item, 7-point scoring	Single dimension	Self-report	Schultz, 2001
Nature Relatedness of Cognitive Type	7	Implicit Connections with Nature, ICN	The degree of implicit connection between humans and nature.	Implicit Association Test, IAT	IAT	Single dimension	IAT	Schultz et al., 2004
	8	Connectivity with Nature, CWN	The perceived identity of humans with nature, the individual's perceived commonality with the natural environment. Represents the extent to which individuals incorporate nature into their selves and the extent to which people see themselves as members of nature.	Connectivity with Nature Scale, CWNS	4 items, 5-point scoring, and 1 graphical multiple choice item	Single dimension	Self-report	Dutcher et al., 2007
	9	Disposition to Connect with Nature, DCN	The individual's attitude towards nature includes the individual's activities related to nature and their evaluation of nature.	Disposition to Connect with Nature Scale, DCN	Rating 50 behaviors, 5-point scoring	Single dimension	Self-report	Brugger et al., 2011

Continued

The type of Nature Relatedness	Serial number	Noun	Concept	The name of the measuring tool	Number of items and scoring	Dimensions of measurement	Method of measurement	Author and year
Nature Relatedness of Multidimensional Relationship Type	10	Environmental Identity, EID	The extent to which the natural environment plays an important role in self-definition. Environmental identity includes emotional connection and identification with nature, as well as approval of policies to protect the environment, and the extent to which people interact with nature.	Environmental Identity Scale, EID	28 items, 5-point scoring	Three dimensions	Self-report	Clayton & Opotow, 2003
	11	Nature Relatedness, NR	The level of an individual's cognitive, emotional and experiential connection with nature includes identification with nature, nature-related world view, familiarity with nature, comfort in nature, and how much he or she is willing to be in nature.	Nature Relatedness Scale, NRS	21 items, 5-point scoring	Three dimensions	Self-report	Nisbet et al., 2009
	12	Nature Relatedness, NR-6		NRS-6	6 items, 5-point scoring	Two dimensions	Self-report	Nisbet & Zelenski, 2013
	13	Emotional Connection to Nature (ECN)	Assess attitudes and willingness to protect nature.	Emotional Connection to Nature Scale, ECNS	20 items, 5-point scoring	Three dimensions	Self-report	Silvas & Daniel, 2013

Table 2. 4 provides a summary and description of different types of measurements for Nature Relatedness and their characteristics. Based on the information organized in the table, the following aspects can be analyzed and summarized as follows:

1. Nature Relatedness Types

(1) Emotional Type: Measures emotional affinity, connectedness, love, care, and empathy towards nature. (2) Cognitive Type: Measures the inclusion of nature in self-concept, implicit connections, connectivity, and disposition to connect with nature. (3) Multidimensional Relationship Type: Measures environmental identity and Nature Relatedness across cognitive, emotional, and experiential dimensions.

2. Measuring Tools

(1) Each Nature Relatedness type has specific scales to measure its dimensions, such as Emotional Affinity toward Nature Scale, Connectedness to Nature Scale, Love and Care for Nature Scale, etc. (2) The number of items, scoring methods (e.g., 5-point or 7-point scoring), and dimensions vary across different scales.

3. Method of Measurement

(1) Self-report: Most measures rely on individuals' self-assessment through questionnaires. (2) Implicit Association Test (IAT): Measures implicit connections with nature. (3) Rating of Behaviors: Evaluates individuals' attitudes and activities related to nature.

4. Dimensions of Measurement

(1) Single dimension: Some measures focus on one specific dimension, such as emotional affinity or inclusion of nature in self. (2) Two dimensions:

Certain measures, like Commitment to Nature Scale, assess psychological attachment and value orientation as separate dimensions. (3) Three dimensions: Measures like Environmental Identity Scale and Nature Relatedness Scale assess cognitive, emotional, and experiential connections with nature.

In summary, the Nature Relatedness measures capture individuals' emotional, cognitive, and multidimensional relationships with nature. The scales vary in terms of their focus, dimensions, scoring methods, and the nature-related aspects they assess. These measures provide valuable tools for assessing individuals' affinity, connectedness, and identity with nature, contributing to the understanding of human-nature relationships.

2. 3. 3   Previous Research on Instruments for Assessing Trait Mindfulness

It can be seen that although mindfulness has widely accepted operational definitions, it is still a concept composed of multiple elements. Therefore, there is a rich variety of measurement tools for mindfulness. In existing research on mindfulness, self-report questionnaires or objective measurements of individual physiological indicators are mostly used to measure mindfulness.

The Mindfulness Attention Awareness Scale (MAAS) is one of the most commonly used scales in current research, developed by Brown and Ryan (2003). The scale consists of 15 items, scored on a 6-point Likert Scale. The project rating ranges from 1 (almost always) to 6 (almost never) , and a higher total score reflects a higher level of mindfulness. However, due to its single dimension, it only focuses on attention and awareness, and lacks attention to other key elements of mindfulness.

The Toronto Mindfulness Scale (TMS) is also a measuring tool, consisting of 13 items, divided into two dimensions of curiosity and decentering (Lau et al., 2006). Curiosity refers to the degree of openness to internal and external stimuli, and decentering refers to an individual's ability to perceive their experiences from a broader perspective. However, this scale mainly measures an individual's mindfulness state at the moment and is not suitable for groups that require sustained participation in mindfulness training (Yang, 2022).

Among many measurement tools, the Five Facet Mindfulness Questionnaire (FFMQ) is relatively more commonly used for measuring Trait Mindfulness (Carpenter et al., 2019; Truong et al., 2020). It is developed based on existing questionnaire items and comprises five dimensions: observing, describing, acting with awareness, non-judging, and non-reactivity. The scale consists of 39 items, and there is also a shorter version containing 24 items (Baer et al., 2008). Deng has revised the Chinese version, and the fit of each dimension with the original English version of the questionnaire is good, and it has been widely used by domestic researchers in China (Deng, 2009; He & Lian, 2018; Zhong et al., 2015). Therefore, this study selects this scale as the measuring tool for measuring university students' Trait Mindfulness.

2.4   Previous Research on Character Strengths, Nature Relatedness and Trait Mindfulness

2.4.1   Previous Research on Character Strengths

2.4.1.1   Research on Character Strengths in Western Countries

1. The Beneficial Results of Character Strengths

Many scholars have explored the relationship between Character Strengths and physical and mental health, as well as other beneficial outcomes, based on different groups of people. This section briefly summarizes these positive outcomes from two perspectives: individuals and organizations.

From an individual perspective, Character Strengths play a particularly important role in positively affecting an individual's subjective experience (life satisfaction, sense of meaning, happiness. Park et al. (2004) found that Character Strengths such as hope, enthusiasm, gratitude, contribute to enhancing life satisfaction, and a sense of humor is closely related to life meaning, while curiosity and perseverance are significantly related to life engagement. An empirical study of adolescents also found that strengths such as love, honesty, and perseverance could significantly predict life satisfaction (Blanca Mena et al., 2017). At the same time, researchers found many Character Strengths were important in promoting healthy behaviors (Proyer et al., 2013). Peterson et al. (2006) analyzed a large-scale adult character strength survey and found that courage and humor can improve physical conditions such as chronic pain and obesity, while appreciation of beauty and love of learning can improve mental issues such as depression and anorexia. Harzer (2016) found that Character Strengths such as enthusiasm, hope, and curiosity were associated with environmental adaptation, self-identity, and psychological well-being, including personal growth.

From an organizational perspective, Character Strengths can also have a positive influence on the organization. For example, honesty, perseverance, and love can improve interpersonal relationships and work satisfaction, while gratitude and hope can improve the overall work environment (Lounsbury et al., 2005). Moreover, honesty, love, and courage can contribute to the development of a positive organizational culture, and overall enhance the performance of the organization (Parker & Collins, 2010). Additionally, creativity and originality can inspire innovation and improve organizational efficiency (Mumford & Gustafson, 1988).

In conclusion, Character Strengths have a wide range of positive influences on both individuals and organizations, and are worth studying and developing.

2. Factors Affecting the Development of Character Strengths

Reviewing the existing research, researchers found that most of the current research focus on Character Strengths and their positive outcomes (such as happiness, satisfaction), and few studies focus on the possible influencing factors of Character Strengths. In recent years, positive psychologists have pointed out that Character Strengths can be developed and changed within individuals. There are many factors that influence changes in personality traits, such as normative changes in genes, predictable changes in social status and roles (such as getting married and having children), and non-normative changes (such as joining the military, experiencing trauma, and other events). For example, some researchers have found that genetics and non-shared environment can affect the development of individual personality advantages (Steger & Kashdan, 2007), and certain Character Strengths such as leadership, creativity, and kindness can be genetically influenced (Johnson et al., 2004; Waller & Zavala, 1993). In addition, some research have shown that deliberate interventions that target certain personality traits can lead to beneficial personality improvements, which don't have to take years (Hudson & Fraley, 2015; Roberts et al., 2017; Yeager & Dweck, 2012). For example, individuals' humor level could be improved through short-term intervention on humor (Wellenzohn et al., 2016b). As for the density distribution model of personality psychology, Fleeson (2001) provided a powerful explanation for these results. He pointed out that there are significant and stable differences in Character Strengths between individuals.

However, within-person traits can be affected by external situations and time changes and show different degrees of Character Strengths (Blackie et al., 2014; Fleeson, 2004). As stated by this model, psychologists speculated that people have a wide range of possibilities to develop their traits, especially Character Strengths. Bright et al. (2014) also pointed out that virtue is a second nature trait that can be cultivated and acquired through one's own intentions and efforts.

2. 4. 1. 2   Research on Character Strengths Among Chinese University Students

The research on Character Strengths among Chinese university students primarily include the following aspects: measuring Character Strengths in university students, studying the levels and characteristics of Character Strengths, exploring the correlations between Character Strengths and other variables, investigating the secondary dimensions of Character Strengths, analyzing the cognition and utilization of Character Strengths, and conducting intervention studies on Character Strengths.

1. Measurement of Character Strengths Among Chinese University Students

In the context of Chinese culture, the structural validity of the Values in Action Inventory of Strengths (VIA-IS) showed inadequacies (Peterson & Seligman, 2006). To address this, Duan et al. (2012) employed a mixed-method approach to select and refine the original 240 items of the VIA-IS, resulting in the development of the Chinese Virtues Questionnaire (CVQ-96). The CVQ-96 comprises 24 categories of Character Strengths, with each strength assessed by four items, making a total of 96 items. The questionnaire retained the classification of Character Strengths from the original VIA-IS and underwent both quantitative testing and qualitative interviews, confirming its applicability to the socio-cultural context of China and its suitability for measuring Character Strengths among Chinese university students. Additionally, to address the issues of lengthy items and limited applicability of CVQ-96, Duan and Bu (2017) followed the criteria proposed by Marsh et al. (2005) to construct the Three-dimensional Inventory of Character Strengths (TICS), consisting of 15 items. The application of TICS in university students adhered to the standards of psychometric assessment.

2. The Levels and Characteristics of Character Strengths Among Chinese Students

Research conducted among Chinese university students indicates that the most commonly observed Character Strengths are authenticity, kindness, love, and fairness, while creativity, perspective, bravery, social intelligence, and modesty are the least common (Zhang, 2009). Another study found that the top five Character Strengths are love, fairness, gratitude, teamwork, and integrity, while the bottom five are self-regulation, love of learning, perspective, creativity, and social intelligence (Li, 2015).

3. Related Studies on Character Strengths Among Chinese University Students

(1) Research on the Relationship Between Character Strengths and Other Variables Among Chinese University Students

Research on the relationship between Character Strengths and other variables among Chinese university students primarily focus on exploring the association between Character Strengths and subjective well-being. For instance, Li (2015) investigated the impact of Character Strengths on subjective well-being among university students, while Zhou and Liu (2011) also conducted a study on this topic. Additionally, there are other relevant studies, such as Yang (2022) exploring the influence of mindfulness on Character Strengths through exploratory and intervention research, Li (2015) conducting a survey on the relationship between Character Strengths and psychological well-being among university students, Cao (2015) examining the relationship between future self-continuity, Character Strengths, and health behaviors among university students, and Ai et al. (2020) studying the mediating role of Character Strengths in the relationship between minority university students' family care and life satisfaction. Furthermore, there are studies investigating the relationship between Character Strengths and factors such as parenting styles and psychological harmony among university students (Duan, 2011; Duan et al. , 2012).

(2) Research on the Secondary Dimensions of Character Strengths Among Chinese University Students

There are also studies that do not focus on the overall level of Character Strengths but instead investigate the secondary dimensions of Character Strengths, primarily concentrating on dimensions such as gratitude and hope. Regarding research on gratitude, Cai and Zheng (2014) studied the psychological mechanisms of gratitude, Zuo et al. (2019) explored the relationship between gratitude and psychological well-being, Liao et al. (2015) investigated the association between gratitude and subjective well-being, and Li (2016) examined the impact of gratitude on negative life events and the sense of meaning in life among university students, along with the mediating effects involved. As for research on the character strength of hope, Peng and Hao (2020) investigated the influence of hope on university students' attitudes towards professional psychological help, Li (2019) studied the intervention effect of hope-based group psychological counseling on exam anxiety among university students, Guo (2018) explored the state of hope and its influencing factors among university students.

4. Cognitive and Utilization of Character Strengths

Researchers have combined the cognitive and utilization aspects of Character Strengths into a single ability called " strengths awareness and application." In intervention studies, participants were first assisted in enhancing their awareness of their own Character Strengths and then encouraged to apply these strengths in their daily lives. Research indicated that both aspects of intervention contribute to promoting the well-being of first-year university students and reducing negative emotions (Duan et al. , 2012).

Moreover, some researchers suggested that the cognitive awareness and utilization of Character Strengths play a mediating role in the relationship between mindfulness and Character Strengths (Yang, 2022).

5. Intervention Studies on Character Strengths

Duan (2012) conducted a longitudinal intervention experiment based on Character Strengths to enhance the well-being of university students. Meanwhile, Yang (2022) employed two intervention models, namely, the Mindfulness-Based Strengths Practice (MBSP) and the traditional Character Strengths Intervention (CSI), to intervene in university students' Character Strengths. During the intervention process, participants were assisted in recognizing and becoming aware of their own Character Strengths, and they were encouraged to apply these strengths in their daily lives. The research findings demonstrated that both intervention approaches had positive effects on the well-being of first-year university students and also helped alleviate negative emotions (Yang, 2022).

2.4.1.3 Research on Character Strengths Among Malaysian University Students

1. Overview of Research on Character Strengths of Asian College Students

Most of the research on Character Strengths of college students has been conducted on Western samples (Chui, 2017). However, there have been studies focusing on college student samples from other Asian countries, including China, Singapore (Chou et al., 2021), Indonesia (Listiyandini & Akmal, 2017), Pakistan (M. N. Kalyar & H. Kalyar, 2018), and Thailand (Pimthong, 2015). Nevertheless, direct research on Character Strengths of college students in Malaysia is relatively scarce. Existing studies primarily involved comparative research on Character Strengths between college students in Malaysia and Thailand, as well as investigations into the Character Strengths of managerial staff and teachers among Malaysian college students, and the examination of personality traits of college students in Malaysia.

Chou et al. (2021) conducted a study on a sample of 231 Singaporean university students and revised the 240-item Values in Action Inventory of Strengths (VIA-IS) developed by Peterson and Seligman (2004). They created a 24-item Values in Action Semantic Differential Scales (VIA-SDS) and conducted a psychometric test, providing support for the effectiveness of VIA-SDS as a concise clinical assessment tool for evaluating Character Strengths among clinical doctors and researchers in Singapore.

Listiyandini and Akmal (2017) examined resilience and Character Strengths among Indonesian university students. M. N. Kalyar and H. Kalyar (2018) investigated the driving factors of creativity among Pakistani college students and explored the relationship between wisdom Character Strengths and stress. The study conducted by Cornet (2019) in Cambodia indicated that Character Strengths among Cambodian university students were mainly reflected in traits such as honesty, kindness, fairness, teamwork, and leadership.

Furthermore, hope and gratitude have shown significant advantages in reducing students' psychological distress, indicating the need for corresponding interventions. Pimthong (2015) conducted a survey on 360 Malaysian undergraduate students and 364 Thai undergraduate students, examining and comparing the structural equation model of psychological and social factors related to excessive consumption behavior. The study revealed that Malaysian students scored higher than Thai students in terms of Character Strengths and other related factors.

2. Study on Character Strengths Among Malaysian University Faculty and Administrators

In Malaysian universities, while there is limited direct research on

Character Strengths among university students, the focus has been on Character Strengths among university administrators and faculty members. Yin and Majid (2018) investigated the Character Strengths of Malaysian teachers and explored the application of these strengths in positive education. Nawi et al. (2015) studied the Big Five Personality Traits and their impact on emotional intelligence among personnel in Malaysian public schools. Chui (2017) emphasized the significance of conducting research on Character Strengths in samples like Malaysia, where such studies were not commonly explored. By reviewing the VIA classification of Character Strengths and their relationship with positive outcomes, it was suggested that Character Strengths typically enhance life satisfaction, flourishing, and leadership abilities. Furthermore, Character Strengths have been found to have significant associations with stress coping, mastery of online educational systems, and recovery from addictive behaviors.

3. Indirect Research on Character Strengths Among Malaysian University Students: Studies on Personality Traits

Although direct research specifically focusing on Character Strengths among Malaysian university students is limited, researchers can draw insights from studies on their personality traits. For instance, Yong et al. (2022) conducted a systematic review on the personality traits of Malaysian university students and their influences, encompassing research published between 2013 and 2022 that used personality traits as independent variables. The study found that personality traits among Malaysian university students influenced various outcomes, such as academic performance, motivation, coping strategies, language learning, stress levels, and happiness. These outcomes may be influenced by other latent factors and mediators.

McCrae and Terracciano (2005) tested the hypothesis regarding the universality of personality traits and validated the existence of differences in personality traits among college students from Botswana, Malaysia, and South Korea. Karim et al. (2009) explored the relationship between internet ethics and the Big Five Personality Traits among college students. The results indicated significant negative correlations between certain personality traits, such as agreeableness, conscientiousness, and emotional stability, and unethical internet behaviors among college students. Abdollahi et al. (2022) found that courage acted as a mediating factor between personality traits and social anxiety among a large group of Malaysian undergraduate students. Pei-Lee et al. (2011) discussed whether the Big Five Personality Traits of Malaysian university students influenced knowledge-sharing behavior, while Bazkiaei et al. (2020) concluded that undergraduate students from public universities scored higher in extraversion and lower in neuroticism. These findings suggested the potential for interventions targeting personality traits at the university level, which could be of significant importance for educators and practitioners.

Moreover, Mustapha and Hyland (2017) investigated the relationship between personality traits and the importance of values among students in Malaysian higher education. The results indicated positive correlations between agreeableness and conscientiousness with conservative values and self-transcendence values, while openness showed negative correlations with these two types of values. Emotional stability displayed negative correlations with self-transcendence values. Rofa (2022) conducted a study on the entrepreneurial potential and entrepreneurial personality traits of Malaysian vocational college students, examining the moderating effect of entrepreneurial mentors. Adawiyah (2023) researched the relationship between smartphone addiction, personality traits, and internet loafing behavior among Malaysian university students. Mey et al. (2014) employed quantitative research methods to analyze and monitor the personality traits of graduate and undergraduate students in a research-oriented Malaysian university. They utilized the Behavioral Management Information System (BeMIS) online assessment tool to depict the personality traits of these individuals and tracked the positive changes in their preferred traits during the rapid institutional transformation process. The researchers emphasized the significance of monitoring students' psychological well-being through changes in their personality traits during the transformation process of Malaysian research-oriented universities, to facilitate positive interventions and help students cope with the demands of learning and research.

2.4.2   Previous Research on Nature Relatedness

Research on Nature Relatedness span across various regions. In Western countries, studies primarily focus on the role of Nature Relatedness in improving cognitive functions, relieving psychological symptoms, and promoting behavioral control. In China, there is a lack of direct research on Nature Relatedness, with studies often substituting this with research in the field of Nature Connectedness. Notably, substantial progress has been made in the measurement, correlation, and functional intervention research on Nature Connectedness among university students. In Malaysia, there is a lack of direct studies on Nature Relatedness, so the scope has been expanded to include Asia. Research on Nature Connectedness among Asian and Malaysian university students, as well as studies by Malaysian researchers on children's Nature Connectedness, have been reviewed.

2.4.2.1   Research on Nature Relatedness in Western Countries

Multiple empirical studies have shown a significant correlation between Nature Relatedness and happiness. Research had found that the closer individuals are to nature, the more likely they are to engage with nature and thus receive positive psychological experiences and increase their happiness. For example, researchers used multiple scales of Nature Relatedness, and found a significant correlation between Nature Relatedness and happiness when measuring Canadian university students (Howell et al., 2011). Nisbet et al.

(2009) found that the relationship between Nature Relatedness and happiness was significant in university students from both countries and business samples and that environmental education can change people's Nature Relatedness and enhance individual vitality. Li (2016) conducted a survey based on a sample of Chinese college students, which further confirmed that Connectedness to Nature were significantly related to happiness among Chinese college students. In addition, based on the meta-analysis of 30 research samples and 8,523 subjects, researchers found that there was a significantly positive correlation between nature connectedness and happiness, and the correlation coefficient was 0.19, indicating that nature connectedness and happiness were indeed correlated (Capaldi et al., 2014).

The relationship between Nature Relatedness and human happiness is mainly reflected in the positive effects of natural elements on human physical and mental functions: natural elements have positive effects on improving individual cognitive functions, relieving psychological symptoms, and promoting behavior control, details are as follows:

1. Improving Cognitive Functions

Natural elements help individuals recover attention functions. In the study by Berto (2005), the participants first completed a series of tasks that required sustained attention (SART task), then they were asked to view either restorative natural pictures (such as green plants) or non-restorative artificial pictures (such as cars), and then performed the sustained attention task test again. Compared to the participants who viewed non-restorative pictures, the participants who viewed restorative pictures showed a significant improvement in reaction time and accuracy in the SART task. The researchers further confirmed that walking in parks and viewing natural pictures can improve an individual's cognitive performance (digit span task and attention recovery). In addition to natural elements having the ability to restore attention, research had also found that natural associations can improve creativity and memory functions (Berman et al., 2008). Leong et al.'s (2014) research revealed a significant correlation between individuals' natural associations and their cognitive styles. Atchley et al.'s (2012) experimental study confirmed that people had better creative performance in natural environments. Holden and Mercer (2014) compared the effects of listening to lectures in environments that were embedded with a lot of natural elements and artificial elements. They found that students in the natural environment group had better learning outcomes in the lecture, indicating that natural elements helped improve memory functions.

2. Relieving Psychological Symptoms

Nature is referred to as a natural and side-effect-free method of treating psychological symptoms, and has a unique effect in reducing stress and improving physical and mental indicators. For example, green spaces near living environments can effectively relieve the stress of residents and promote physical and mental health (Van Den Berg et al., 2010; White et al., 2013). Thompson's analysis revealed a significant relationship between the green plant coverage of residents' actual living environment and the cortisol content in their saliva. By examining the green plant coverage of residents' actual living environment and using cortisol content from their saliva as a stress indicator, Thompson (2012) found compelling evidence of this association. Ulrich et al. (1991) found that the subjects exposed to natural environments recovered from stress faster and more completely than those exposed to artificial environments. They conduct a study where 120 subjects first watch a movie that induces stress, and then watch six different videos of either natural or artificial environments. The researchers analyzed the self-reported emotional state and physiological stress indicators such as heart rate, blood pressure, muscle tension, skin electrical conductivity and pulse.

Further studies by Hartig et al. (2003) confirmed that the natural elements in protected areas of wild flora and fauna could significantly reduce blood pressure, improve attention, increase positive emotions, and reduce negative emotions. These above studies provided evidence of the positive influence of visual natural elements on human physical and mental health, and the researchers also explored the influence of natural auditory information on humans. For example, experiments have shown that natural sounds promote the recovery of the sympathetic nervous system excited by psychological stress, and natural sounds (auditory) help with emotional recovery (Alvarsson et al. , 2010; Benfield et al. 2014).

Additionally, Bratman et al. (2012) found that walking in natural environments improved cognitive and emotional functions in individuals with depression. They suggested the integration of nature into depression treatment methods. In comparison to artificial environments, individuals report reduced rumination after walking in natural environments for an hour and a half. Moreover, there is a decrease in activity in the prefrontal cortex, which is closely associated with rumination (Bratman et al. , 2015). People who have more contact with natural environments have higher natural associations and less unnecessary anxiety (Martyn & Brymer, 2016). The field of psychology is gradually recognizing the healing effects of nature in alleviating physical and mental symptoms. Clinical psychologists are increasingly applying nature-based psychological treatment methods, such as nature-oriented therapy, gardening therapy, and adventure therapy, in clinical practice (Burns, 1999; Clatworthy et al. , 2013; Bowen et al. , 2016).

3. Promoting Behavioral Control

The earliest origins of research on Nature Relatedness come from environmental protection. People who view themselves as one with nature are more likely to protect the environment. Many researchers studying Nature

Relatedness measured the relationship between Nature Relatedness and environmental attitudes and behaviors. Various Nature Relatedness indices and pro-environmental attitude and behavior scales are significantly related (Mayer & Frantz, 2004; Nisbet et al., 2009). Contact with the environment (environmental education, tourism) can improve an individual's nature connectedness, thereby promoting more pro-environmental behavior. Even mindfulness exercises imagining being in a green environment can help individuals enhance their Nature Relatedness and increase their pro-environmental behavior tendencies (Barbaro & Pickett, 2016). Environmental behavior is inherently pro-social, and Nature Relatedness can also promote pro-social behavior. Experiments have shown that when people immerse themselves in nature, they behave more generously and are more concerned with others (Weinstein et al., 2009).

Additionally, researchers had demonstrated that the natural environment has the potential to reduce impulsiveness (Berry et al., 2014) and improve self-control abilities (Taylor et al., 2002). For example, a study by Kuo and Taylor (2004) found that natural elements could reduce the symptoms of Attention Deficit Hyperactivity Disorder (ADHD) in children. When people are exposed to the natural environment, they can better control their unreasonable impulsive behavior and emotions, and increase their preference for social value (Joye & Bolderdijk, 2014). The research by Berry et al. (2014) indicated that having subjects observe natural pictures could reduce impulsive behavior decisions: university students were randomly divided into three groups, observing natural pictures (such as forests), artificial pictures (such as buildings), and geometric shapes (such as triangles), and then were asked to complete a delay discount task based on hypothetical monetary stimulation, for example, choosing to receive 10 dollars now or 100 dollars in a week. The results showed that the number of choices made by subjects who observed natural pictures was higher than the other two groups, indicating less impulsive decision-making.

Nature Relatedness also had the following functions: communities that live in environments rich in natural elements had lower crime rates (Kuo & Sullivan, 2001), and perhaps people who were exposed to a rich natural environment were more willing to cooperate rather than compete (Zelenski et al., 2015). Viewing natural images can effectively reduce an individual's aggressiveness (Poon et al., 2016).

4. Nature Connection Intervention

The existing research has demonstrated the significant role of Nature Relatedness in enhancing physical and mental health, focusing on three aspects: improving cognitive functions, relieving psychological symptoms, and promoting behavioral control. It is noteworthy that, with the development of positive psychology theory, scholars have increasingly regarded nature connection intervention as a specific form of positive psychology intervention, further exploring its application in enhancing well-being and mental health.

(1)Theoretical Background of Nature Connection Intervention

With the continuous development of positive psychology theory over the past two decades, a series of intervention methods derived from its core principles have emerged. Positive Psychology Interventions (PPI) were born in this theoretical context, serving as a concrete embodiment of transforming positive psychology theory into psychological interventions or therapeutic techniques. Positive psychology interventions refered to a series of intervention techniques and activities developed based on the fundamental principles of positive psychology, aiming to enhance individual psychological well-being (Proyer et al., 2015). Through long-term research and practice, positive psychology interventions have developed four core strategies: recognizing and utilizing positive traits, perceiving and appreciating positive experiences, training positive thinking patterns, and establishing and maintaining positive interpersonal relationships (Duan et al., 2018). Among them, the natural environment, as an important part of human life, had been shown to have a significant impact on individuals' positive experiences. For example, pleasant climates can enhance mood and broaden cognition (Keller et al., 2005), and connection with nature helps promote overall well-being in physical, mental, and spiritual aspects. Research showed that nature was not only an important source of happiness but also helped individuals restore attention and alleviate stress (Capaldi et al., 2015). Therefore, nature connection intervention is considered an important component of positive psychology interventions, serving as an effective pathway to promote mental health by enhancing individuals' interaction with nature.

(2) Strategies of Nature Connection Intervention

As a form of positive psychology intervention, nature connection intervention mainly aims at enhancing individuals' awareness of the benefits of nature and improve their nature connection level, thereby promoting happiness and environmental protection behaviors. The relevant intervention strategies mainly include the following three types:

Environmental Education Intervention Strategy is typically initiated by government agencies or social organizations, encouraging individuals to immerse themselves in natural environments and realize the benefits of nature through firsthand experience, thereby enhancing their nature connection and promoting environmental protection behaviors. For example, environmental education aimed at youth has been shown to effectively improve their environmental knowledge, emotional connection to nature, and environmental consciousness (Erdogan, 2015). Cognitive Intervention Strategy starts by changing people's understanding of the "human-nature relationship" and correcting their erroneous cognitive patterns about nature (Wang et al., 2016). Methods include mindfulness practices and anthropomorphized environmental campaigns, aiming at reshaping individuals' cognition and emotions regarding nature (Tam et al., 2013). Experiential Intervention Strategy emphasizes direct interaction between humans and nature. Through outdoor activities, individuals immerse themselves in natural environments to experience the positive psychological effects brought by nature (Nisbet et al., 2009; Mayer et al., 2009). This immersive natural experience not only enhances individual happiness but also effectively strengthens their emotional connection to nature (Nisbet, 2014).

The empirical research above showed that Nature Relatedness had a positive impact on both physical and mental health. The more individuals were exposed to the natural environment, the better their physical and mental health were, and the more rational their behavior became. As the material foundation for human survival, the natural environment provides all the necessary resources for life and development. Nature connection intervention is proposed within this theoretical framework, emphasizing the improvement of individuals' well-being by strengthening their connection to nature. The strategies of nature connection intervention mainly include environmental education, cognitive interventions, and experiential interventions. These strategies aim at increasing individuals' awareness of the benefits of nature, promoting direct contact with nature, and ultimately improving their physical and mental health. Individuals who maintain a strong connection to nature can experience a wide range of positive physical and mental benefits, which is one of the reasons why Nature Relatedness is significantly correlated with positive psychological qualities.

2. 4. 2. 2   Research on Nature Relatedness Among Chinese University Students

Research on the Nature Connectedness of Chinese university students can be divided into three aspects: measurement research on the Nature Connectedness of Chinese university students, correlational research on Nature Connectedness, and functional and intervention research on Nature Connectedness.

1. Measurement Research on the Nature Connectedness of Chinese University Students

Li (2016) revised the Connectedness to Nature Scale (Mayer & Frantz, 2004) to create a Chinese version and validated its validity and reliability for measuring the Nature Connectedness of Chinese university students. The scale consists of 14 items and adopts a unidimensional structure to measure the extent to which individuals feel integrated with nature. The Chinese version of the scale also demonstrated good reliability and validity, making it suitable for evaluating the nature connectedness of Chinese university students. Higher scores indicate a stronger sense of connection to nature.

2. Correlational Research on the Nature Connectedness of Chinese University Students

Researchers explored the associations between Nature Connectedness and various aspects of university students, including their happiness, self-esteem, depressive emotions, life satisfaction, pro-environmental behaviors, body appreciation, and sense of life meaning. For instance, Wang et al. (2022) found that nature connectedness played a mediating role in the relationship between envy on social media and life meaning. Conversely, C. Y. Wang and C. Z. Wang (2018) found a correlation between nature connectedness and self-esteem and depressive emotions. Gan et al. (2023) demonstrated that mindfulness influenced university students' life satisfaction, with Nature Connectedness serving as a mediator. Chen and Huang (2022) investigated the influence of awe emotions on pro-environmental behavior in university students, and found that nature connectedness mediated this relationship, with environmental values acting as a moderator. Wang et al. (2020) explored the relationship between nature connectedness and life meaning experience in university students, finding that nature appreciation played a mediating role. Li (2016) conducted a study with Chinese university students and found that mindfulness level acted as a mediator between trait nature connectedness and happiness. Li (2016) conducted a study with Chinese university students and found that mindfulness mediated the relationship between trait nature connectedness and happiness. The results further confirmed that connectedness to nature was significantly associated with happiness among Chinese college students.

3. Functional and Intervention Research on the Nature Connectedness Among Chinese University Students

Some researchers focused on how intervention measures could influence the nature connectedness of university students. Yang et al. (2017) conducted a review of the concept and measurement of nature connectedness, and further reviewed the functions and interventions related to nature connectedness. Passmore et al. (2022) conducted a study titled "An extended replication study of the well-being intervention, the noticing nature intervention (NNI)," involving 173 Chinese university undergraduates in a 2-week nature intervention experiment. The results showed that the increase in happiness and decrease in distress among the participants were solely due to their attention to the nature they encountered in their daily lives. This study provided further empirical support for the effectiveness of the noticing nature intervention as a well-being intervention. In addition, Li et al. (2018) also conducted a review of the functions and promotion of nature connectedness.

2.4.2.3 Research on Nature Relatedness Among Malaysian University Students

1. Study on the Natural Connectedness of Asian University Students

Kleespies and Dierkes (2023) conducted an empirical study across 41 countries, investigating the natural connectedness of university students in the environmental field. The study covered regions such as South Asia (e.g., India or Pakistan), East Asia (China or Japan), Southeast Asia (Thailand or Singapore), and West Asia (e.g., Saudi Arabia).

Prasetyo et al. (2018) conducted a survey in Indonesia through the UI GreenMetric, an organization that assesses current environmental conditions and policies of universities, targeting highly-ranked university students. The results indicated that environmental conditions, such as the "greenness" of the campus, did not predict students' connectedness to nature. However, the study found that students from higher-ranked green campuses held stronger nature-related perspectives compared to those from medium- and lower-ranked green campuses.

2. Study on the Natural Connectedness of Malaysia University Students

Jing (2018) adapted Nisbet's (2009) Nature Connectedness Scale and Dunlap et al.'s (2000) New Environmental Paradigm Scale (NEPS) to conduct a survey among Malaysian Chinese university students. The research aimed at exploring the natural connectedness of Malaysian Chinese youth in higher education and its influence on pro-environmental behaviors. The author hoped to promote environmental education through educational communication, extending beyond ecological tourism and natural resource management.

Roslan et al. (2022) conducted an experiment by recruiting 160 Muslim university students from the Centre of Foundation Studies for Agricultural Science, Universiti Putra Malaysia. The study revealed that Muslim students benefited significantly from zikr meditation and nature exposure, and spending time outdoors was an effective way to enhance their spiritual and ecological self-value. Sahak (2018) studied school students in Johor Bahru, Malaysia, investigating the mediating factors of spirituality between nature contact, connectedness to nature, and psychological well-being of the students.

3. Study on the Natural Connectedness of Malaysian Children

Mustapa et al. (2016) conducted a comprehensive review of the fundamental structure of children's connectedness to nature, aiming to provide a detailed description of how this connectedness is constructed. The review draws from existing tools designed for both adults and children to better understand the underlying constructs of nature connectedness. Additionally, they addressed key conceptual issues, including challenges in defining and measuring connectedness to nature, and explored the ongoing debate about whether this construct should be considered single-dimensional or multi-dimensional. The authors also proposed future research directions, highlighting the need for more refined instruments and a clearer theoretical framework to deepen the understanding of nature connectedness, particularly in children. However, this research was a review conducted by Malaysian researchers on children's nature connectedness, without specifying the age range of the research subjects and without conducting empirical research.

2.4.3   Previous Research on Mindfulness and Trait Mindfulness

2.4.3.1   Research on Mindfulness and Trait Mindfulness in Western Countries

For over a decade, mindfulness research has become a thriving field in Western countries. Many studies have shown that mindfulness not only has positive effects on individuals' perceptual, memory, and thinking patterns but also helps reduce stress, alleviate depression, and has significant value for emotional regulation. Additionally, many studies have shown that mindfulness can help alleviate pain in chronic patients and reduce negative behaviors such as tobacco and drug addiction (J.W. Creswell & J. D. Creswell, 2017).

However, the above studies have focused on the research of mindfulness to improve negative psychology, and only a few studies have begun to focus on the promoting effect of mindfulness on individuals' positive qualities and positive psychological functions, in order to promote people's potential, enhance individual happiness, and promote self-realization (Baer, 2015; Baer & Lykins, 2011; Ivtzan & Lomas, 2016; Malinowski, 2013). For example, Randal et al. (2015) investigated the relationship between mindfulness and self-esteem as well as the influence of mindfulness intervention (MBI) on self-esteem, and the researchers found a significant positive correlation between mindfulness and self-esteem, and most studies on mindfulness intervention (MBI) significantly increased individuals' self-esteem (Randal et al., 2015). The book, *Mindfulness and Character Strengths: A Practical Guide to Flourishing*, focuses on the relationship between mindfulness and Character Strengths, discusses how to combine the two to help individuals achieve psychological and emotional prosperity, and provides practical techniques and tools to help people apply mindfulness and Character Strengths to improve their quality of life and happiness (Niemiec, 2013).

Some researchers have focused on Trait Mindfulness and conducted related studies. The individual inclination of mindfulness exists as a trait tendency. Trait Mindfulness is positively correlated with variables such as self-esteem, mental health, emotion regulation, and life satisfaction. It is negatively correlated with variables such as perceived life stress, negative emotions, anxiety, and depression. In the professional domain, Trait Mindfulness contributes to increased job satisfaction, performance, and interpersonal relationships, while reducing feelings of burnout and work withdrawal (Mesmer-Magnus et al., 2017). Trait Mindfulness is relatively stable, but can be improved after mindfulness intervention. During the intervention, the meditative state mindfulness trajectory predicts the change of Trait Mindfulness, which is also the process from a state to a trait (Kiken et al., 2015).

Trait Mindfulness has been found to have a positive predictive effect on positive emotions, optimism, resilience and self-efficacy (Carleton et al., 2018; Charoensukmongkol & Suthatorn, 2018). Moreover, Trait Mindfulness has been shown to positively predict certain Character Strengths such as love, kindness and compassion (Teper et al., 2013).

2.4.3.2   Research on Mindfulness and Trait Mindfulness Among Chinese University Students

Relevant research on mindfulness among Chinese university students covers the following aspects: the measurement of mindfulness among Chinese university students, studies investigating the relationship between mindfulness and various psychological factors, and research on the training and intervention of mindfulness.

1. Measurement of Mindfulness Among Chinese University Students

Deng (2009) revised the Chinese version of the Five Facet Mindfulness Questionnaire (FFMQ) developed by Baer et al. (2008), making it suitable for measuring Trait Mindfulness among Chinese university students.

2. Studies on the Relationship Between Mindfulness and Chinese University Students

Research on the relationship between mindfulness and subjective well-being is relatively extensive. Liu et al. (2015) found that mindfulness among university students influenced subjective well-being, with emotional regulation and psychological resilience acting as mediators. Liu and Tang (2019) explored the relationship between mindfulness levels and subjective well-being among university students, while Ding (2012) and Yang (2014) investigated the effects of mindfulness practices and training on mindfulness levels and subjective well-being. Studies have also revealed that mindfulness training has a positive impact on university students' life satisfaction, with the experience of nature connection serving as a mediator (Gan, 2023; Li, 2016). The relationship between mindfulness and anxiety/aggression among university students is mediated by psychological resilience (Yu et al., 2022). Duan (2016) examined the impact of individual mindfulness on psychological health, with individual strengths playing a mediating role. Yang (2022) investigated the influence of mindfulness on Character Strengths, and Xu (2020) explored the relationship between mindfulness levels, coping efficacy, stress perception, and intervention research. Chen (2018) focused on the association between university students' mindfulness and life satisfaction, finding that nature connection plays a mediating role in this relationship.

3. Training and Intervention Research on Mindfulness Among Chinese University Students

Mindfulness Training and Intervention among Chinese university students have also received considerable attention. Researchers have explored the effects of mindfulness on university students' psychological health, subjective well-being, and psychological resilience. Many studies have focused on mindfulness interventions to improve individuals' mental and physical well-being, promoting psychological health, and alleviating negative emotions such as anxiety and depression. For example, Shen et al. (2022) found that mindfulness training could improve university students' attention bias and reduce smartphone dependence. Lu et al. (2023) indicated that mindfulness training had an intervention effect on university students' social anxiety. Jia (2019), Chen (2018), Li (2016), and Cheng (2024) applied mindfulness training to address issues such as academic stress, depressive emotions, and sleep disturbances among university students. Their findings provided essential theoretical and practical support for implementing mindfulness interventions in this population.

2.4.3.3　Research on Mindfulness and Trait Mindfulness Among Malaysian University Students

Malaysian university students' mindfulness research can be categorized into the following areas: studies on the level and characteristics of mindfulness among Malaysian university students, research on related variables, and intervention studies on mindfulness.

1. Studies on the Level and Characteristics of Mindfulness Among Malaysian University Students

Ahmadi et al. (2014) conducted a study with 273 first-semester undergraduate students as participants, using the Mindfulness Attention Awareness Scale. The results showed that the average level of mindfulness among the respondents was 3.77. There was no significant correlation between mindfulness level and age, gender, religion, ethnicity, family, as well as educational background. The field of study did not have an impact on this level. There was a correlation between mindfulness level and health condition. In another study, Ahmadi (2016) investigated the level of mindfulness among university students in Malaysia, specifically focusing on students from the Universiti Teknologi Malaysia. The Mindful Attention Awareness Scale (Brown & Rayan, 2003) was utilized, and the findings revealed that the average mindfulness level among Malaysian university students was 3.77, which was lower than the general population's average score of 3.86. The study also explored the influence of mindfulness on Malaysian university students concerning faculty and demographic factors. This research investigated the relationship between mindfulness levels and demographic factors among university students in Malaysia.

2. Research on Related Variables of Mindfulness Among Malaysian University Students

Ramli et al. (2018) explored the relationship between academic stress, self-regulation, and mindfulness among Malaysian undergraduate students. The results indicated that mindfulness played a mediating role between academic stress and self-regulation in Malaysian undergraduate students. Jayaraja et al. (2017) investigated the predictive effects of mindfulness and procrastination on the psychological well-being of Malaysian university students. The study revealed significant correlations among mindfulness, procrastination, and psychological well-being in Malaysian university students. In a study by Ramli (2018), 384 undergraduate students from Klang Valley, Malaysia, were selected to investigate the influence of academic stress, self-regulation, and mindfulness. The study confirmed that mindfulness acted as a mediator between academic stress and self-regulation. Rosenstreich and Margalit (2015) selected university students from Sultan Idris Education University as participants to explore the relationship between loneliness, mindfulness, and academic achievement. The study also investigated the moderating effect of mindfulness on this relationship. Tan et al. (2021) examined the hypothetical positive relationship between mindfulness and meaning in life among undergraduate participants from Australia, Indonesia, Malaysia, as well as the potential mechanisms underlying this relationship. These findings provided evidence for the positive association between mindfulness and meaning in life across different cultural backgrounds.

3. Intervention Studies on Mindfulness Among Malaysian University Students

In intervention studies on Mindfulness among Malaysian university students, the majority of research focused on students from Malaysian medical schools. Medical students in Malaysia face significant stress (Ramli, 2018). To assist medical students in coping more effectively with stress, Keng et al. (2015) explored the impact of a brief mindfulness-based intervention on the psychological symptoms and well-being of Malaysian medical students in a controlled study. The results indicated that mindfulness played a statistically significant mediating role in the effects on psychological symptoms and well-being. The study also examined whether changes in mindfulness would affect psychological symptoms and well-being and validated whether changes in Trait Mindfulness mediated the effects of the Mindful-Gym (a mindfulness training program) on psychological symptoms and well-being. Phang et al. (2016) also selected a sample of medical students from various ethnic groups in Malaysia to validate the factor validity and psychometric properties of the Mindful Attention Awareness Scale (MAAS). They explored the effects of a brief group mindfulness-based cognitive therapy aimed at reducing stress among medical students in Malaysia, verifying the applicability of Mindfulness Intervention in Malaysia.

2.5 Previous Research on the Relationship Between Nature Relatedness and Character Strengths

2.5.1 Research on Nature Relatedness and Some Character Strengths

Most researchers focused on the positive effects of Character Strengths (such as job satisfaction), but few studies have focused on the factors that promote the change of Character Strengths (Yang, 2022). Connectedness to Nature is a hot topic in the research of environmental psychology, previous researchers studies the concept, measuring, function, intervention, and about the connectedness to nature to alleviate psychological symptoms, promoting happiness, improve cognitive function, promote the behavior control. However, there are few studies on the direct influence of connectedness to nature on Character Strengths. Several studies have found that connectedness to nature can improve some individual Character Strengths of individuals (Yang et al., 2017; Li et al., 2018; Merino et al., 2020), but some studies have found that natural bonds can enhance certain Character Strengths, as shown in Table 2.5.

Table 2.5　**Research on the Relationship Between Nature Relatedness and Some Character Strengths**

Serial number	Research viewpoints	Key words	Corresponding Character Strengths	Author and year
1	Watching videos of natural environments promoted cooperative behavior	Cooperative behavior	Cooperative	Zelenski et al., 2015
2	People are more creative in natural environments	Expression of creativity	Creativity	Atchley et al., 2012
3	Contact with nature can enhance the individual's aesthetic	Aesthetic	Appreciation of beauty	Frumkin, 2001
4	Exposure to nature also promotes people's prosocial and other-focused values, leading them to become more loving	More loving	Love	Weinstein et al., 2009
5	Contact with nature can make the relationship between community residents more harmonious	Harmonious	Social intelligence	Wakefield et al., 2007
6	The natural environment enhances self-control	Self-control	Self-regulation	Taylor et al., 2002
7	Contact with nature can also increase vitality	Vitality	Zest	Ryan et al., 2010
8	Exposure to nature improves students' academic performance and a more positive evaluation of the course	Academic performance, positive evaluation	Love of learning	Benfield et al., 2015

Continued

Serial number	Research viewpoints	Key words	Corresponding Character Strengths	Author and year
9	Contact with nature has the potential to enhance a range of positive psychological qualities or abilities such as awe, gratitude, forgiveness, responsibility, and spirituality	Gratitude, forgiveness, and other positive psychological qualities	Gratitude, forgiveness	Yang et al., 2017
10	Our results thus point to these Character Strengths (appreciation of beauty, creativity, love of learning, and zest) as the signature strengths for Nature Relatedness.	Appreciation of beauty, creativity, love of learning, and zest	Appreciation of beauty, creativity, love of learning	Merino et al., 2020

As can be seen from Table 2.5, researchers have conducted empirical studies on some Character Strengths of individuals based on Nature Relatedness, such as cooperative (Zelenski et al., 2015), creativity (Atchley et al., 2012), appreciation of beauty (Frumkin, 2001), love (Weinstein et al., 2009), social intelligence (Wakefield et al., 2007), self-regulation (Taylor et al., 2002), zest (Ryan et al., 2010), love of learning (Benfield et al., 2015). From these studies, it can be speculated that connectedness to nature may have a promoting effect on improving the overall Character Strengths. However, the existing studies are scattered and single-dimensional studies, there is currently no study that has proposed the influence of Nature Relatedness on overall Character Strengths, which is a research gap. Therefore, this study fills the gap by comprehensively verifying the influence of Nature Relatedness on Character Strengths from an overall perspective.

2.5.2   Research on Nature Relatedness and Overall Character Strengths

Currently, a study has been conducted on the relationship between Nature Relatedness and Character Strengths, rather than the impact of Nature Relatedness on overall Character Strengths. The researchers use the Values in Action Inventory of Strengths (VIA-IS) and the Nature Relatedness Scale (NRS) to assess participants' Character Strengths and level of connection to nature. The results showed that people with stronger connections to nature generally exhibited more Character Strengths, particularly intellectual strengths related to appreciation of beauty, love of learning, and curiosity. The research also explored the influence of factors such as gender, age, education, and cultural background on this relationship. This research provides new insights into understanding the connection between humans and nature, and can contribute to advancing research and practices in environmental protection and sustainable development. However, the research only examined the relationship between Nature Relatedness and Character Strengths, attempting to use Character Strengths as a predictor variable and Nature Relatedness as an outcome variable. The research design limited the ability to determine the direction and causality of the relationship between the two variables (Amparo Merino et al., 2020).

2.6   The Influence of Nature Relatedness on Character Strengths: The Mediating Effect of Trait Mindfulness

Through analyzing previous literature, this study proposed that Nature Relatedness may have a predictive influence on Character Strengths, with Trait Mindfulness potentially serving as a mediator between the two variables. The influence of Nature Relatedness on Character Strengths can be understood as a process whereby sustained connection with nature fosters positive character traits. This influence is often mediated, and in this study, researcher interpret this mediation as Nature Relatedness indirectly enhancing Character Strengths by promoting Trait Mindfulness. The relationship among these three variables is shown in Figure 2.1, with further explanation provided below.

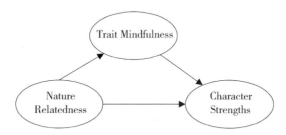

Figure 2.1   The Relationship Between the Three Variables

2.6.1   Research on the Relationship Between Nature Relatedness and Trait Mindfulness

Some researchers have explored the relationship between Nature Relatedness and mindfulness from various perspectives. For example, at the trait level, Nature Relatedness is positively correlated with Trait Mindfulness (Barbaro & Pickett, 2016). The researchers, by using two different measures of Nature Relatedness, found that they were associated with higher levels of mindfulness (Howell et al., 2011); Li (2016) found that mindfulness played a mediating role between Nature Relatedness and happiness in Chinese university students. The level of Nature Relatedness itself reflects the ability of individuals to incorporate environmental experiences into their cognition. Individuals with higher levels of Nature Relatedness are more likely to pay attention to subtle and novel changes in the natural environment, which may lead to higher levels of mindfulness. The association between Trait Mindfulness and a stronger connection to nature is reflected in curiosity, openness and acceptance of experience within mindfulness.

Some aspects of Trait Mindfulness, such as attentional abilities (Mayer et al., 2019) and interoceptive awareness (Leary et al., 2008), are related to Nature Relatedness. Researchers had found a significant correlation between mindfulness and a stronger connection to nature (Howell et al., 2011; Barbaro & Pickett, 2015). The relationship between the two variables may be that Nature Relatedness is beneficial to Trait Mindfulness.

2.6.2   Research on the Relationship Between Trait Mindfulness and Character Strengths

The reasons why mindfulness can positively predict individuals' overall level of Character Strengths are as follows:

First, early research on the relationship between mindfulness and personality traits indirectly supports this point. Researchers have found an overlap between Trait Mindfulness and the Five Factor Model (FFM) of personality, such as a meta-analysis research showing a negative correlation between Trait Mindfulness and neuroticism and a positive correlation with conscientiousness (Giluk, 2009). A cross-sectional research found that individuals with mindfulness meditation experience had higher scores in openness, lower scores in neuroticism, and higher scores in extraversion than those without meditation experience (Van Den Berg & Custers, 2011). As described by the Big Five Personality Traits, high extraversion, low neuroticism, high openness, high conscientiousness, and high agreeableness are positive personality traits that play an important role in promoting individuals' adaptive and healthy personality functions. Character Strengths represent a series of positive personality traits, so based on the above empirical research, researchers can infer that individuals with high Trait Mindfulness are likely to have a higher overall level of Character Strengths.

Second, from a theoretical perspective, there are some similarities between the concepts of mindfulness and Character Strengths. Reviewing the operational definition of mindfulness by Bishop et al. (2004), mindfulness refers to individuals' continuous awareness of their internal and external stimuli, and the ability to use mindfulness to gently bring their attention back to the present moment when interfering stimuli occur, while maintaining a curious, open, and accepting attitude towards the current experience. In this definition, researchers can see positive attitudes such as curiosity, openness, and self-control, which all belong to the 24 Character Strengths. The observational component of mindfulness also emphasizes the importance of observing and paying attention to internal and external stimuli, which is also a key aspect of Character Strengths such as appreciation of beauty. Therefore, mindfulness may promote the growth of these positive qualities. In addition, research by Ferguson showed that individuals who had received mindfulness training had higher psychological resilience when facing physical discomfort, mental symptoms, and neurological stress, and could maintain their physical and mental health to the greatest extent. Therefore, mindfulness may help to cultivate positive Character Strengths (Chapman et al., 2013; Roberts et al., 2007).

Third, in many empirical studies, numerous scholars had found that individuals who received mindfulness intervention showed varying degrees of improvement in certain Character Strengths. For example, many mindfulness meditations can promote an individual's wise mind (Linehan, 1993), and the concept of wisdom meditation had been proposed. Individuals who had received mindfulness training were more curious, creative, and insightful (Kristeller, 2003). Mindfulness-Based Stress Reduction (MBSR, Kabat-Zinn, 1990) and Mindfulness-Based Cognitive Therapy (MBCT, Segal et al., 2018), widely used today, are not created to enhance Character Strengths, but improvements in participants' Character Strengths can be observed in these programs. For example, MBSR emphasizes patience, openness, and letting go, which are closely related to Character Strengths such as self-regulation, curiosity, open-mindedness, and forgiveness. Researchers have applied MBSR to clinical patients to help them cope with chronic pain and have found that participants who underwent Mindfulness-Based Stress Reduction training demonstrated Character Strengths such as persistence, courage, and good self-regulation (Kabat-Zinn, 2003). The MBCT manual also explicitly emphasizes the enhancement of participants' love, kindness, and compassion through mindfulness courses (Segal, et al., 2018).

Fourth, experimental research on mindfulness-based interventions for Character Strengths was conducted. Based on prior findings from questionnaire surveys confirming that mindfulness positively predicts the overall level of Character Strengths, researchers further employed a randomized controlled trial design. Participants were randomly assigned to one of three groups: the Mindfulness-Based Strengths Practice Program (MBSP), the Character Strengths-Based Intervention (CSI), and a waitlist control group. The MBSP group integrated mindfulness as a core element, whereas the CSI group did not include any mindfulness component. The aim was to investigate the differential effects of incorporating mindfulness into Character Strengths interventions. Results showed that compared to the CSI group, the MBSP group achieved significantly greater improvements in the overall level of Character Strengths (Yang, 2022).

Section 2.5 discusses the relationship between Nature Relatedness and specific Character Strengths, as well as the relationship between Nature Relatedness and overall Character Strengths. Numerous studies have shown that Nature Relatedness is significantly related to Character Strengths and that Nature Relatedness is likely to have a positive predictive effect on Character Strengths. Based on the definition of the mediating effect (Wen et al., 2004), the hypothesis is proposed that Trait Mindfulness may mediate the relationship between Nature Relatedness and Character Strengths, which also represents a research gap.

2.7　Theoretical Framework

Figure 2.2 illustrates the theoretical framework of this research, which is based on the Attention Restoration Theory and the Mindful Personality Theory. The Attention Restoration Theory supports that Nature Relatedness enhances Trait Mindfulness by promoting the restoration of attention, enabling individuals to consciously focus on the present moment with openness and acceptance. Meanwhile, the Mindful Personality Theory combines aspects of mindfulness with personality traits, explaining how mindfulness strengthens positive psychological qualities, such as Character Strengths.

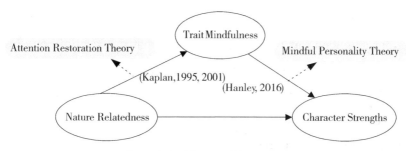

Figure 2.2　Theoretical Framework

2.7.1　Attention Restoration Theory

The theoretical framework demonstrates that Nature Relatedness promotes Trait Mindfulness and is primarily based on the Attention Restoration Theory (ART). Proposed by Kaplan (1995), this theory suggests that exposure to natural environments provides opportunities for the restoration and replenishment of attentional resources. Natural elements, tranquility, and beautiful scenery in natural environments can attract individuals' attention and help them recover from fatigue and stress (Kaplan, 1995; Kaplan, 2001). This theory suggests that daily work tasks and environmental distractions deplete an

89

individual's directed attention resources, leading to attention fatigue. Urban environments offer a "hard fascination" to people, where they relax by engaging in stimulating activities, such as some behavior of racing, and sports, etc. However, such intense stimuli only facilitate partial and superficial attention restoration. In contrast, natural environments provide a "soft fascination" that doesn't consume all cognitive resources. Along with providing aesthetic enjoyment, this soft fascination allows room for reflection and contributes to the restoration of focused attention resources (Chen, 2018).

The Attention Restoration Theory is supported by numerous empirical studies (e.g., Alvarsson et al., 2010; Berman et al., 2008; Berto, 2005; Van Den Berg et al., 2010). For instance, research has shown that individuals perform better in cognitive tasks (such as digit span tasks) after exposure to nature, whether it is real or simulated (Berman et al., 2015). Some studies have further extended this theory by suggesting that the level of connectedness to nature may be related to creative thinking (Lenog et al., 2014). Additionally, classrooms with abundant natural elements have been found to enhance students' learning outcomes during lectures compared to typical artificial environments (Holden and Mercer, 2014).

Attention is an important component of mindfulness, as Kabat-Zinn (2003) defined mindfulness as paying attention in a particular way. Bishop et al. (2004) proposed that self-regulation of attention was a crucial component of Trait Mindfulness, involving an individual's active engagement with internal and external stimuli and the ability to redirect attention when distracted. Furthermore, other researchers had confirmed aspects of mindfulness such as attentional abilities (Mayer et al., 2009) and inner awareness (Leary et al., 2008) were related to Nature Relatedness.

Based on these studies, it can be inferred that Nature Relatedness can enhance levels of attention, thus promoting Trait Mindfulness. This provides indirect evidence for the facilitative role of Nature Relatedness in Trait

Mindfulness.

Other studies serve as direct evidence for the enhancement of Mindfulness through Nature Relatedness, as research has found a significant correlation between mindfulness and stronger Nature Relatedness (Howell et al., 2011; Barbaro & Pickett, 2016). Nature Relatedness, by increasing individual's sense of relatedness to themselves and the world, redirects their focus towards the natural world, enhancing present-moment experiences and promoting higher levels of mindfulness. Nature Relatedness enriches individuals' experiences and vitality, and an enhanced connection to nature enables individuals to consciously attend to the present moment with openness and acceptance, bringing attention and awareness to their relationship with the natural world, thereby elevating levels of mindfulness (Li, 2009). Nature Relatedness has the potential to be beneficial for mindfulness (Howell et al., 2011). In summary, the relationship between humans and nature can facilitate attention restoration, and this restoration of attentional resources contributes to the cultivation and support of Trait Mindfulness.

2.7.2 Mindful Personality Theory

From the theoretical framework diagram, it can be seen that the theoretical foundation for the association between Trait Mindfulness and Character Strengths is derived from the Mindful Personality Theory (Hanley, 2016). This theory builds upon the Five Factor Model (FFM) and integrates it with the five aspects of Mindfulness. As stated by Baer et al. (2006), the five aspects of Mindfulness include observing, describing, acting with awareness, non-judging, and non-reactivity to inner experiences. The FFM proposed by John, Naumann, and Soto encompasses neuroticism, extraversion, openness, agreeableness, and conscientiousness, which is considered the most widely researched personality conceptual model (John et al., 2008). Hanley's (2016) "Mindful Personality Theory" demonstrates the association between Trait Mindfulness and Personality, but it does not include neuroticism. Extraversion, openness, agreeableness, and conscientiousness are considered Character Strengths. This theory serves as one of the foundational frameworks for this study.

There are additional studies that indirectly support the relationship between Mindfulness and Personality Traits. Some researchers have found overlaps between Trait Mindfulness and the Five Factor Model of Personality (McCrae & Costa, 1987). For example, a meta-analysis study indicated a negative correlation between Trait Mindfulness and neuroticism, and a positive correlation with conscientiousness (Giluk, 2009). A cross-sectional study by Van Den Hurk et al. (2011) found that individuals with mindfulness meditation experience had higher scores in openness, lower scores in neuroticism, and higher scores in extraversion compared to those without meditation experience. Based on the Five Factor Model of Personality, high extraversion, low neuroticism, high openness, high conscientiousness, and high agreeableness are considered positive personality traits that contribute to adaptive and healthy psychological functioning, representing a range of positive Character Strengths (Yang, 2020). Therefore, based on the aforementioned empirical research, it can be inferred that individuals with high Trait Mindfulness are likely to have higher overall levels of Character Strengths.

2.8   Conclusion

In conclusion, Character Strengths can be cultivated, and studying the influencing factors and mechanisms of Character Strengths is of great value for Character Strengths education. Therefore, the objective of this research is to investigate the influence of Nature Relatedness on Character Strengths among Chinese and Malaysian university students. Furthermore, this research aims at exploring the mediating effect of Trait Mindfulness on this relationship and to provide a theoretical foundation for promoting Character Strengths among Chinese and Malaysian university students.

CHAPTER 3   METHODOLOGY

3.1   Introduction

This research aims at examining the impact of Nature Connectedness on Character Strengths among Chinese and Malaysian university students, and analyzing and confirming the mediating role of Trait Mindfulness between Nature Relatedness and Character Strengths. The study employs a quantitative approach, with primary data derived from a convenient sample of Chinese and Malaysian university students. The findings were quantified, and the relationship between the independent and dependent variable was assessed. Consistent with educational research, the independent variable influenced the dependent variable, and the mediator variable affected the relationship between them (Mills & Gay, 2019).

Drawing from the literature review, Nature Relatedness serves as the independent variable, represented by the total scores of NR-self, NR-perspective, and NR-experience (Nisbet et al., 2009). Character Strengths are the dependent variable, encompassing the total scores of caring, inquisitiveness, and self-control (Duan & Bu, 2017). Trait Mindfulness acts as the mediating variable in this research, measured by the combined scores of five dimensions: observing, describing, acting with awareness, non-judging, and non-reactivity (Baer et al., 2006). In this chapter, the research methodology includes an introduction, research design, sampling procedure, research procedure, research instruments, pilot study, data collection, data analysis, and conclusion.

3.2   Research Design

This research consists of four research stages, primarily utilizing questionnaire survey methods and statistical analysis to explore the research topic. The first stage involves revising the Chinese version of the Nature Relatedness Scale to ensure it meets the measurement criteria and answering research question RQ1. The second stage entails conducting a questionnaire survey to investigate the current status of variables X, Y, and M, analyzing their differences, and addressing research questions RQ2a and RQ2b. The third stage involves analyzing the causal relationship between variables X and Y and answering research questions RQ3a and RQ3b. The fourth stage focuses on examining the mediating relationship of variable M between X and Y and answering research questions RQ4a and RQ4b. The specific nouns corresponding to each variable are as follows: X = Nature Relatedness, Y = Character Strengths, M = Trait Mindfulness. The research framework and methodology are depicted in Figure 3.1.

Study 1 involved the revision of the Chinese version of the Nature Relatedness Scale. This process was conducted under the guidance of the original scale author. It was include translation, back-translation, item analysis, exploratory factor analysis, confirmatory factor analysis, and assessments of validity and reliability to ensure the feasibility of the Chinese version of the scale. A total of 692 valid samples were collected from three Chinese universities. 346 data points were utilized for item analysis and exploratory factor analysis, while another 346 data points were used for confirmatory factor analysis of the Chinese version of the scale, as well as assessments of validity and reliability to ensure the feasibility of the Chinese version of the scale.

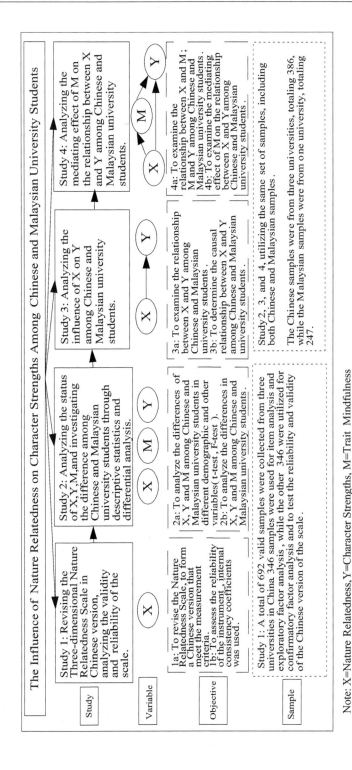

Figure 3.1 Research Design (Quantitative Research)

Note: X=Nature Relatedness, Y=Character Strengths, M=Trait Mindfulness

95

Study 2 used three survey questionnaires, and the questionnaire data was collected from Chinese and Malaysian university students and then analyzed. The Nature Relatedness Scale was used to measure the Nature Relatedness of university students, the Five Facet Mindfulness Questionnaire—Short Form was used to measure the Trait Mindfulness of university students, and the Three-dimensional Inventory of Character Strengths was used to measure Character Strengths of university students. The purpose of the questionnaire study was to understand the current characteristics of the three variables and different findings on demographic variables. It is worth noting that, except for the Nature Relatedness Scale, the other three scales have standardized Chinese revised versions, so English and Chinese questionnaires can be collected equitably, while the standardization of the Chinese version of the Nature Relatedness Scale was conducted in the Study 1.

Study 3 aimed at examining the relationship between Nature Relatedness and Character Strengths and determining whether Nature Relatedness positively predicts Character Strengths.

Study 4 aimed at exploring the mediating effect of Trait Mindfulness on the relationship between Nature Relatedness and Character Strengths.

Studies 2, 3, and 4 utilized the same set of samples, which included both Chinese and Malaysian participants. The Chinese samples were from three universities, totaling 386, while the Malaysian samples were from one university, totaling 247.

3.3   Sampling Procedure

3.3.1   Population

Population is a general term that refers to a larger group from which a sample is selected or to which researchers intend to generalize their findings

(Creswell, 2018; Mills & Gay, 2019). It is a collective term for people, events, or records, including selected data, that can respond to survey questionnaires (Cooper & Schindler, 2008). Additionally, Creswell (2014) explained that a population is a group of people with similar characteristics. The population can be large or small. Researchers must determine which group they wish to include in their research. Quantitative researchers select samples from available individual lists.

3.3.1.1 Target and Reference Population of This Research

Target population or sampling frame is a group of people or a group of organizations with some general defining characteristics that researchers can recognize (Creswell & Poth, 2016). In this research, the population comprises university students in China and Malaysia. The first step is to analyze and compare the population sizes, the number of public universities, and the number of university students in each country. Based on this analysis and the literature review, an estimation of the required sample size can then be made.

In accordance with the data from the National Bureau of Statistics of China, as of December 2022, the total population of China was 1,411,750,000. Based on the data from the Department of Statistics Malaysia, as of February 2021, the population of Malaysia was 32,750,000. As described by the list of higher education institutions in China provided by the Ministry of Education in 2022, there were a total of 849 public undergraduate universities nationwide. Based on the data from the Ministry of Education Malaysia in March 2019, there were currently 20 public undergraduate universities in Malaysia. The total number of university students in China, according to the Ministry of Education of the People's Republic of China, was 36,545,000, while Malaysia has approximately 3,500,000 university students according to the Ministry of Education Malaysia's statistics.

The reference population includes all students in China and Malaysia who are pursuing higher education at the university level. The target population specifically refers to students currently enrolled at universities in China and Malaysia. The source population, or sampling pool, consists of students who are currently attending universities in both countries. The sampling frame is based on the students' database, which is confidential and inaccessible to researchers. However, researchers can obtain an enrollment list of students from the lecturers in charge of the classes. The objectives of this research are to study Nature Relatedness, Trait Mindfulness, and Character Strengths among university students in China and Malaysia. The participants in this study are undergraduate students from both countries. Finally, among the universities that agreed to participate in the sampling process, three public universities in China and one public university in Malaysia approved the administration of this survey.

3.3.1.2   Subject Criteria of This Research

The subject criteria for this questionnaire are as follows: participants must be current undergraduate university students, specifically those enrolled in undergraduate programs at universities in China and Malaysia. Graduates are excluded from the study. Foreign students are also excluded for specific reasons, as this research aims to investigate differences among university students in the two countries. Therefore, in the survey conducted in Malaysia, only students of Malaysian nationality are included, specifically Malay, Malaysian Chinese, and Malaysian Indian, as outlined in the questionnaire instructions. The instructions clarify that foreign students are excluded from the study. Similarly, in the survey conducted in China, foreign students are excluded. Participants must be 18 years of age or older. Additionally, participants must have sufficient English or Chinese reading proficiency to understand and respond to the questionnaire. Only those who meet these criteria are eligible to participate in the survey.

3.3.2 Research Sampling

Research sampling, which refers to the process of selecting participants for the study, includes three sections: sampling technique, study location, and subject recruitment. For practical reasons, convenience sampling was adopted, with testing conducted upon receiving approval from participating universities. The study locations included three universities in China and one in Malaysia. Participants were recruited via two methods: face-to-face and online. Subject recruitment involved different approaches to reach participants; face-to-face recruitment was conducted in classrooms with the assistance of instructors, while online recruitment was facilitated through notifications in WhatsApp and WeChat groups. The recruitment process also ensured unbiased and systematic participant selection by researchers.

3.3.2.1 Sampling Technique

Sampling is the process of selecting a sufficient number of elements from the population so that the properties or characteristics of the sample can be generalized to the population elements (Kumar, et al., 2013). Sampling involves selecting certain features from a population to represent the entire population (Cooper & Schindler, 2008). Sampling design is an important consideration for researchers when sampling from a population (Singleton & Straits, 2012). Sampling has practical reasons, as conducting a comprehensive survey is not feasible when dealing with large population sizes. Sampling helps save time and effort and avoids inaccuracies when dealing with large populations (Zikmund et al., 2014; Creswell & Poth, 2016). Sampling design can be categorized into probability sampling and non-probability sampling. Probability sampling methods include simple random sampling, stratified random sampling, cluster sampling, and systematic sampling, all of which involve random selection processes. Each element in the population has an equal chance of being selected as a sample for the study (Christensen & Bengtsson, 2011). Non-probability sampling methods include purposive sampling and quota sampling, where individuals in the population do not have an equal chance of being selected (Singleton & Straits, 2012).

Christensen and Bengtsson (2011) identified another primary sampling method commonly used in psychological research, which is non-random sampling. Although these methods may be relatively weaker in terms of sampling, they are sometimes necessary due to practical considerations. Convenience sampling is one such non-random sampling method. Convenience sampling involves selecting individuals who are readily available, willing, or easy to recruit as participants. When conducting convenience sampling, researchers simply ask people who are most convenient to participate in the study or choose the most accessible participants. For example, psychologists often select samples from students taking introductory psychology courses (i.e., students who participate in the research project either to earn college credit or out of curiosity about being research participants).

While true random samples are essential for certain research endeavors, studies that utilize non-random samples can also yield valuable insights (Brislin & Baumgardner, 1971). Although methodological literature highlights the advantages of different types of random samples (Festinger & Katz, 1953; Blalock, 1960), cross-cultural psychologists have predominantly relied on non-random samples, often referred to as "clusters" or "convenience samples," when studying individual responses. These clusters consist of readily available subjects from schools, factories, or single villages, with the individual as the unit of analysis rather than culture (Naroll et al., 1970). As pointed out by Campbell (1969), psychology has managed to progress in some way despite the lack of systematic random sampling as a common method, but not without self-criticism. Although many researchers have acknowledged the use of cavalier or problematic samples (Doob, 1960; Price-Williams, 1961; Gay and Cole, 1967;

Osgood, 1960), it is not a valid reason for continuing this approach. The cost, time, and practical challenges associated with random sampling make it highly difficult. While certain studies may require examining the representativeness of the selected samples to infer the unsampled population, other research might not prioritize representativeness and thus researchers may be willing to acknowledge biases introduced by non-random samples. Such studies might aim to investigate psychological processes by testing individuals chosen based on specific criteria (Brislin & Baumgardner, 1971).

Due to the comparative study on Nature Relatedness, Trait Mindfulness, and Character Strengths among Chinese and Malaysian university students, the selection of regions and universities in each country where the questionnaire was administered is critical. To address this issue, a comparative analysis of sample sizes for cross-cultural comparisons targeting university student populations was conducted through a literature review.

Kühnen et al. (2001) investigated cross-cultural variations in identifying embedded figures and selected samples of university students from four countries: the United States, Germany, Russia, and Malaysia. The sample sizes were as follows: 60 students from the University of Michigan, Ann Arbor, in the United States; 80 students from the University of Dortmund in Germany; 107 students from Rostov University in Russia; and 175 students from the International Islamic University of Malaysia (IIUM) in Malaysia. The sample from IIUM only included members of Malaysia's minority ethnic groups and did not include Chinese students from the university. This measure was taken to ensure the resolution of collinearity between collectivism and logographic writing systems. Students from introductory psychology courses or various university campuses were asked to participate in the study. Convenience sampling was used in this research, with sample sizes from the United States, Germany, Russia, and Malaysia being 60, 80, 107, and 175, respectively. Guan et al. (2015) explored the differences in career decision-making patterns

(CDMP) between American and Chinese university students, as well as potential mediating mechanisms supporting these cultural differences. The study included undergraduate student samples from the United States ($n = 929$) and China ($n = 945$) through a questionnaire survey. The sample sizes of American and Chinese university students were nearly 1:1. Hatfield and Sprecher (1995) studied preferences for marriage partners among male and female university students in the United States, Russia, and Japan. The American sample included 970 participants from five different universities: Illinois State University ($n = 470$); Southern Methodist University in Dallas, Texas ($n = 272$); University of Hawaii in Honolulu, Hawaii ($n = 96$); Bradley University in Peoria, Illinois ($n = 78$); and Millikin University in Decatur, Illinois ($n = 54$). The Russian sample consisted of 327 participants from Vladimir Polytechnic Institute. The Japanese sample included 222 participants from two universities: Nanzan University in Nagoya City ($n = 108$) and Tohoku University in Sendai City ($n = 114$). These eight universities were selected because they were the authors' alma mater or had a connection with the authors. Convenience sampling was used, and although non-probability sampling could introduce bias, the familiarity of the questionnaire interviewers provided some control and ensured the validity of the questionnaire administration. The sample sizes for American, Russian, and Japanese university students were 970, 327, and 222, respectively, following the convenience sampling method without a specific pattern. Chen (2017) conducted a cross-cultural study on conscientiousness traits and influencing factors among Chinese and Vietnamese university students. The sample sizes of Chinese and Vietnamese university students were 760 and 750, respectively, which were approximately 1:1. Pimthong (2015) examined and compared the structural equation model of psychological and social factors related to consumer foot behavior among university students in Malaysia and Thailand. The study included a comparison of Character Strengths among Malaysian and Thai university students. For this research, one public

102

university was selected in each country. The sample sizes were 360 undergraduate students from Malaysia and 364 undergraduate students from Thailand.

Through the analysis of sampling methods and the number of university students sampled in cross-cultural comparative studies, it became evident that while there was no fixed pattern, some cross-cultural studies had sample size proportions mostly around 1:1, while others did not follow this ratio. Therefore, for this survey, a convenience sampling method was employed to select participants (Kühnen et al., 2001). Convenience sampling involved selecting individuals who were readily accessible or convenient for data collection, often due to practical considerations such as geographical proximity or ease of contact. In this study, potential participants were recruited from the university campus, utilizing both online (WhatsApp groups or WeChat groups) and offline (classrooms during university lectures) recruitment methods.

Convenience sampling was utilized for the study, thus, this might have affected the generalizability of the findings. This sampling method did indeed have some issues, but some of them had already been addressed. In the ethical review process, data collection consent letters were received from three universities in China. However, this research still had some limitations. In Malaysia, data collection consent was currently only received from one university.

3.3.2.2 Study Location

To facilitate a comparison of university students from two countries, the research is conducted at public universities in China and Malaysia (Pimthong, 2015). The researchers have obtained data collection consent letters from three universities in China: A, B, and C Universities. In Malaysia, consent has been secured only from D University. Although researchers made every effort to select universities from different regions and of various types as research locations, practical constraints have prevented obtaining consent from all intended universities, which introduces some limitations to the research.

In the four research locations mentioned above, two public comprehensive universities stand out as world-class and key national institutions. These are A University in northern China and B University in northern Malaysia. A University is located in Beijing, China, while D University is situated in Penang, Malaysia. Renowned for their excellence, these universities offer a wide range of disciplines, including engineering, science, management, humanities, law, economics, philosophy, education, medicine, and arts. They feature spacious campuses, picturesque surroundings, and are enriched with abundant natural resources. Additionally, there are two more public universities in China: B University, a normal University, and C University, a provincial key university. They are both located in Anhui Province in central China. Data Collection Permission Letters from each university have been signed and stamped prior to the commencement of data collection.

3.3.2.3 Subject Recruitment

1. Recruitment Methods for Participants

Participants were recruited through two methods: face-to-face and online. Face-to-face recruitment took place in classrooms with instructors, while online recruitment was done through notifications in WhatsApp or WeChat groups. Participants were invited to take part in this survey. They were informed about the purpose of the research, the voluntary nature of their participation, and the confidentiality of their responses. Informed consent was obtained from all participants before they commenced the questionnaire. Recruiting samples through social media platforms (WhatsApp, WeChat) involve ethical considerations such as informed consent and privacy protection. These concerns can be addressed through the following methods: clear guidance in questionnaire introduction, begin the questionnaire with prominent instructions clarifying the purpose of the survey, emphasizing its anonymous nature, explaining privacy protection measures, and highlighting voluntary participation. Explicit voluntary participation question: include a dedicated question at the beginning of the questionnaire, such as "Are you willingly participating in this survey?" with response options like "agree" and "not agree," allowing participants to indicate their agreement by checking the appropriate option. The WhatsApp and WeChat groups were identified through two methods: with the assistance of student associations: after approval was obtained from the students' respective schools, the request was made for student organizations sharing the survey links in their WhatsApp and WeChat groups. With the assistance of lecturers: coordination was made with the lecturers of the classes in which students were enrolled, seeking their support to share the survey links in the class groups.

2. Ensuring Unbiased Systematic Recruitment by Researchers

The research employed the following methods: measures were taken to avoid biased recruitment, not just selected samples. Diverse recruitment channels: various recruitment channels, including classes, student organizations, face-to-face, and online, were utilized to ensure sample diversity. Transparent recruitment information: the research purpose and participation criteria were clearly outlined in recruitment materials, emphasizing that university students who met the recruitment criteria were all welcome to participate. Random invitations: members were randomly invited to participate within group settings to minimize selection bias and ensure systematic recruitment. Track sample sources: recruitment quantities from each channel were recorded, potential biases were assessed, and recruitment strategies were adjusted as needed.

3.3.3 Research Sample

To accurately estimate the sample size, the researcher compared three methods and made a comprehensive judgment. These methods were: estimating sample size based on the total population, using the G * Power sample size calculator, and applying psychometric sample size estimation methods.

3.3.3.1 Sample Size Estimation Based on Total Population

The first method involved referring to the table created by Krejcie and Morgan (1970), which provides sample size estimates based on the total population. The second method involved using sample size calculators, which are tools specifically designed for sample calculation. The first method involves estimating the sample size based on the total population. In this study, the researcher referred to Table 3.1, which displays the sample size estimates for populations ranging from 10 to 50,000,000 (Krejcie & Morgan, 1970). This is one of the methods used to determine sample size in random sampling. As illustrated in Table 3.1, it is recommended to have a sample size of 384 for populations within the range of 100,000 to 50,000,000. The total number of university students in China, according to the Ministry of Education, is 36,545,000, while Malaysia has approximately 3,500,000 university students as mentioned above, according to the statistics released by the Ministry of Education Malaysia. They are falling within the range of 100,000 to 50,000,000. Therefore, the total estimated sample size is 384, and any number greater than this is considered valid.

Table 3.1 **Sample Size for Population Within the Range of 10-50,000,000**

N	n	N	n	N	n	N	n	N	n
10	10	110	86	300	169	950	274	4500	354

Continued

N	n	N	n	N	n	N	n	N	n
15	14	120	92	320	175	1000	278	5000	357
20	19	130	97	340	181	1100	285	6000	361
25	24	140	103	360	186	1200	291	7000	364
30	28	150	108	380	191	1300	297	8000	367
40	36	170	118	420	201	1500	306	10000	370
45	40	180	123	440	205	1600	310	15000	375
50	44	190	127	460	210	1700	313	20000	377
55	48	200	132	480	214	1800	317	30000	379
60	52	210	136	500	217	1900	320	40000	380
65	56	220	140	550	226	2000	322	50000	381
70	59	120	144	600	234	2200	327	75000	382
75	63	240	148	650	242	2400	331	100000	384
80	66	250	152	700	248	2600	335	260000	384
85	70	260	155	750	254	2800	338	500000	384
90	73	270	159	800	260	3000	341	1000000	384
95	76	280	162	850	265	3500	346	10000000	384
100	80	290	165	900	269	4000	351	50000000	384

Note: N represents the population size, and n represents the recommended sample size. The sample size is based on a 95% confidence interval.

3.3.3.2 Sample Size Calculation Using G ∗ Power Analysis

The second method involves using sample size calculators for sample calculation. In accordance with the review and recommendation by Christensen and Bengtsson (2011), one of the most popular sample size calculation programs is G ∗ Power (Erdfelder et al. , 1996). G ∗ Power 3.1.9.2 (Faul et al. , 2009) was used to compare with the sample size determination formula by Krejcie and Morgan (1970). G ∗ Power is proficient in calculating five different types of power analyses (Prajapati et al., 2010).

In this study, a prior power analysis was used because it is the most relevant for estimating the sample size. It determines the sufficient sample size for any identified effect size, alpha level, and power. Effect size refers to the degree to which the null hypothesis (H_0) is incorrect, which is measured by the inconsistency between the null hypothesis (H_0) and the alternative hypothesis (H_1). Effect sizes are described as small, medium, and large effects with values of 0.10, 0.30, and 0.50, respectively (Cohen, 1992). In this study, the effect size value was 0.10. Furthermore, Cohen (1992) suggested using a significance level of 0.05 to avoid Type I error, which is incorrectly rejecting the null hypothesis (H_0) when the null hypothesis is true. Meanwhile, a statistical power of 0.80 or 80% is used to avoid Type II error, which is the probability of failing to reject the null hypothesis even though the null hypothesis is false. In other words, there is a 20% possibility of accepting the null hypothesis in error, where beta is 0.20 or 20% (Cohen, 1992).

In the regression analysis of this study, there are two predictor variables, namely Nature Relatedness and Trait Mindfulness. Based on these input parameters, the calculated sample size was 64, as shown in Figure 3.2.

3.3.3.3   Psychometric-Based Sample Size Estimation Method

According to psychometric sample size calculation methods, the required sample size should be 5 to 10 times the number of items in the scale (Hair et al., 2011; Kyriazos, 2018). In this study, the total number of items across all scales used is 71, including: 17 items in the revised Nature Relatedness Scale, 1 item in the Inclusion of Nature in the Self Scale, 14 items in the Connectedness to Nature Scale, 15 items in the Three-dimensional Inventory of Character Strengths, and 24 items in the Five Facet Mindfulness Questionnaire—Short Form. Therefore, the recommended sample size ranges from 355 to 710, indicating sufficient statistical power.

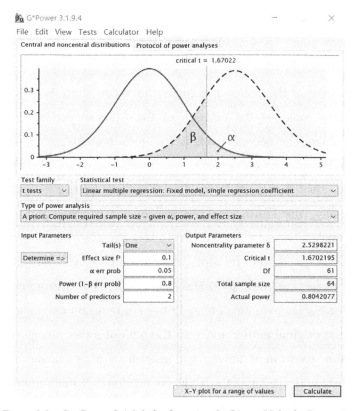

Figure 3.2 G * Power 3.1.9.2 Configuration for Linear Multiple Regression

When comparing the results of all three methods of sample size estimation, i.e., 384 or more (based on population size), 64 or more (based on G * Power analysis), and 355-710 (based on psychometric estimation), all values fall within acceptable ranges. Based on this comparison, and following the principle that a larger sample size allows for more accurate results (Gaskin & Happell, 2014; Gay et al., 2011), the ideal sample size in this study was determined to be 384 for both Chinese and Malaysian university students. Ultimately, questionnaires were distributed as widely as possible based on actual circumstances. However, if practical limitations occurred, a combined total of more than 355 valid responses from Chinese and Malaysian university students would still be considered acceptable.

3.4   Research Procedure

As mentioned in the research design, the entire study is divided into four stages. The first stage is the revision of the Chinese version of the Nature Relatedness Scale. The second stage is the questionnaire survey and analysis, focusing on exploring the differences among variables. The third stage involves studying the relationship between independent variables and dependent variables. Finally, the fourth stage focuses on constructing and validating the mediation model.

The first stage is the revision of the Chinese version of the Nature Relatedness Scale, answering RQ1a. First, the researcher contacted the developer of the scale, via email to seek her consent and assistance. Under the guidance of the original author and with the help of a psychology professor and four Ph.D students from B University, as well as a psychology measurement professor from A University, the Chinese version of the Nature Relatedness Scale underwent translation and back-translation. Then, a questionnaire comprehensibility test was conducted at B University in China. Following this, the questionnaires were distributed at A, B, and C Universities in China, where standardized item analysis, exploratory factor analysis, confirmatory factor analysis, validity analysis, and reliability analysis were performed. The second stage is the questionnaire survey and analysis, answering RQ2a and RQ2b. It includes the following four steps: First, the researchers obtained consent from the original developers and Chinese version revisers of the three scales and collected both the Chinese and English versions of the scales. Second, data collection was requested from A, B, and C Universities in China and D University in Malaysia. Third, after obtaining approval, trained interviewers read the instructions and conducted the survey. The questionnaire was administered collectively, using both online and offline methods, and questionnaires were distributed. Before the test, the subjects were informed that the survey results would be kept strictly confidential and used only for scientific research purposes. If necessary, the test results can be provided to the subjects themselves. Finally, the aim is to analyze the differences in Nature Relatedness, mindfulness, and Character Strengths among university students of different genders, majors, grades, and urban-rural backgrounds, etc. Subsequently, an analysis was conducted to examine the differences in Nature Relatedness, Trait Mindfulness, and Character Strengths among Chinese and Malaysian university students.

The third stage involves studying the relationship between independent variables and dependent variables, addressing RQ3a and RQ3b. First, the relationship between Nature Relatedness and Character Strengths is analyzed. Then, it is determined whether Nature Relatedness positively predicts Character Strengths.

The fourth stage focuses on constructing and validating the mediation model, addressing RQ4a and RQ4b. First, the relationship between Nature Relatedness and mindfulness, as well as mindfulness and Character Strengths, is examined. Then, a full mediation model is established, and structural equation modeling is used to examine the mediating effect of Trait Mindfulness on the relationship between Nature Relatedness and Character Strengths. The established full mediation model is depicted in Figure 3.3.

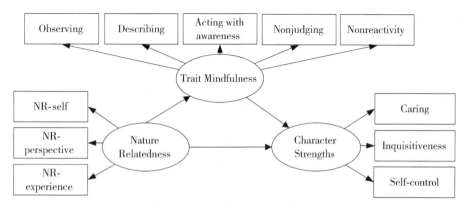

Figure 3.3 Full Mediation Model

3.5   Research Instruments

This research includes three variables: one independent variable, one mediating variable, and one dependent variable. Three measurement tools are selected for each variable: the Nature Relatedness Scale, Five Facet Mindfulness Questionnaire—Short Form, and a Three-dimensional Inventory of Character Strengths. The subscales of each measurement tool are shown in Figure 3.4.

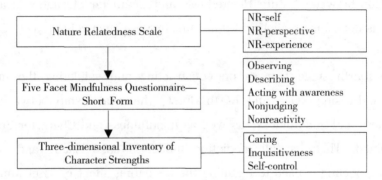

Figure 3.4   The Subscales of Each Instrument

A pilot study was conducted in this research to validate these three instruments. In the second part of the pilot study, internal consistency and split-half coefficients were used as indicators to examine the reliability of the instruments.

3.5.1   Nature Relatedness Scale

This study employed the Nature Relatedness Scale (NRS) developed by Nisbet et al. (2009), a 21-item measure assessing three dimensians (NR-perspective, and NR-experience) using a 5-point Likert scale. There are eight reverse-scored items on this scale, which comprehensively measure individuals' relationship with nature. The internal consistency reliability of the entire scale is 0.87, and the reliability of the three subscales are 0.84, 0.66, and 0.80, respectively. The test-retest reliability after an interval of 6-8 weeks is 0.85, indicating good reliability. The scale is effective in predicting environmental behavior and well-being, demonstrating good validity. Subsequently, Nisbet and Zelenski (2013) selected six items from the original 21 items (four from the self subscale and two from the experience subscale) to create a short version of the scale (NR-6), which does not include any reverse-scored items. The reliability and validity of NR-6 are also satisfactory. Since this study aims at comprehensively measuring Nature Relatedness, the 21-item version from 2009 was used. The scale has been widely used in English-speaking countries, and in China, some researchers have translated and used parts of the scale without following standardized procedures for psychological measurement. Therefore, it is necessary to revise and validate the Chinese version of the Nature Relatedness scale, which was conducted under the guidance of the original scale author Nisbet et al. (2009). This involved translation, back-translation, exploratory factor analysis, confirmatory factor analysis, and testing of validity and reliability. Table 3.2 displays the 5-point Likert scale for all items in the Nature Relatedness Scale tool, including reverse-scored items.

Table 3.2   **Likert Scale For Nature Relatedness Scale Items**

Likert scale	Disagree strongly	Disagree a little	Neither agree nor disagree	Agree a little	Agree strongly
Nature Relatedness scale items: 1,4,5,6,7,8,9,12,16,17, 19,20,21	1	2	3	4	5
Reverse score item: 2,3,10,11,13,14,15,18	5	4	3	2	1

Note: From the Nature Relatedness Scale: Linking individuals' connection with nature to environmental concern and behavior (Nisbet et al., 2009).

Furthermore, the Nature Relatedness Scale can measure three types of NR-self, NR-perspective, and NR-experience. The arrangement of items in the Nature Relatedness scale instrument is listed in Table 3.3. The Item Examples of the English and Chinese Versions in the Nature Relatedness Scale are listed in Table 3.4.

Table 3.3   **Items in the Nature Relatedness Scale/Subscales**

Nature Relatedness scale/subscales	Items	Number of items
NR-self	5, 7, 8, 12, 14, 16, 17, 21	8
NR-perspective	2, 3, 11, 15, 18, 19, 20	7
NR-experience	1, 4, 6, 9, 10, 13	6
Total Nature Relatedness		21

Note: From the Nature Relatedness scale: Linking individuals' connection with nature to environmental concern and behavior (Nisbet et al., 2009).

Table 3.4   **Item Examples of the English and Chinese Versions in the Nature Relatedness Scale**

Subscales	Items	Item examples of the English and Chinese versions
NR-self	5	I always think about how my actions affect the environment. 我总是考虑自己的行为是如何影响环境的。
NR-perspective	2	Some species are just meant to die out or become extinct. 有些物种注定要消亡或逐渐灭绝。
NR-experience	1	I enjoy being outdoors, even in unpleasant weather. 即使在糟糕的天气里,我也喜欢待在户外。

Note: From the Nature Relatedness scale: Linking individuals' connection with nature to environmental concern and behavior (Nisbet et al., 2009).

3.5.2   Three-dimensional Inventory of Character Strengths

This study uses the Three-dimensional Inventory of Character Strengths developed by Duan and Bu (2017) to measure the Character Strengths of college students. The scale consists of three sub-scales, namely, caring, inquisitiveness, and self-control, with a total of 15 items, with 5 items in each sub-scale. The scale uses a 5-point Likert scale (1 represents "not like me at all", and 5 represents "very much like me"), and there are no reverse-scored items. The scale was developed using a sample of 1,074 college students studying in China (518 Asian samples and 556 Western samples). Exploratory factor analysis and item selection were conducted using the Asian samples, while confirmatory factor analysis was conducted using the Western samples to ensure cross-cultural validity. Both the total scale and sub-scales can be scored by using either the total score or the average score. Higher scores indicate more prominent Character Strengths. The Cronbach's alpha coefficients for the three sub-scales were 0.74, indicating good internal consistency. The alpha values of the Caring sub-scale were 0.82 and 0.86 in the community and patient samples, respectively, the alpha values of the Inquisitiveness sub-scale were 0.79 and 0.80, and the alpha values of the Self-control sub-scale were 0.83 and 0.85. The scale has good construct validity and meets psychometric standards when used with university students, adults, community residents, and patient groups. The structure validity of the scale was verified in a sample of Western international students, and the measurement invariance and predictive validity of the scale were verified in samples of community residents and general surgical inpatients. Table 3.5 displays the 5-point Likert scale for all items in the Three-dimensional Inventory of Character Strengths, there is no reverse-scored item.

Furthermore, the Short Three-dimensional Inventory of Character Strengths can measure three types of caring, inquisitiveness, and self-control, and arrangement of items in the Short Three-dimensional Inventory of Character Strengths is listed in Table 3.6. The item examples of the English and Chinese Versions in the Short Three-dimensional Inventory of Character Strengths are listed in Table 3.7.

Table 3.5   **Likert Scale For the Short Three-dimensional Inventory**
of Character Strengths Items

Likert scale	Very much unlike me	Unlike me	Neutral	Like me	Very much like me
Items: 1,2,3,4,5,6,7,8,9,10,11,12,13,14,15	1	2	3	4	5
None reverse score item					

Note: From the development and initial validation of a short Three-dimensional Inventory of Character Strengths (Duan & Bu, 2017).

Table 3.6   **Items in the Three-dimensional Inventory of Character Strengths/Subscales**

Three-dimensional Inventory of Character Strengths/Subscales	Items	Number of Items
Caring	11,12,13,14,15	5
Inquisitiveness	3,5,7,8,9	5
Self-control	1,2,4,6,10	5
Total		21

Note: From the development and initial validation of a short Three-dimensional Inventory of Character Strengths (Duan & Bu, 2017).

Table 3.7   **Item Examples of the English and Chinese Versions in the Three-**
dimensional Inventory of Character Strengths

Subscales	Items	Item examples of the English and Chinese versions
Caring	11	I enjoy being kind to others. 我享受善待他人的感觉。
Inquisitiveness	3	I have the ability to make other people feel interesting. 我有能力令其他人对一些事物产生兴趣。
Self-control	1	I am a highly disciplined person. 我是一个高度自律的人。

Note: From the development and initial validation of a short Three-dimensional Inventory of Character Strengths (Duan & Bu, 2017).

3.5.3   Five Facet Mindfulness Questionnaire—Short Form

In this research, Trait Mindfulness was measured to represent the level of mindfulness. Among the numerous instruments on mindfulness, the Five Facet Mindfulness Questionnaire (FFMQ) is widely used. It is a multidimensional structured scale for assessing Trait Mindfulness (Kiken et al., 2015). The scale was based on items from existing scales, consisting of five dimensions: observing, describing, acting with awareness, non-judging, and non-reactivity. It contains 39 items, scored on a 5-point scale ranging from 1 (never or very rarely true) to 5 (very often or always true). Higher total scores on the scale indicate higher levels of mindfulness (Baer et al., 2006).

Five Facet Mindfulness Questionnaire—Short Form (FFMQ-SF) was selected for this research. The scale was based on the FFMQ-SF and consisted of 24 items. The questionnaire includes five subscales that assess different aspects of mindfulness: (1) observing (4 items), (2) describing (5 items), (3) acting with awareness (5 items), (4) non-judging (5 items), and (5) non-reactivity (5 items) (Bohlmeijer et al., 2011).

Participants were asked to indicate on a 5-point Likert scale how true each item was for them in general, ranging from 1 (almost never true) to 5 (very often or always true). Examples of items for each subscale are as follows: (1) "I usually notice sounds, such as the ticking of a clock, birds chirping, or the sound of a car driving." (2) "I am good at finding words to describe my feelings." (3) "I find it difficult to pay attention to what is happening in the present moment (reverse coded)." (4) "I tell myself that I should not be feeling the way I'm feeling (reverse coded)." and (5) "I observe my feelings without getting lost in them." Using the total and subscale scores of the FFMQ-SF, higher scores indicate higher levels of internal mindfulness. The Cronbach's alpha for the total score was 0.82, while the Cronbach's alpha for subscales 1 to 5 were 0.74, 0.79, 0.80, 0.75, and 0.66, respectively (Bohlmeijer et al., 2011;

Boekhorst & Duijndam, 2023). In China, the Chinese version of the FFMQ-SF was revised by Deng and showed a good fit with the original English version on each dimension. It has been widely used by domestic researchers (Deng et al., 2011; Li, 2020; He et al., 2018; Zhong et al., 2016). Table 3.8 displays the 5-point Likert scale for all items in the Five Facet Mindfulness Questionnaire—Short Form, including reverse-scored items.

Furthermore, the Five Facet Mindfulness Questionnaire—Short Form can measure five types of observing, describing, acting with awareness, non-judging, and non-reactivity. The arrangement of items in the Five Facet Mindfulness Questionnaire—Short Form instrument is listed in Table 3.9. The Item Examples of the English and Chinese Versions are listed in Table 3.10.

Table 3.8   **Likert Scale For Five Facet Mindfulness Questionnaire—Short Form Items**

Likert Scale	Never or very rarely true	Rarely true	Sometimes true	Often true	Very often or always true
Five Facet Mindfulness Questionnaire—Short Form Items: 1,2,3,6,9,10,13,15,16,18, 20,21	1	2	3	4	5
Reverse score item: 4,5,7,8,11,12,14,17,19,22,23,24	5	4	3	2	1

Note: From the Psychometric properties of the Five Facet Mindfulness Questionnaire in depressed adults and development of a short form. Assessment (Bohlmeij et al., 2011).

Table 3.9   **Items in the Five Facet Mindfulness Questionnaire—Short Form/Subscales**

Five Facet Mindfulness Questionnaire—Short Form/Subscales	Items	Number of items
Observing	6, 10,15, 20	4
Describing	1,2, 5,11, 16	5
Acting with awareness	8,12,17,22,23	5

Continued

Five Facet Mindfulness Questionnaire—Short Form/Subscales	Items	Number of items
Non-judging	4,7,14,19,24	5
Non-reacting	3,9,13,18,21	5
Total Nature Relatedness		24

Note: From the Psychometric properties of the Five Facet Mindfulness Questionnaire in depressed adults and development of a short form. Assessment (Bohlmeijer et al, 2011).

Table 3.10 **Item Examples of the English and Chinese Versions in the Five Facet Mindfulness Questionnaire—Short Form**

Subscales	Items	Item examples of the English and Chinese versions
Observing	6	I pay attention to physical experiences, such as the wind in my hair or sun on my face. 我会注意我的一些感觉,比如:微风吹拂我的头发、阳光照在我的脸上的感觉。
Describing	1	I'm good at finding words to describe my feelings. 我擅长于用言语描述我的情感。
Acting with awareness	8	I find it difficult to stay focused on what's happening in the present moment. 我难以把注意力集中在当前发生的事情上。
Non-judging	4	I tell myself I shouldn't be feeling the way I'm feeling. 我告诉自己,我不应该以我现在的这种方式来感受此时的情感。
Non-reacting	3	I watch my feelings without getting carried away by them. 我观察自己的情绪,而不迷失其中。

Note: From the Psychometric properties of the Five Facet Mindfulness Questionnaire in depressed adults and development of a short form. Assessment (Bohlmeijer et al., 2011); The Five Facet Mindfulness Questionnaire: psychometric properties of the Chinese version. Mindfulness (Deng et al., 2011); The Construct Validity Test of the Brief Chinese Five Facet Mindfulness Questionnaire among College Students and Athletes (Zhong et al., 2016).

3.5.4 Inclusion of Nature in the Self Scale (INS)

To directly measure individuals' subjective sense of inclusion with nature, Schultz (2001) adapted the scale originally developed by Aron et al. (1991) for assessing interpersonal closeness, creating the single-item Inclusion of Nature in the Self Scale (INS). This scale consists of seven pairs of gradually overlapping circles labeled "Self" and "Nature," representing varying degrees of overlap from completely separate to almost fully merged. The greater the overlap between the two circles is, the stronger the perceived integration of self and nature is. Participants select the pair of circles that best represents their relationship with nature. Due to its single-item format, the scale is easy to administer, as illustrated in Figure 3.5. Previous studies have shown that the INS demonstrates good validity and has been widely used (Yang, et al., 2017). The scale has also been found to be significantly correlated with variables such as biospheric concern (Mayer & Frantz, 2004), environmental attitudes and behaviors (Schultz et al., 2004), and connectedness to nature (Mayer & Frantz, 2004; Li, 2016). In this study, the INS was used as one of the comparison measures to assess the convergent validity of the Chinese version of the Nature Relatedness Scale.

3.5.5 Connectedness to Nature Scale (CNS)

Mayer and Frantz (2004) developed the Connectedness to Nature Scale (CNS), a unidimensional scale consisting of 14 items, each rated on a 5-point Likert scale (1 = strongly disagree, 5 = strongly agree). The scale measures individuals' emotional connection to nature (Sample item "I often feel a sense of oneness with the natural world around me") and has demonstrated high internal consistency ($\alpha = 0.84$) and test-retest reliability ($r = 0.79$). It has also been shown to be significantly correlated with biocentric values, the new ecological paradigm, perspective taking, environmental attitudes, ecological

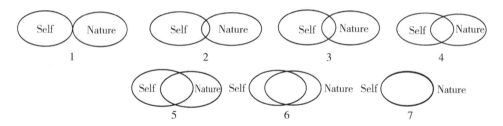

Figure 3.5 The Inclusion of Nature in the Self Scale

behavior, and life satisfaction (Schultz, 2001; Stern & Dietz, 1994; Geng et al., 2015). The CNS had been translated into multiple languages and was widely used (Yang et al., 2017). In China, Zhou (2013) was the first to adopt the Simplified Chinese version revised by Tam (2013a) in Hong Kong and validated it among Chinese university students, confirming its reliability and validity and further demonstrating a significant association between CNS scores and pro-environmental behavior.

Building upon this, Li (2016) further revised the Chinese version of the scale. This study adopts this revised version, which contains the same 14 items as the original English version, rated on a 5-point Likert scale, including three reverse-scored items (Sample item in Chinese: "我常感觉与大自然融为一体。"). Higher CNS scores indicate a stronger connection with nature. The revised Chinese version demonstrated good psychometric properties, with internal consistency reliability of 0.783, test-retest reliability of 0.901 (p<0.01), and convergent validity of 0.491 (p<0.01), meeting statistical standards and supporting its use as a valid tool for assessing individuals' connection to nature. In this study, the Chinese version of the CNS was used as the second comparison measure to evaluate the convergent validity of the Chinese version of the Nature Relatedness Scale.

3.6   Pilot Study

Before entering the actual implementation stage of the questionnaire survey research, a pilot study was conducted in this study. The pilot study overall included two aspects: validity and reliability of the scales. It should be noted that the reliability of the Chinese version of the Nature Relatedness Scale designed in this study needs to be calculated after the revision of the scale. Therefore, the calculation of this scale was not conducted here. Malaysian university student participants were involved in the administration of the English version of the scale, so the internal consistency of the English version of the Nature Relatedness Scale was calculated in the pilot study.

3.6.1   Validity of the Scales

Validity is one of the fundamental characteristics of constructing psychological measurement tools. Validity testing refers to measuring what it claims to measure (DeVellis & Thorpe, 2021). In this research, content validity was used as the validity indicator.

First, surface content validity of the Nature Relatedness Scale, Five Facet Mindfulness Questionnaire—Short Form and Three-dimensional Inventory of Character Strengths were examined using student pre-tests. Before using the questionnaires for formal testing, students were asked to try out the questionnaires and provide feedbacks on their understanding of the questionnaire items from their perspective. As stated by Gay et al. (2012), it is sufficient to have three to four people read the questionnaire to identify problems. Therefore, the researchers randomly selected 48 participants (24 males and 24 females) from the research population in the central region of China to distribute the Nature Relatedness Scale, Five Facet Mindfulness Questionnaire—Short Form and Three-dimensional Inventory of Character

Strengths. The selected sample size accounted for approximately 5.3% of the total survey participants, and the questionnaire items were designed with high precision to assist respondents in providing reliable data. The implementation time was about 10 minutes. The random selection was based on the convenience and practicality of the researcher's location, as recommended by Creswell (2013).

This study asked the participants to read the validated questionnaires and provide feedbacks on whether they understood all the instructions and items in the questionnaire during the questionnaire completion process. After receiving feedbacks from 48 Chinese university students and 24 Malaysian university students, it was found that they all had a good understanding of the Chinese and English questionnaires. Table 3.11 provides specific information about the Chinese sample, while Table 3.12 contains details about the Malaysian sample.

Table 3.11   **Sample of the Pilot Study in China**

School	Specialization	Gender		
		Female	Male	Total
School of Biological Engineering	Landscape Architecture	12	12	24
School of Education	Elementary Education	12	12	24
Total		24	24	48

Table 3.12   **Sample of the Pilot Study in Malaysia**

School	Specialization	Gender		
		Female	Male	Total
School of Educational Studies	Educational Psychology &Counselling	3	3	6
	Counselling	3	3	6
	Special Education	3	3	6
	Sports psychology	3	3	6
Total		12	12	24

Second, an expert group was established to review the instruments required for measurement, to evaluate the validity of the tools used to measure the required variables (Allen & Yen, 2001). These measuring tools were handed over to a group of experts in the field of psychology for validation. As part of the validation process, expert recommendations were sought to assess the content validity of the measuring tools. Questionnaire content evaluations were conducted by 6 Malaysian psychology experts and 8 Chinese psychometric experts, all of whom considered the Chinese and English questionnaires to be well-validated and suitable for use in this study.

Table 3.13   **The Distribution of Specialist Responses to the Three Scales by Area of Expertise**

Institution	Area of expertise	Bill
Universiti Sains Malaysia (USM, Malaysia)	Educational Psychology & Counselling	3
Universiti Sains Malaysia (USM, Malaysia)	Counseling	3
Beihang University (BUAA, China)	Psychological Measurement	2
Huainan Normal University (China)	Applied Psychology	4
Anhui University of Traditional Chinese Medicine (China)	Counselling	2
Total		14

3.6.2 Reliability of the Scales

In this research, the internal consistency coefficient (Gay et al., 2011), can be used to reflect the reliability of the Five Facet Mindfulness Questionnaire—Short Form and Three-dimensional Inventory of Character Strengths. Internal consistency: a portion of the sample data is used to calculate Cronbach's alpha coefficient. By doing so, the acceptability level of each reliability indicator can be determined, and the reliability of the scales can be tested.

Table 3. 14 shows that the Chinese versions of the Nature Relatedness Scale, Five Facet Mindfulness Questionnaire—Short Form and the Three-dimensional Inventory of Character Strengths demonstrate good internal consistency, with coefficients of 0.910, 0.790 and 0.844, respectively, both of which are relatively high. The internal consistency coefficients of the English versions of the three scales are 0.848, 0.753, and 0.943, the internal consistency coefficient of the Five Facet Mindfulness Questionnaire—Short Form in English is acceptable, while the internal consistency coefficients of the other two scales are very high.

Table 3.14   **Reliability of the Scales in This Research**

Scale	Cronbach's alpha coefficient (Chinese samples)	Cronbach's alpha coefficient (Malaysian samples)
Nature Relatedness Scale	0.910	0.848
Five Facet Mindfulness Questionnaire—Short Form	0.790	0.753
Three-dimensional Inventory of Character Strengths	0.844	0.943

3.7   Data Collection

An email was sent to each university for seeking permission to carry out the survey and get the signature or stamped data collection permission letter. The purpose of the research as well as the required information was stated in the letter. After obtaining permission, the questionnaires were distributed. Regarding the distribution method, the study used the same approach in both Malaysia and China. In China, trained examiners, professional psychology lecturers, and doctoral students were utilized to distribute the questionnaires. In Malaysia, Ph. D students and lecturers with backgrounds in psychology and counseling were asked to distribute the questionnaires. During the questionnaire distribution process, doctoral students actively participate as the main testers in data collection. However, due to time and resource constraint, data collection needed assistance from other individuals with a background in psychology. These assistants are friends of the author and are not provided with any incentives. Nevertheless, the author expressed gratitude to these individuals in the Afterword of the book.

The questionnaire distribution takes two forms: face-to-face and online. The instructions section of both types of questionnaires clearly outlines the research purpose and content as required by the informed consent form, ensuring that participants voluntarily engage in the survey. Participants were asked to check the option to confirm whether they agree to voluntarily participate in the questionnaire survey. For face-to-face distribution, the main tester conducted it centrally in classrooms where university students attend classes. To ensure consistency and high-quality data, survey participants were required to answer all questions. Simultaneously, for online surveys, leaders of university student unions and class teachers were commissioned to distribute online surveys to participating students through WeChat, with the instructions prominently displayed.

The survey questionnaire includes demographic information (including gender, grade, major, and urban-rural backgrounds et al.) as well as scales measuring Nature Relatedness, Trait Mindfulness, and Character Strengths. The content and arrangement of the questionnaire are shown in Figure 3.6. At the end of the questionnaire, there was a reminder for participants to check if they have completed all the questions and an expression of gratitude for their participation in the survey.

Regarding the duration of participant involvement, previous studies indicate that each question requires approximately 5 seconds. The questionnaire for this study comprises a total of 71 items. The theoretical calculation suggests around 355 seconds, roughly 6 minutes. Considering the time for reading instructions

126

and final checks, a total duration of 10-15 minutes may be deemed reasonable. The author included time testing during the pilot study, serving as a crucial reference for the official testing time.

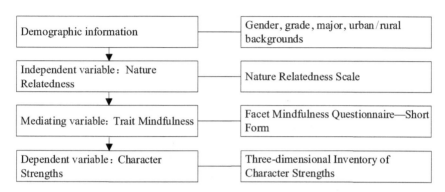

Figure 3.6   Content and Order of Survey Measures

3.8   Data Analysis

A diagrammatic illustration was provided to visually depict the process and the study workflow: First, the measuring instruments were revised and selected. Second, questionnaires were distributed to the target group, and survey data was collected. Subsequently, the survey data was organized and processed. Third, data analysis was conducted by using SPSS 28.0. Fourth, mediating effects were examined using Model 4 of the PROCESS SPSS plugin provided by Hayes (2018) for manifesting variable mediation analysis, followed by further refinement of latent variable analysis using AMOS 28.0 (Wen et al., 2004). The process flow of research data analysis was illustrated in Figure 3.7.

The quantitative data analysis in this study was conducted using the computer programs social science statistical software packages SPSS 28.0, PROCESS macro and AMOS 28.0. After the questionnaire survey and data compilation, the study tested the raw data using the SPSS statistical software version 28. 0. SPSS which was chosen because of its popularity in academic circles, making it the most widely used software package of its kind. SPSS is a versatile software package that allows for many different types of analysis, data transformation, and forms of output. In short, these methods are sufficient for the purposes of this research (Arkkelin, 2014).

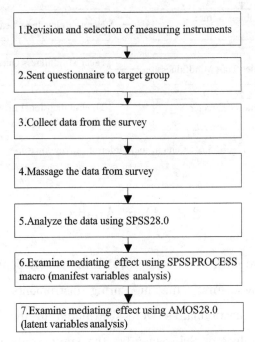

Figure 3.7   Process Flow of Research Data Analysis

As the questionnaire did not collect the names or specific identities of the participants, the researcher was not required to blind the information from the questionnaires. As mentioned earlier, the data collected from the three scales were integrated and populated into the SPSS 28. 0 data editor and later underwent data cleaning or processing (Wen et al., 2004; Wu, 2003).

The researcher conducted several quantitative analysis based on the research questions. The researcher used the guidelines provided by Sekaran and Bougie (2009) for data analysis. The scope of this quantitative analysis included scale revision techniques, independent samples t-test, one-way ANOVA, correlation analysis, regression analysis, and model testing for mediation effect using the Model 4 of the PROCESS macro and structural equation modeling of AMOS (Mills & Gay, 2019; Wen et al., 2004; Wu, 2003). Scale revision techniques included item analysis, exploratory factor analysis, confirmatory factor analysis, validity analysis, and reliability analysis (DeVellis & Thorpe, 2021; Wen et al., 2004). Detailed statistical analysis can be found in Table 3.15.

Table 3.15　**Summary of Research Questions and Statistical Analysis Used**

N	Research questions	Statistical analysis
RQ1a	Does the Chinese version of the Three-dimensional Nature Relatedness Scale have high validity and reliability?	Scale Revision Techniques: Item Analysis, Exploratory Factor Analysis, Confirmatory Factor Analysis, Validity Analysis, Reliability Analysis
RQ2a	Are there differences in Nature Relatedness, Trait Mindfulness, and Character Strengths among Chinese and Malaysian university students of different genders, majors, and urban-rural backgrounds?	Independent samples t-test, One-way ANOVA
RQ2b	Are there differences in Nature Relatedness, Trait Mindfulness, and Character Strengths among Chinese and Malaysian university students?	Independent samples t-test
RQ3a	Is there a significant correlation between Nature Relatedness and Character Strengths among Chinese and Malaysian university students?	Correlation analysis
RQ3b	Does Nature Relatedness predict Character Strengths positively among Chinese and Malaysian university students?	Path coefficient analysis(AMOS)
RQ4a	Is there a significant correlation between Nature Relatedness and Trait Mindfulness, Trait Mindfulness, and Character Strengths among Chinese and Malaysian university students?	Correlation analysis
RQ4b	Does Trait Mindfulness have a mediating effect on the relationship between Nature Relatedness and Character Strengths among Chinese and Malaysian university students?	Regression analysis (PROCESS macro), Structural equation modeling (AMOS)

3.9   Ethical Considerations and Ethical Code

3.9.1   Participant Vulnerability

No serious assessment of participants is required because this is just a questionnaire. The participants are undergraduate students from both Chinese and Malaysian universities. The purpose of the questionnaire survey was explained to participants before they fill it out to ensure informed consent, and participation will not be compulsory. In the research process, it is ensured that the samples are volunteers, and they do not have any very severe mental issues. Therefore, if they have any of these significant issues, they would be not included as samples. Additionally, the researcher provided the contact number in the questionnaire instructions. If participants have issues of vulnerability, they can contact the researcher, and the researcher would assist them in withdrawing from this study.

The data from the questionnaire survey was kept independently and was not be disclosed to the university's management authorities. It was also not used for academic or course-related assessments or decisions.

3.9.2   Declaration of Absence of Conflict of Interest

There are no conflicts of interest and the research did not receive any compensation from companies or other organizations. Although the data for this study were obtained from three universities in China and USM in Malaysia, the ownership of the data belongs to the doctoral researchers and USM. The ownership is clearly defined because, in the data collection request letter for this study, the researcher explicitly stated that the survey results would be used for the researcher's doctoral thesis, without any data-sharing agreements signed with other universities. Therefore, there are no potential disputes or intellectual property controversies.

All data is confidential, and participants' names or details are not required. The research was committed to ensuring the study's integrity by maintaining independence in professional judgment and actions and taking appropriate measures to uphold this integrity. This includs accurate data collection and analysis to ensure objective and reliable findings. Furthermore, adherence to research ethics principles that ensured the privacy and rights of participants were properly safeguarded.

3.9.3 Privacy and Confidentiality

In the university student questionnaire survey for this study, strict data confidentiality measures can be implemented to ensure the privacy and data security of participants. The privacy and confidentiality statement are as follows:

Firstly, all questionnaire forms are anonymous, with no personal information related to the identity of the participants being collected or stored. Responses are ensured to be completely anonymous and not linked to any personal identifying information.

Secondly, the collected data is entered into SPSS 28.0 software, a tool specifically used for data analysis, with passwords set for the files. Access and processing of this data are restricted to research team members, who strictly adhere to data confidentiality regulations.

Thirdly, during data presentation and analysis, the researcher ensures that data is presented in aggregated form, and individual participant identities are not identifiable. This helps protect the privacy of the participants. Participants can't get access to the results. During data presentation and analysis, data is presented in aggregated form, ensuring that individual participant identities are not identifiable. This approach helps protect the privacy of the participants. Participants do not have access to the results.

3.9.4   Community Sensitivities and Benefits

In this study, the research tool is a normal questionnaire that does not cause any distress, anxiety, or social sensitivities among participants. Participants may obtain the following benefits from participating in this study:

Firstly, benefit to individual: individuals have the opportunity to gain in-depth insights into research on Nature Relatedness, Character Strengths, and mindfulness.

Secondly, benefit to community: the results of this study have a positive impact on the community by offering crucial insights into how Nature Relatedness, Character Strengths, and mindfulness influence individuals and communities. These findings help improve mental health support and educational programs.

Thirdly, benefit to university: this study contributes to expanding research in the areas of Nature Relatedness, Character Strengths, and mindfulness among Chinese and Malaysian university students. The university leverages the outcomes of this study, including data analysis and reports, to support further research efforts and community collaboration projects.

3.9.5   Honorarium and Incentives

No gifts or transportation expenses are offered to the participants. However, participants have the option to access their questionnaire results. Their participation is highly valued, and their contribution is vital to the research.

3.9.6   Ethics Statement and Ethical Code

This study adheres to the principles outlined in the 1964 Declaration of Helsinki and its subsequent amendments. Approval was granted by the Universiti Sains Malaysia's official Ethics Committee, Jawatankuasa Etika Penyelidikan

Manusia (JEPeM), before commencement (Ethical code: USM/JEPeM/PP/ 23100795). To ensure participants' informed consent, written agreements were obtained prior to their involvement in the study. These agreements confirmed not only their willingness to participate but also their consent for the publication of study findings without revealing their identities. Participation was restricted to adults, specifically college students aged 18 years and older, eliminating the necessity for parental consent. Informed consent was directly obtained from all participants involved.

3.10   Conclusion

This chapter has discussed the introduction, research design, sampling procedure, research procedure, research instruments, pilot study, data collection, data analysis, and ethical considerations. The pilot study includes revising and testing the validity and reliability of the Chinese version of the standardized Nature Relatedness Scale, as well as examining the validity and reliability of other scales, such as the Five Facet Mindfulness Questionnaire— Short Form and the Three-dimensional Inventory of Character Strengths. Overall, the methods used in this research are crucial to systematically carry out this research, answer all research questions, test research hypotheses, and ensure the achievement of research objectives.

CHAPTER 4   RESULTS OF THE STUDY

4.1   Introduction

This study aims at exploring the influence of Nature Relatedness on Character Strengths among Chinese and Malaysian university students and investigating the underlying mediating mechanisms. This chapter displays the results of the study through quantitative analysis. The data were analyzed to answer the research questions stated in Chapter 1. The analysis included the revision of the Chinese version of the Three-dimensional Nature Relatedness Scale, answering the RQ1. Next, this study performed descriptive statistics and differential analysis, addressing RQ2a, and RQ2b. This was followed by an analysis of the influence of Nature Relatedness on Character Strengths among Chinese and Malaysian university students, answering RQ3a, and RQ3b. It further discusses the result from the analysis of the mediating effect of Trait Mindfulness on the role of Nature Relatedness on Character Strengths among Chinese and Malaysian university students, answering RQ4a, and RQ4b. At the end of the chapter, the findings are summarized with a conclusion from the analysis.

Data were obtained through questionnaire surveys, and the following statistical analysis methods were employed: descriptive statistical analysis, independent samples t-test, F-test, correlation analysis, regression analysis, and model testing for the mediation effect using structural equation modeling.

The research results and findings in this chapter provide answers to RQ1, RQ2a, RQ2b, RQ3a, RQ3b, RQ4a, and RQ4b, designed in the research questions of Chapter 1. Detailed research questions and statistical analyses can be found in Table 4.1.

Table 4.1   **Summary of Research Questions and Statistical Analysis Used**

N	Research questions	Statistical analysis	Sub-subsection heading
RQ1	Does the Three-dimensional Nature Relatedness Scale have high validity and reliability?	Scale Revision Techniques: Item Analysis, Exploratory Factor Analysis, Confirmatory Factor Analysis, Validity Analysis, Reliability Analysis	4.2
RQ2a	Are there differences in Nature Relatedness, Trait Mindfulness, and Character Strengths among Chinese and Malaysian university students in different demographic and other variables?	Descriptive statistical methods, Independent samples t-test, F-test	4.3.4
RQ2b	Are there differences in Nature Relatedness, Trait Mindfulness, and Character Strengths among Chinese and Malaysian university students?	Independent samples t-test	4.3.5
RQ3a	Is there a significant correlation between Nature Relatedness and Character Strengths among Chinese and Malaysian university students?	Correlation analysis	4.4.1
RQ3b	Does Nature Relatedness predict Character Strengths positively among Chinese and Malaysian university students?	AMOS path coefficient validation	4.4.2
RQ4a	Is there a significant correlation between Nature Relatedness and Trait Mindfulness, Trait Mindfulness, and Character Strengths among Chinese and Malaysian university students?	Correlation analysis	4.5.1
RQ4b	Does Trait Mindfulness have a mediating effect on the relationship between Nature Relatedness and Character Strengths among Chinese and Malaysian university students?	Exploration and Verification of AMOS Model	4.5.2

4.2 Revision of the Chinese Version of the Three-dimensional Nature Relatedness Scale (Answering RQ1)

RQ1: Does the Three-dimensional Nature Relatedness Scale have high validity and reliability?

As there is currently no standardized Chinese version of the Nature Relatedness Scale, revision work was carried out on the Chinese version first. Before entering the actual implementation stage of the questionnaire survey research, a revision of the Chinese version of the Nature Relatedness Scale was conducted in this study. The researcher emailed the creator of the Nature Relatedness Scale, to request her permission and assistance in translating and back-translating the Chinese version of the scale and revising it into a standardized form. The specific steps were as follows:

Based on Tam's (2013b) suggestion, this study selected the 21-item Nature Relatedness Scale, which is frequently used in foreign literature, for Chinese revision and validity testing. The Chinese version of the Nature Relatedness Scale was revised for Chinese university students as the research sample, and its validity and reliability were tested in the context of Chinese culture, providing an effective measurement tool for future research on Nature Relatedness. The specific revision process was presented in the following sequence: research sample, translation and back-translation, item analysis, exploratory factor analysis, confirmatory factor analysis, validity analysis, and reliability analysis.

4.2.1 Translation and Back-translation

To adapt to Chinese culture and consider language as a potential issue, the researcher translated the Nature Relatedness Scale into Chinese. The translation was based on the back-translation technique (Brislin, 1970), translating research tools in cross-cultural studies is not easy. Translation means converting ideas and concepts from one language to another, whether orally or in writing, without changing the interpretive process to avoid different connotations. He proposed that the translation process should follow five stages. First, the research tool should be translated. Second, back-translation should be performed by a language expert who is proficient in both languages but unfamiliar with the tool. Third, the accuracy of both the translated and back-translated versions should be assessed, along with their consistency with the original tool. Fourth, a pilot study should be conducted. Fifth, the final stage involves evaluating the pilot study data. In this study, the entire process was overseen by relevant experts and the creator of the original scale.

The accuracy of the translation was validated using a 3-point Likert scale from 1 to 3, as shown in Table 4.2. In addition, experts provided suggestions to revise items that were found to be inaccurate in the translation.

Table 4.2   **Scales for Evaluating the Accuracy of Nature Relatedness Scale Translation**

Item	Scale / Score
Very Accurate	3
Accurate	2
Inaccurate	1

Based on these criteria, items that were translated very accurately received 3 points, items that were accurately translated received 2 points, and items that were inaccurately translated by experts received 1 point each. The results of translation accuracy were presented using descriptive methods. Table 4.3 shows the results of six experts' assessment of the translation accuracy of the Nature Relatedness Scale.

Table 4.3   **The Distribution of Specialist Responses to Nature Relatedness**
Scale Translated Version by Area of Expertise

Institution	Area of expertise	Number of experts
Universiti Sains Malaysia (USM)	Psychology	2
Universiti Sains Malaysia (USM)	Counseling	1
Beihang University (BUAA)	Psychological Measurement	1
Universiti Sains Malaysia (USM)	English Language	1
Universiti Sains Malaysia (USM)	Chinese Language	1
Total		6

Table 4.4 shows that 13 items (61.9%) in the list were responded to by the six experts as "very accurate" in their translations. 5 items (23.8%) were responded as "accurate" in their translations, while 3 items (14.3%) were responded as "not very accurate" in their translations. In other words, the translated version validated by experts in Table 4.4 indicates that the 13 items listed are very accurate and acceptable without further modification.

Table 4.4   **The Results of the Translation Accuracy on Nature Relatedness Scale Items**
According to the Number of Raters(Specialists)

Nature Relatedness Scale Translation	Number of items (and %)	List of items	Number of rater (Specialist)
Very Accurate	13(61.9%)	2,3,4,5,6,7,8,12,13,15,18,19,20	6
Accurate	5(23.8%)	9,10,11,14,16	6
Inaccurate	3(14.3%)	1,17,21	6
Total	21(100%)		

On the one hand, five items (23.8%) in the 21-item tool were rated as basically accurate by six experts and needed adjustments. The inaccuracies pointed out by the experts in items 9, 10, 11, 14, and 16 have been corrected, as shown in Table 4.5.

Table 4.5 **Revision on Translated Chinese Version of Nature Relatedness Scale Items According to Feedback from Raters (Specialists)**

Item	Original English version and translated Chinese version	Revision of the translated Chinese version
9	I take notice of wildlife wherever I am. 无论身处何地,我都会关注野生动物。	无论身处何地,我都会留意野生动物。
10	I don't often go out in nature. 我不经常去进行户外活动。	我不经常到大自然中去。
11	Nothing I do will change problems in other places on the planet. 无论我怎么做都不能改变环境问题。	我做什么都不能改变地球上其他地方的环境问题。
14	My feelings about nature do not affect how I live my life. 我对自然的看法不会影响我的生活方式。	我对大自然的感受不影响我怎样生活。
16	Even in the middle of the city, I notice nature around me. 即使在城市中心,我也会关注身边的自然环境。	即使在城市中心,我也会留意身边的自然环境。
1	I enjoy being outdoors, even in unpleasant weather. 即使在糟糕的天气里,我也喜欢户外。	即使在糟糕的天气里,我也喜欢户外运动。
17	My relationship to nature is an important part of who I am. 我与自然的关系是自我中的重要部分。	我与自然的关系是自我认知中的重要部分。
21	I feel very connected to all living things and the earth. 我感觉自己与所有的生物体和地球都有紧密联结。	我感觉自己与所有的生物和地球都有紧密的联系。

On the other hand, there were 3 items (14.3%) which some experts responded as "inaccurate" in translation. Among them, 2 experts responded that item 1 and item 17 were "inaccurate," and 1 expert responded that item 21 was "inaccurate." The inaccuracies in items 1, 17, and 21 pointed out by the experts have been corrected, as shown in Table 4.6.

Table 4.6 **Revision on Back Translated Nature Relatedness Scale Items According to Feedback from the Original Author of the Scale**

Item	Original version	Back translated version (English) and translated version (Chinese)	Suggestions highlighted by the original author	Revised back translated version (English) and revised translated version (Chinese)
1	I enjoy being outdoors, even in unpleasant weather.	I enjoy outdoor activities even in bad weather. 即使在糟糕的天气里,我也喜欢户外运动。	There may be a subtle difference here, from the original in that activities means "doing" something, adversely being outdoors. For example, one could be sitting which is not really an activity (or maybe some people would consider that to qualify as an "activity"?) I think the goal here is to capture how people may be willing to be outdoors or not when the weather might be less than ideal, but it doesn't necessarily involve a specific "activity."	I enjoy being outdoors, even in unpleasant weather. 我喜欢待在户外,即使在令人不愉快的天气。
17	My relationship to nature is an important part of who I am.	My relationship with nature is an important part of my self-awareness. 我与自然的关系是自我认知中的重要部分。	Perhaps in your language, the meaning is different, but to me, self-awareness is not the same as identity (who we are). Being aware of one's self is not quite the same as the concept of self-identity or just the self. This is not a huge distinction but perhaps may need adjustment, depending on what the translation means in your language.	My relationship to nature is an important part of who I am. 我与自然的关系是"我是谁"的重要组成部分。
21	I feel very connected to all living things and the earth.	I feel a close connection to all living beings and the earth. 我感觉自己与所有的生物和地球都有紧密的联系。	I am not sure how this comes across in your language but "being" to me implies something different than living things. I would think of a plant as a living thing, for example, whereas "beings" makes me think of only people or animals. Is that the same in your language?	I feel a very close connection to all living things and the earth. 我感觉与所有生物和地球都有着密切的联系。

After completing the revisions mentioned above, the next step was to back-translate the entire Chinese version of the Nature Relatedness Scale into English. The back-translation was performed by another language expert who is proficient in both English and Chinese but is not familiar with the tool. Finally, after completing all necessary steps, the translated Chinese version of the Nature Relatedness Scale and the back-translated English version was sent to the original author for validation as requested. The original author's feedback emphasized several items in the back-translated Nature Relatedness Scale that needed to be revised again, which the researchers revised based on the comments summarized by experts in Table 3.15, and these revised items were listed in Table 4.6.

The above is the final draft of the literal translation work of the scale, which has been evaluated and revised by experts. Subsequently, the scale will undergo back-translation work (Brislin, 1970). Back-translation and literal translation are two different translation processes, differing in their purposes and methods. Back-translation involves translating a previously translated text back into the original language. In the back-translation process, a different translator, separate from the original translator, is typically employed to perform the reverse translation to assess the accuracy and consistency of the translation. The purpose of back-translation is to validate the quality of the translation, ensuring that the translated version aligns with the original text without significant deviations in important information or meaning. The results of back-translation can be compared to the original text to identify any potential issues, errors, or differences in meaning, allowing for further improvements and adjustments to the translation. Back-translation is a commonly used and reliable validation method in the localization and cross-cultural research of scales (Brislin, 1970; Edunov et al., 2018). Through the process of back-translation, researchers can further refine the previous literal translation work, resulting in an improved translation version for use.

Table 4.6 clearly shows that each item has been revised accordingly based on suggestions from experts and the original author. The revised back-translated English version and the revised Chinese version were sent to the original author for a second round of validation. Finally, the author of the scale granted permission for the researcher to use the translated Chinese version of the Nature Relatedness Scale in an email. The example of comments on translation and back-translation of the Nature Relatedness Scale is illustrated in Appendix A. The approval letter from the original scale developer for the Chinese version of the Nature Relatedness Scale is illustrated in Appendix B. In the translation and back-translation process of the "Nature Relatedness Scale," a review was conducted on the definition of Nature Relatedness and its operational definition, as well as an examination of the scale. Subsequently, the scale was translated and back-translated by three Ph. D scholars proficient in both Chinese and English. These translations were then evaluated by five experts and the original scale's creator. Some modifications were made, resulting in the production of the initial test version and the creation of the Chinese version of the "Nature Relatedness Scale." as illustrated in Table 4.7.

Table 4.7　**The Initial Test Chinese Version of the Nature Relatedness Scale**

Item	Original version	Chinese initial test version
1	I enjoy being outdoors, even in unpleasant weather.	我喜欢待在户外,即使在令人不愉快的天气。
2	Some species are just meant to die out or become extinct.	有些物种注定要消亡或逐渐灭绝。
3	Humans have the right to use natural resources any way we want.	人类有权利随心所欲地使用自然资源。
4	My ideal vacation spot would be a remote, wilderness area.	遥远的原生态区域是我理想的度假胜地。

Continued

Item	Original version	Chinese initial test version
5	I always think about how my actions affect the environment.	我总是考虑自己的行为是如何影响环境的。
6	I enjoy digging in the earth and getting dirt on my hands.	我喜欢挖掘泥土,并享受双手沾满泥土的感觉。
7	My connection to nature and the environment is a part of my spirituality.	我与自然和环境的联系,是我精神世界的一部分。
8	I am very aware of environmental issues.	我很清楚环境问题。
9	I take notice of wildlife wherever I am.	无论身处何地,我都会留意野生动物。
10	I don't often go out in nature.	我不经常到大自然中去。
11	Nothing I do will change problems in other places on the planet.	我做什么都不能改变地球上其他地方的环境问题。
12	I am not separate from nature, but a part of nature.	我不是与自然分离的,而是自然的一部分。
13	The thought of being deep in the woods, away from civilization, is frightening.	深入森林,远离城市的想法是可怕的。
14	My feelings about nature do not affect how I live my life.	我对大自然的感受不影响我怎样生活。
15	Animals, birds and plants should have fewer rights than humans.	动物、鸟类和植物应该比人类拥有更少的权利。
16	Even in the middle of the city, I notice nature around me.	即使在城市中心,我也会留意身边的自然环境。
17	My relationship to nature is an important part of who I am.	我与自然的关系是"我是谁"的重要组成部分。
18	Conservation is unnecessary because nature is strong enough to recover from any human impact.	没有必要保护自然,因为自然足够强大,能从任何人类影响中恢复。
19	The state of non-human species is an indicator of the future for humans.	非人类物种的状况预示着人类的未来。

Continued

Item	Original version	Chinese initial test version
20	I think a lot about the suffering of animals.	我对动物所承受的痛苦考虑得比较多。
21	I feel very connected to all living things and the earth.	我感觉与所有生物和地球都有着密切的联系。

4.2.2   Evaluation of Item Comprehensibility

Based on the criteria of "understand" or "did not understand," participants assessed the meaning of 21 items in the preliminary version of the "Chinese Nature Relatedness Scale" formed after translation and back-translation. The comprehensibility rates of these items were determined. A survey on the comprehensibility of the questionnaire was conducted in classrooms at B University, with 64 questionnaires distributed and all 64 deemed valid, resulting in a 100% validity rate. The participants included 17 males and 47 females, with 14 students from the humanities and 50 from the sciences.

The questionnaire was titled "Scale Item Comprehensibility Assessment," and the instructions provided were as follows: "亲爱的参与者,欢迎参与我们的研究。这是对量表项目'可理解性'的评估。对于每个项目,请仔细阅读问题,然后评估您是否能理解问题的含义。本问卷是匿名的,请真实回答。您的参与对我们的研究非常宝贵。"(Dear participant, welcome to our research. This is an evaluation of the "comprehensibility" of scale items. For each item, please carefully read the question and then evaluate whether you can understand the meaning of the question. This questionnaire is anonymous, so please answer truthfully. Your participation is highly valuable for our research.)

For each item, participants had two options: ①我能理解这个句子的含义(I can understand the meaning of this sentence); ②我不能理解这个句子的含义(I cannot understand the meaning of this sentence). See Table 4.8 for the analysis results of item comprehensibility in the preliminary version of the "Chinese Nature Relatedness Scale."

Table 4.8 **Analysis Results of Item Comprehensibility in the Preliminary Version of the Chinese Nature Relatedness Scale**

Item	Comprehension rate (%)	Item	Comprehension rate (%)	Item	Comprehension rate (%)
1	71.88%	8	92.19%	15	42.19%
2	87.5%	9	87.5%	16	96.88%
3	23.44%	10	53.13%	17	93.75%
4	76.56%	11	29.69%	18	26.56%
5	87.5%	12	100%	19	79.69%
6	56.25%	13	48.44%	20	82.81%
7	98.44%	14	53.13%	21	96.88%

There are a total of 8 reverse-scored items in this scale, identified as follows: 2, 3, 10, 11, 13, 14, 15, 18. Through Table 4.8, it is observed that the comprehensibility of the reverse-scored items is consistently below 60%. Additionally, random interviews revealed that participants tend to misinterpret the comprehensibility of reverse-scored items during the answering process, often confusing it with formal answering and leading to judgmental thinking, thereby affecting the accurate assessment of comprehensibility. Consequently, after discussions with experts, the researcher decided to convert all reverse-scored items into forward-scored items. For items with scores greater than 60% but less than 90%, slight adjustments were made to the wording. Items with scores exceeding 90% did not require modification.

Following the comprehensibility assessment, revisions were made to the preliminary version of the questionnaire. The original English items, Chinese preliminary version items, Chinese revised version, and revision explanations are detailed in Table 4.9.

Table 4.9   **Comparison Between the Preliminary Version and Revised Version of the Scale**

Serial number	Original version	Chinese preliminary version	Chinese revise modification	Revision explanations
1	I enjoy being outdoors, even in unpleasant weather.	我喜欢待在户外，即使在令人不愉快的天气。	我喜欢待在户外，即使天气不好。	Fine-tune the statement
2	Some species are just meant to die out or become extinct.	有些物种注定要消亡或逐渐灭绝。	一些物种有望继续存续或逐渐繁衍。	Convert to positive scoring item
3	Humans have the right to use natural resources any way we want.	人类有权利随心所欲地使用自然资源。	人类应当合理使用自然资源。	Convert to positive scoring item
4	My ideal vacation spot would be a remote, wilderness area.	遥远的原生态区域是我理想的度假胜地。	我理想的度假胜地是远离城市的自然原生态区域。	Fine-tune the statement
5	I always think about how my actions affect the environment.	我总是考虑自己的行为是如何影响环境的。	我常常思考自己的行为如何对环境产生影响。	Fine-tune the statement
6	I enjoy digging in the earth and getting dirt on my hands.	我喜欢挖掘泥土，并享受双手沾满泥土的感觉。	我喜欢踩泥坑，并享受双脚踩泥坑的感觉。	Modify with vocabulary suitable for the Chinese context. In traditional Chinese education, using hands to dig soil is considered unhygienic and has a negative connotation. Therefore, changing "挖掘泥土" (digging soil) to "踩泥坑" (treading mud puddles) is more fitting for the Chinese cultural expression.

Continued

Serial number	Original version	Chinese preliminary version	Chinese revise modification	Revision explanations
7	My connection to nature and the environment is a part of my spirituality.	我与自然和环境的联系，是我精神世界的一部分。	我与自然和环境的联系，是我精神世界的一部分。	No modification needed
8	I am very aware of environmental issues.	我很清楚环境问题。	我很清楚环境问题。	No modification needed
9	I take notice of wildlife wherever I am.	无论身处何地，我都会留意野生动物。	无论身处何地，我都会留意野生动物。	No modification needed
10	I don't often go out in nature.	我不经常到大自然中去。	我经常到大自然中去。	Convert to positive scoring item
11	Nothing I do will change problems in other places on the planet.	我做什么都不能改变地球上其他地方的环境问题。	哪怕我只做一点点环保的事，都有可能对地球上的环境产生作用。	Convert to positive scoring item
12	I am not separate from nature, but a part of nature.	我不是与自然分离的，而是自然的一部分。	我不是与自然分离的，而是自然的一部分。	No modification needed
13	The thought of being deep in the woods, away from civilization, is frightening.	深入森林，远离城市的想法是可怕的。	"远离城市，深入森林"的想法并不令人害怕。	Convert to positive scoring item
14	My feelings about nature do not affect how I live my life.	我对大自然的感受不影响我怎样生活。	我对大自然的感受会对我的生活产生影响。	Convert to positive scoring item

147

Continued

Serial number	Original version	Chinese preliminary version	Chinese revise modification	Revision explanations
15	Animals, birds and plants should have fewer rights than humans.	动物、鸟类和植物应该比人类拥有更少的权利。	动物、鸟类和植物不应该比人类拥有更少的权利。	Convert to positive scoring item
16	Even in the middle of the city, I notice nature around me.	即使在城市中心，我也会留意身边的自然环境。	即使在城市中心，我也会留意身边的自然环境。	No modification needed
17	My relationship to nature is an important part of who I am.	我与自然的关系是"我是谁"的重要组成部分。	我与自然的关系是"我是谁"的重要组成部分。	No modification needed
18	Conservation is unnecessary because nature is strong enough to recover from any human impact.	没有必要保护自然，因为自然足够强大，能从任何人类影响中恢复。	保护自然是必要的，因为它没有强大到能从每一次人类的影响中恢复。	Convert to positive scoring item
19	The state of non-human species is an indicator of the future for humans.	非人类物种的状况预示着人类的未来。	"非人类物种"的状况是人类未来发展的一个指标。	Fine-tune the statement
20	I think a lot about the suffering of animals.	我对动物所承受的痛苦思考比较多。	我会较多地关注动物所承受的痛苦。	Fine-tune the statement
21	I feel very connected to all living things and the earth.	我感觉与所有生物和地球都有着密切的联系。	我感觉与所有生物和地球都有着密切的联系。	No modification needed

148

For the revised questionnaire, a further assessment of the comprehensibility of questionnaire items was conducted. Questionnaires were distributed in elective course classrooms, with 40 questionnaires distributed and all 40 collected, resulting in a 100% response rate. The participants included 15 males and 25 females.

As shown in Table 4.10, the comprehensibility of the items in the revised version of the scale all reached 95% or higher, which is considered excellent.

Table 4.10   **Analysis Results of Item Comprehensibility in the Revised Version of the Chinese Nature Relatedness Scale**

Item	Comprehension rate (%)	Item	Comprehension rate (%)	Item	Comprehension rate (%)
1	100%	8	100%	15	97.5%
2	97.5%	9	100%	16	100%
3	100%	10	100%	17	100%
4	100%	11	100%	18	97.5%
5	100%	12	100%	19	95%
6	97.5%	13	100%	20	100%
7	100%	14	97.5%	21	100%

4.2.3   Item Analysis

In this section of the study, the researcher conducted the distribution, identification, and exclusion of invalid questionnaires for the revised version, and then utilized two methods for item analysis: high/low group comparison and correlation between items and total score.

Using the Wenjuanxing platform, the lecturers delivering the mental health course displayed the QR code on the classroom screen. Students scanned the code using WeChat, and a total of 770 invitations were sent. Applying techniques for controlling and identifying subjects who did not answer the

149

questionnaire seriously (Zhong et al., 2021), a total of 78 questionnaires were deleted. These exclusions were based on the following criteria: 13 questionnaires were removed due to undergraduate participants selecting a grade higher than the fourth year; 5 questionnaires were excluded due to significant differences in grade and age; 10 questionnaires were removed due to extremely high or low scores on the same dimension with a clear pattern; 36 questionnaires were deleted based on excessively long or short completion times; and 14 questionnaires were excluded based on Mahalanobis distance calculations exceeding 16.75. After excluding invalid questionnaires, a total of 692 valid questionnaires were collected. This sample data was then divided into two halves, named Sample 1 (346 responses) and Sample 2 (another 346 responses). Sample 1 was used for item analysis and exploratory factor analysis, while Sample 2 was used for exploratory factor analysis.

4.2.3.1   High/Low Group Comparison

The participants in Sample 1 were ranked based on their total scores on the scale, with the top 27% forming the high-scoring group and the bottom 27% forming the low-scoring group. Independent sample t-tests were performed on the scores of the high-scoring and low-scoring groups on the 21 items. If the t-value reached the significance level, it indicated a significant difference between the two groups of participants. The item was considered effective in distinguishing the response levels of different participants. Conversely, if the t-value did not reach the significance level, it indicated that the item could not distinguish the response level of different participants and should be deleted or revised (DeVellis & Thorpe, 2021).

In Sample 1, 346 samples were sorted based on the total scores obtained from the scale. The top 27% of individuals were grouped into the high-score group, and the lowest 27% were grouped into the low-score group. Specifically, the top 1-93 samples with scores above 86 (the 93rd position scored 86) constituted the high-score group, and samples numbered 254-346 with scores below 70 (the 254th position scored 70) formed the low-score group. An independent samples t-test was conducted on the scores of participants in the high-score and low-score groups across the 21 items. If the t-value reached the significance level, it indicated a significant difference between the two groups of participants, suggesting that the item could differentiate the reaction levels of different participants and was an effective item. Conversely, if not, it suggested that the item could not distinguish the reaction levels of different participants and should be deleted. The results showed that there were significant differences in scores between the two groups for each item (all $p<0.001$), with t-values ranging from 5.760 to 20.275. Using the critical values obtained from the independent samples t-test of high and low groups, when the test was significant, it indicated good discriminative ability for the item. Therefore, no items needed to be deleted.

4.2.3.2   Using the Correlation Coefficient Between Items and Total Score to Represent Item-Total Correlation

The correlation between each item and the total score of the scale was calculated. The correlation coefficients between each item and the total scale ranged from 0. 379 to 0. 765, all reaching significance at the 0. 001 level. Therefore, no items needed to be deleted.

4.2.4   Exploratory Factor Analysis

Exploratory factor analysis was performed on the 21 items of the official scale using the data from Sample 1. The KMO (Kaiser-Meiyer-Olkin) value and Bartlett's sphericity test were used to determine whether the data were suitable for factor analysis. After principal component analysis and orthogonal rotation, the three-factor structure of the original English scale was determined to be appropriately based on the criterion that the eigenvalues were greater than 1 and the scree plot (Kline, 2015; DeVellis & Thorpe, 2021).

Utilizing data from 346 samples, an exploratory factor analysis was conducted on the 21 items formally administered. Due to the comprehensive theoretical framework of the Three-dimensional Scale and the established structural validity of its English version across multiple administrations, Hierarchical Factor Analysis was conducted separately at the subscale level. The "Varimax" method with orthogonal rotation was used, incorporating each subscale of the scale separately in each analysis. The Kaiser-Meyer-Olkin (KMO) measure of sampling adequacy was employed, where a larger KMO value indicates more common factors between variables and is more suitable for factor analysis. As per Kaiser's (1974) suggestion, if the KMO value is less than 0.5, factor analysis is less appropriate. Additionally, if the χ^2 value from Bartlett's sphericity test is significant, it indicates the presence of common factors in the population's correlation matrix, making it suitable for factor analysis.

In this study, an exploratory factor analysis was conducted using a stratified panel approach. First, based on the results of KMO and Bartlett's tests, it was determined whether each level was suitable for factor analysis. Then, based on principal component analysis and gravel plot, how many common factors can be extracted from the subscale, and observe the cumulative explanatory power of the common factors. Then, based on the "rotated component matrix", examine whether the subscale can retain only one factor. Table 4.11 displays the KMO values of each subscale and the statistical values of Bartlett's sphericity test.

Table 4.11   **KMO Values of Each Subscale and Statistical Values of Bartlett's Sphericity Test**

Subscale	KMO	χ^2	Df	p
NR-self	0.916	1176.913	28	0.000
NR-perspective	0.846	631.865	21	0.000
NR-experience	0.737	362.202	15	0.000

4.2.4.1 Exploratory Factor Analysis of the NR-self Subscale

For the NR-self subscale, items 5, 7, 8, 12, 14, 16, 17, and 21 were included, totaling 8 items. KMO = 0.916 (>0.5), indicating suitability for factor analysis. The statistic X^2 from Bartlett's sphericity test reached 1176.913 (df = 28, p = 0.000), signifying significance and confirming the appropriateness of data for factor analysis. Through principal component analysis and orthogonal rotation, based on the eigenvalue greater than 1 criterion and scree plot, it was determined that extracting one factor was most appropriate. Thus, one factor was fixed, explaining 55.080% of the total variance.

4.2.4.2 Exploratory Factor Analysis of the NR-perspective Subscale

For the NR-perspective subscale, items 2, 3, 11, 15, 18, 19, and 20 were included, totaling 7 items. KMO = 0.846 (>0.5), indicating suitability for factor analysis. The statistic X^2 from Bartlett's sphericity test reached 631.865 (df = 21, p = 0.000), signifying significance and confirming the appropriateness of data for factor analysis. Through principal component analysis and orthogonal rotation, based on the eigenvalue greater than 1 criterion and scree plot, it was determined that extracting one factor was most appropriate. Thus, one factor was fixed, explaining 45.928% of the total variance.

4.2.4.3 Exploratory Factor Analysis of the NR-experience Subscale

For the NR-experience sub-scale, items 1, 4, 6, 9, 10, and 13 were included, totaling 6 items. NR-perspective subscale KMO = 0.737 (>0.5), indicating suitability for factor analysis. The statistic X^2 from Bartlett's sphericity test reached 362.202 (df = 15, p = 0.000), signifying significance and confirming the appropriateness of data for factor analysis. Through principal component analysis and orthogonal rotation, based on the eigenvalue greater than 1 criterion and scree plot, it was determined that extracting 2 factors was most appropriate.

Although there are only 6 items, two common factors were extracted, and the cumulative explained variance of the two common factors was 58.293%. Thus, one factor was fixed, explaining 41.558% of the total variance.

In the structure matrix, it is observed that within the two common factors, the first common factor includes items 1, 6, 9, and 10, while the second common factor includes items 4 and 13. As the first common factor encompasses a larger number of items, retaining the first factor is more practical.

Upon finding the original and Chinese version of items 4 and 13, it is revealed that in item 4, the original statement is: "My ideal vacation spot would be a remote, wilderness area." and the Chinese translation is: "我理想的度假胜地是远离城市的自然原生态区域。" In Chinese culture, due to the long-term influence of safety education on students, the experience of vacationing in a natural wilderness area is not very common.

Similarly, in item 13, the original statement is: "The thought of being deep in the woods, away from civilization, is frightening." and the Chinese translation is: "深入森林, 远离城市的想法是可怕的。" Due to cultural differences in safety education in China, the idea of being frightened by the thought of being deep in the woods and away from civilization does not resonate as strongly. Therefore, in predicting and addressing the issues reflected in reverse-scored items, a reinterpretation into forward-scored items such as "The idea of being away from the city and deep in the woods" is not considered frightening in the Chinese cultural context. Considering the comprehensive interpretation and results of exploratory factor analysis, it is deemed appropriate to delete items 4 and 13. Therefore, the 21-item scale with three dimensions was revised into a 19-item scale, with the three dimensions remaining unchanged. Based on this, the 19-item original model was constructed using AMOS, laying the foundation for confirmatory factor analysis, as shown in Figure 4.1.

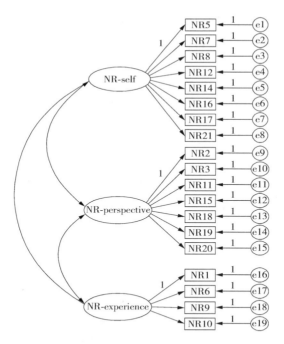

Figure 4.1 The 19-item Original Model

4.2.5 Confirmatory Factor Analysis

CFA is a statistical test that is concerned with the measurement models as part of structural equation modeling, which is the relationship between indicators or items and the latent variables or factors of a certain scale/construct (Brown, 2015). This relationship is specified based on the primary theoretical framework (Kline, 2015). A confirmatory factor analysis was conducted on the data from Sample 2 to evaluate the goodness of fit of the three-dimensional model of the Chinese version of the Nature Relatedness Scale using the following indices: $X^2/$ df, RMSEA, GFI, NFI, CFI, IFI, and TLI (Kline, 2015). The purpose was to verify whether the revised Chinese version of the Nature Relatedness Scale was still a three-dimensional structure and to evaluate its construct validity. Conducting confirmatory factor analysis on Sample 2 data.

The factor loadings for item 3 and item 6 are 0.24 and 0.23, both below 0.3.

Therefore, it is recommended to delete items 3 and 6, the revised scale retains the original three dimensions but with a reduced total of 17 items. The model was then revised, and a first-order model (as depicted in Figure 4.2) and a second-order model (as illustrated in Figure 4.3) were constructed. The results reveal that the fit indices of the second-order model for the formal data of the Nature Relatedness Scale are relatively good. This indicates that the revised Nature Relatedness Scale remains a three-dimensional linear scale with good structural validity, as shown in Table 4.12.

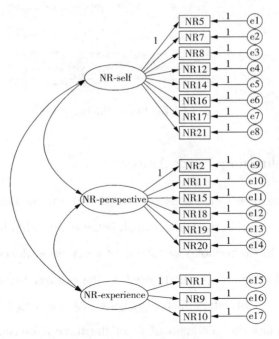

Figure 4.2   First-Order Model

4. 2. 6   Validity Analysis of the Chinese Version of the Nature Relatedness Scale

This study assessed the validity of the Chinese version of the Nature Relatedness Scale using two indicators: congruent validity and construct validity

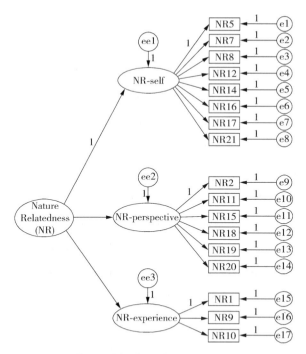

Figure 4.3   Second-Order Model

Table 4.12   **Various Indices of Confirmatory Factor Analysis Conducted by AMOS**

Model	X^2/df (Acceptable within 1-5; Preferably 1-3)	NFI	RFI	IFI	TLI	CFI	RMSEA
First-Order Model	254.738/111 = 2.295<3	0.877	0.850	0.922	0.904	0.921	0.066
Second-Order Model	280.857/112 = 2.508<3	0.888	0.863	0.934	0.918	0.933	0.061

(Kline, 2015). Congruent validity was examined by administering the Chinese version of the Nature Relatedness Scale alongside the Inclusion of Nature in the Self Scale and the Connectedness to Nature Scale. Based on data from Sample 2, Pearson correlation coefficients were calculated between the total score of the Nature Relatedness Scale and the scores of the Inclusion of Nature in the Self Scale and the Connectedness to Nature Scale. If the correlation coefficient between the total score of the Nature Relatedness Scale and the Inclusion of

Nature in the Self Scale reaches a significant level (p<0.01), it indicates that the Chinese version of the Nature Relatedness Scale possesses a certain level of congruent validity. Construct validity was assessed based on the results of the confirmatory factor analysis mentioned earlier.

Convergent Validity: Based on data from Sample 2, congruent validity was tested using Pearson correlation analysis. The results showed that the correlation coefficient between the Nature Relatedness Scale and the Inclusion of Nature in the Self Scale was 0.35, indicating a moderate correlation, and the correlation with the Connectedness to Nature Scale was 0. 71, indicating a strong correlation. Both correlations reached statistical significance (p<0.001), suggesting that the Chinese version of the Nature Relatedness Scale has high convergent validity, as displayed in Table 4.13.

Table 4.13 **Convergent Validity (Pearson Correlation)**

Scale	Inclusion of Nature in the Self Scale (INS)	Connectedness to Nature Scale(CNS)
Nature Relatedness Scale (NRS-C)	0.35 ***	0.71 ***

Note: * p<0.05, **p<0.01, ***p<0.001

Construct validity refers to the extent to which the scores of a measurement instrument or questionnaire align with the researcher's theoretical expectations, that is, whether the instrument accurately measures the intended latent construct (DeVellis & Thorpe, 2021). Construct validity focuses on whether the construct proposed by the researcher is reflected in the observed scores. Since latent constructs cannot be measured directly, observed scores or indicators play a crucial role in indirectly assessing these constructs (Kline, 2015). In this study, construct validity was examined through confirmatory factor analysis. The results showed acceptable fit indices, indicating good structural validity of the scale. This supports the scale's effectiveness in measuring the degree of participants' Nature Relatedness (see Table 4.12).

4. 2. 7   Reliability Analysis of the Chinese Version of the Nature Relatedness Scale

The reliability of a measurement refers to the consistency of the results obtained. In measurement theory, reliability is defined as the ratio of the true variance of a set of measurement scores to the total variance. This ratio is called the reliability coefficient. In actual measurement, since the true value is unknown, the reliability coefficient can only be estimated based on a set of obtained data. The main reliability coefficients include test-retest reliability, alternate-form reliability, split-half reliability, and internal consistency reliability (Gay et al., 2011; Wu, 2003). This study used two indicators, internal consistency reliability to reflect the reliability of the revised Chinese version of the Nature Relatedness Scale. Internal consistency reliability was assessed by calculating Cronbach's alpha coefficient using data from Sample 2. The internal consistency coefficients of the three subscales, NR-Self, NR-Perspective, and NR-Experience, are shown in Table 4.14, which are 0.88, 0.75, and 0.71, respectively, all greater than 0.7, indicating acceptable reliability. The internal consistency coefficient of the total scale is relatively high, at 0.91, indicating high overall scale reliability.

Table 4.14   **Internal Consistency Coefficients for the Overall**

Scale and Three Subscales

Nature Relatedness Scale Subscales	Items	Cronbach's Coefficient Value
NR-self	5, 7, 8, 12, 14, 16, 17, 21	0.88
NR-perspective	2, 11, 15, 18, 19, 20	0.75
NR-experience	1, 9, 10	0.71
Total Nature Relatedness		0.91

4.3 Descriptive Statistics and Differential Analysis
(Answering RQ2a, RQ2b)

4.3.1 Study Participants

Utilizing the same set of samples, including both Chinese and Malaysian samples. The Chinese samples came from 3 universities, totaling 386 (65 samples from A University, 170 samples from B University, and 151 samples from C University). However, the Malaysian samples came from D university, totaling 247 (see Table 4.15).

Table 4.15　　　　　　　　**Distribution of Study Participants**

(**Chinese N=386 / Malaysian University Students N=247**)

Demographic variables		Number	Ratio(%)	Number	Ratio(%)
		Chinese University Students		Malaysian University Students	
Gender	Male	156	40.4	50	20.2
	Female	230	59.6	197	79.8
Age	18	109	28.2	0	0
	19	128	33.2	0	0
	20	87	22.5	26	10.5
	21	38	9.8	55	22.3
	22	18	4.7	49	19.8
	23	6	1.6	57	23.1
	>23	0	0	60	24.3
Current academic year	Year 1	178	46.1	85	34.4
	Year 2	128	33.2	54	21.9
	Year 3	41	10.6	50	20.2
	Year 4	39	10.1	58	23.5

Continued

Demographic variables		Number	Ratio(%)	Number	Ratio(%)
		Chinese University Students		Malaysian University Students	
Major	Humanities and Social Sciences	53	13.7	247	100
	Science and Engineering	292	75.6	0	0
	Arts and Sports	41	10.6	0	0
Only Child Status	only child	113	29.3	16	6.5
	Not an only child	273	70.7	231	93.5
Family location	Urban	162	42	112	45.3
	Rural	224	58	135	54.7
Mindfulness experience	Yes	94	24.4	97	39.3
	No	292	75.6	150	60.7
Time in nature one week	① Less than half an hour	43	11.1	14	5.7
	② 0.5-1 hour	45	11.7	16	6.5
	③ 1-2 hours	55	14.2	51	20.6
	④ 2-3 hours	63	16.3	46	18.6
	⑤ 3-4 hours	61	15.8	0	0
	⑥ 4-5 hours	26	6.7	52	21.1
	⑦ 5-6 hours	15	3.9	27	10.9
	⑧ 6-7 hours	15	3.9	10	4
	⑨ 8 hours or more	63	16.3	11	4.5
Times in nature one week	① 0 time	28	7.3	13	5.3
	② 1 time	51	13.2	19	7.7
	③ 2 times	67	17.4	59	23.9
	④ 3 times	65	16.8	40	16.2
	⑤ 4 times	39	10.1	42	17
	⑥ 5 times	44	11.4	31	12.6
	⑦ 6 times	29	7.5	10	4
	⑧ 7 times	63	16.3	9	3.6
	⑨ 8 times or more	0	0	24	9.7

Continued

Demographic variables		Number	Ratio(%)	Number	Ratio(%)
		Chinese University Students		Malaysian University Students	
Activities types in nature	① Walking	200	51.8	129	52.2
	② Running	49	12.7	13	5.3
	③ Cycling	33	8.5	9	3.6
	④ Hiking	10	2.6	19	7.7
	⑤ Gardening	3	0.3	7	2.8
	⑥ Meditation	7	2.3	9	3.6
	⑦ Sightseeing	35	9.1	28	11.3
	⑧ Others	49	12.7	32	13.4
Emotional experience in nature	1 Negative	3	0.3	0	0
	2	3	0.3	0	0
	3	3	0.8	0	0
	4	3	0.3	4	1.6
	5	22	7.3	15	6.1
	6	42	10.9	23	9.3
	7	124	32.1	33	13.4
	8	87	22.5	56	22.7
	9 Positive	99	25.6	116	47

4.3.2   Common Method Bias Test

Due to the self-report nature of the data in this study obtained through university students' self-report questionnaires, there may be the presence of common method bias, potentially impacting the accuracy of the research results (Malhotra et al., 2006). To mitigate common method bias during the questionnaire design and survey process, several methods were employed. Clear instructional language: during questionnaire distribution, uniform instructions were provided, emphasizing the importance of truthful and honest responses at the beginning of the questionnaire to reduce potential response biases. Emphasis on anonymity: the questionnaire design ensured anonymity to minimize response biases arising from social expectations. Randomization of question order: questions in the questionnaire were randomly arranged to reduce the likelihood of respondents answering in a specific pattern. Design of reverse-scoring items: several reverse-scoring items were included in the questionnaire to assess whether participants were responding attentively. In total, there were 20 reverse-scoring items in this questionnaire.

Following the questionnaire survey, Harman's Single-Factor Test was employed to examine the potential presence of common method bias in the research data (Zhou & Liu, 2011; Malhotra et al., 2006). Principal component analysis (exploratory factor analysis without rotation) was performed on the 70 items of the questionnaire. In the data of Chinese university students, the results showed that there were 5 factors with eigenvalues greater than 1, and the first primary factor explained 17.337% of the variance, which is below the critical threshold of 40%. Therefore, this data did not exhibit common method bias issues. In the data of Malaysian university students, the results showed that there were 13 factors with eigenvalues greater than 1, and the first primary factor explained 26.829% of the variance, which is below the critical threshold of 40%. Therefore, this data did not exhibit common method bias issues.

4.3.3 Descriptive Statistics

Table 4.16 presents the three sub-scales of the Nature Relatedness Scale and its total score, the five subscales of the Five Facet Mindfulness Questionnaire—Short Form along with the Trait Mindfulness total score, and the three subscales of the Three-dimensional Inventory of Character Strengths and the Character Strengths total score. Except for Chinese university students scoring below than the mean on the non-judging and non-reactivity mindfulness subscales, all other subscales and total scores are above average.

Table 4.16   **Distribution of Descriptive Statistics of the Scores for the Three Main Variables and Their Dimensions（Chinese N=386 / Malaysian University Students N=247）**

Number	Variables	Chinese or Malaysian University Students	M	SD	Scale items	Scoring method	Total score	Mean score
1	NR-self	CUS	31.36	4.34	8	5	40	20
		MUS	32.46	4.29				
2	NR-perspective	CUS	23.88	3.37	6	5	30	15
		MUS	21.94	3.05				
3	NR-experience	CUS	9.92	1.99	3	5	15	7.5
		MUS	11.61	1.75				
4	Nature Relatedness	CUS	65.15	8.36	17	5	85	42.5
		MUS	66	7.43				
5	Observing	CUS	14.41	2.54	4	5	20	10
		MUS	15.78	2.68				
6	Describing	CUS	15.58	2.85	5	5	25	12.5
		MUS	17.78	2.46				
7	Acting with awareness	CUS	14.97	3.06	5	5	25	12.5
		MUS	16.02	2.45				
8	Non-judging	CUS	8.32	1.83	5	5	25	12.5
		MUS	14.85	1.94				
9	Non-reactivity	CUS	10.09	1.93	5	5	25	12.5
		MUS	18.52	2.83				
10	Trait Mindfulness	CUS	63.38	6.36	24	5	100	50
		MUS	82.94	6.9				
11	Caring	CUS	19.83	2.71	5	5	25	12.5
		MUS	21.12	3.67				
12	Inquisitiveness	CUS	16.95	2.88	5	5	25	12.5
		MUS	19.33	3.55				
13	Self-control	CUS	16.11	3.02	5	5	25	12.5
		MUS	19.5	3.27				
14	Character Strengths	CUS	52.89	6.74	15	5	75	32.5
		MUS	59.95	9.51				

4.3.4   Differences of Nature Relatedness, Trait Mindfulness, and Character Strengths Among Chinese and Malaysian University Students in Different Demographic and Other Variables (Answering RQ2a)

RQ2a: Are there differences in Nature Relatedness, Trait Mindfulness, and Character Strengths among Chinese and Malaysian university students in different demographic and other variables?

Significant differences in Nature Relatedness, Trait Mindfulness, and Character Strengths were found among Malaysian university students across demographic factors (gender, academic year, only-child status, family location) and other variables (mindfulness experience, activities, and emotional experiences in nature). Chinese university students showed significant differences in these traits only in terms of emotional experiences in nature.

4.3.4.1   Differences in Gender

As illustrated in Table 4.17, gender had no significant impact on the Nature Relatedness, Trait Mindfulness, and Character Strengths of Chinese university students. Gender had no significant influence on the Nature Relatedness and Trait Mindfulness of Malaysian university students, but had a significant influence on their Character Strengths. The Character Strengths of female university students (60.55 ± 9.23) were higher than that of male university students (57.54 ± 10.18).

4.3.4.2   Differences in Age

Based on the F-test results in the following Table 4.18, age had no significant effect on Nature Relatedness, Trait Mindfulness, and Character Strengths among Chinese and Malaysian university students. However, an interesting phenomenon emerged during the survey of Chinese and Malaysian university students: there were no participants aged 18 and 19 among Malaysian university students, while among Chinese university students, there were no participants over the age of 23.

165

This phenomenon will be discussed in detail in Chapter 5.

Table 4.17   **The t-test of Nature Relatedness, Trait Mindfulness,**
and Character Strengths on Gender

Variables	Gender	Chinese University Students				Malaysian University Students			
		Number	Mean	SD	t	Number	Mean	SD	t
Nature Relatedness	Male	156	64.28	8.82	−1.69	50	63.64	8.27	0.31
	Female	230	65.74	7.99	p=0.09	197	66.6	7.08	p=0.76
Trait Mindfulness	Male	156	63.47	6.28	0.24	50	81.62	6.19	0.21
	Female	230	63.31	6.42	p=0.82	197	83.31	7.04	p=0.84
Character Strengths	Male	156	53.33	6.88	1.06	50	57.54	10.18	−2.07*
	Female	230	52.59	6.64	p=0.29	197	60.55	9.23	p=0.04 (Male<Female)

Note: * p<0.05, **p<0.01, ***p<0.001

4.3.4.3 Differences in Academic Year

Table 4.18   **The F-test of Nature Relatedness, Trait Mindfulness,**
and Character Strengths on Academic Year

Variables	Academic Year	Chinese University Students				Malaysian University Students			
		Number	Mean	SD	F	Number	Mean	SD	F
Nature Relatedness	Year 1	178	66.29	8.97	2.46 p=0.06	85	67.4	7.29	3.23* p=0.02 (Year1>Year2; Year1>Year4; Year 3>Year 4)
	Year 2	148	63.90	8.01		54	64.65	7.78	
	Year 3	41	65.44	6.85		50	67.16	6.43	
	Year 4	19	63.63	6.85		58	64.21	7.61	
Trait Mindfulness	Year 1	178	63.44	6.73	0.61 p=0.61	85	83.72	7.97	1.37 p=0.25
	Year 2	148	63.05	5.90		54	81.57	7.01	
	Year 3	41	63.46	5.95		50	83.74	5.77	
	Year 4	19	65.11	7.19		58	82.52	5.84	
Character Strengths	Year 1	178	53.70	7.45	2.119 P=0.10	85	61.79	9.34	7.02 p=0.000
	Year 2	148	51.89	6.07		54	56.3	8.54	
	Year 3	41	52.59	6.42		50	63.14	9.63	
	Year 4	19	53.84	4.13		58	57.88	9.03	

Note: * p<0.05, **p<0.01, ***p<0.001

In accordance with the F-test results in the following Table 4.19, academic year's Nature Relatedness for Chinese university students, Trait Mindfulness, and Character Strengths had no significant effect. The academic year had no significant influence on Malaysian university students' Trait Mindfulness and Character

Table 4.19 **The F-test of Nature Relatedness, Trait Mindfulness, and Character Strengths on Age**

Variables	Age	Chinese University Students				Malaysian University Students			
		Number	Mean	SD	F	Number	Mean	SD	F
Nature Relatedness	18	109	66.72	9.52	1.62 p=0.15	0	0	0	0.58 p=0.68
	19	128	64.00	8.19		0	0	0	
	20	87	65.20	7.52		26	67.08	8.1	
	21	38	64.89	7.81		55	66.45	7.04	
	22	18	63.17	6.35		49	65.67	7.74	
	23	6	68.00	6.75		57	66.47	7.3	
	>23	0	0	0		60	64.93	7.38	
Trait Mindfulness	18	109	63.38	6.92	0.86 p=0.51	0	0	0	0.24 p=0.92
	19	128	63.21	6.16		26	82.69	10.07	
	20	87	63.26	5.92		55	83.49	7.3	
	21	38	62.84	6.02		49	82.43	6.55	
	22	18	64.67	5.88		57	83.37	5.88	
	23	6	68.00	9.55		60	82.68	6.19	
Character Strengths	18	109	53.55	7.05	0.97 p=0.44	0	0	0	1.26 p=0.29
	19	128	52.34	7.17		26	60.85	10.56	
	20	87	52.43	6.95		55	59.95	9.13	
	21	38	53.18	4.74		49	59.06	8.97	
	22	18	53.06	4.67		57	61.98	10.15	
	23	6	57.17	1.47		60	58.33	9	

Strengths. But the academic year had a significant effect on the Nature Relatedness of Malaysian university students. After the LSD post-mortem multiple comparisons, the scores of Year 1 (67.4±7.29)>Year 2 (64.65±7.78); Year 1 (67.4 ±7.29)>Year 4 (64.21±7.61); Year 3 (67.16±6.43)>Year 4 (64.21±7.61).

4.3.4.4   Differences in Major

In line with the F-test results in Table 4.20, the major had no significant effect on the correlation, Trait Mindfulness, and Character Strengths among Chinese university students. In the survey sample in Malaysia, the statistics of each major did not meet statistical standards, so no analysis and comparison were conducted on this.

Table 4.20   **The F-test of Nature Relatedness, Trait Mindfulness, and Character Strengths on Major Among Chinese University Students**

Variables	Major	Number	Mean	SD	F
Nature Relatedness	Humanities and Social Sciences	53	66.45	8.65	0.75 (p=0.47)
	Science and Engineering	292	64.97	8.25	
	Arts and Sports	41	64.78	8.75	
Trait Mindfulness	Humanities and Social Sciences	53	63.57	5.50	0.60 (p=0.55)
	Science and Engineering	292	63.21	6.51	
	Arts and Sports	41	64.34	6.31	
Character Strengths	Humanities and Social Sciences	53	52.96	5.87	1.26 (p=0.29)
	Science and Engineering	292	52.66	6.72	
	Arts and Sports	41	54.44	7.83	

Note: *p<0.05, **p<0.01, ***p<0.001

4.3.4.5   Differences in Only Child Status

As stated by Table 4.21, Only Child Status did not have a significant impact on

168

Chinese university students' Nature Relatedness, Trait Mindfulness, and Character Strengths. Only Child Status did not have a significant impact on Malaysian university students' Trait Mindfulness, Character Strengths, but had a significant impact on Nature Relatedness. The Nature Relatedness level of Malaysian university students who are not only children at home (66.32 ± 66.32) is higher than that of Malaysian university students who are only children at home (61.31 ± 61.31).

Table 4.21   **The t-test of Nature Relatedness, Trait Mindfulness, and Character Strengths on Only Child Status**

Variables	Only Child Status	Chinese University Students				Malaysian University Students			
		Number	Mean	SD	t	Number	Mean	SD	t
Nature Relatedness	Only Child	113	66.19	9.82	1.48	16	61.31	61.31	−4.12 ***; p=0.000 (Only child<Not an only child)
	Not An Only Child	273	64.72	7.65	p=0.16	231	66.32	66.32	
Trait Mindfulness	Male	113	63.97	7.00	1.12	16	80.25	80.25	−1.64; p=0.10
	Female	273	63.13	6.07	p=0.26	231	83.16	83.16	
Character Strengths	Male	113	53.49	6.90	1.12	16	56.63	56.63	−1.45; p=0.15
	Female	273	52.64	6.67	p=0.27	231	60.17	60.17	

Note: * p<0.05, **p<0.01, ***p<0.001

4.3.4.6   Differences in Family Location

As stated in Table 4.22, Family Location Status did not have a significant impact on Chinese university students' Nature Relatedness, Trait Mindfulness, and Character Strengths. Family Location Status did not have a significant impact on Malaysian university students' Nature Relatedness, or Trait Mindfulness, but has a significant impact on Malaysian university students' Character Strengths. Rural Malaysian university students (61.07 ± 9.71) had higher

169

Character Strengths than in Urban (58.58±9.07).

Table 4.22　　**The t-test of Nature Relatedness, Trait Mindfulness, and Character Strengths on Family Location Status**

Variables	Family Location	Chinese University Students				Malaysian University Students			
		Number	Mean	SD	t	N	Mean	SD	t
Nature Relatedness	Urban	162	9.31	0.73	0.68	112	66.16	7.81	0.31,
	Rural	224	7.61	0.51	p=0.50	135	65.87	7.09	p=0.76
Trait Mindfulness	Urban	162	6.28	0.49	1.11	112	83.07	7.39	0.21,
	Rural	224	6.41	0.43	p=0.27	135	82.89	6.49	p=0.84
Character Strengths	Urban	162	6.88	0.54	1.28	112	58.58	9.07	−2.07*, p=0.04
	Rural	224	6.63	0.44	p=0.20	135	61.07	9.71	(Urban<Rural)

Note: * p<0.05, **p<0.01, ***p<0.001

Table 4.23　The T-test of Nature Relatedness, Trait Mindfulness, and Character Strengths on Mindfulness Experience

Variables	Mindfulness Experience	Chinese University Students				Malaysian University Students			
		Number	Mean	SD	t	Number	Mean	SD	t
Nature Relatedness	Experienced	94	64.15	8.29	−1.34	97	67.58	7.87	2.72**,p=0.007 (Experienced> Inexperienced)
	Inexperienced	292	65.47	8.37	p=0.18	150	64.98	6.94	
Trait Mindfulness	Experienced	94	64.18	6.26	1.41	97	84.86	6.89	3.53***,p=0.000 (Experienced> Inexperienced)
	Inexperienced	292	63.12	6.38	p=0.16	150	81.75	6.65	
Character Strengths	Experienced	94	52.88	6.23	−0.014	97	63.32	9.1	4.68***,p=0.000 (Experienced> Inexperienced)
	Inexperienced	292	52.89	6.91	p=0.99	150	57.76	9.12	

Note: * p<0.05, **p<0.01, ***p<0.001

4.3.4.7   Differences in Mindfulness Experience

As shown in Table 4.23, mindfulness experience had no significant impact on Chinese university students' Nature Relatedness, Trait Mindfulness, and Character Strengths. However, mindfulness experience had a significant influence on Malaysian university students' Nature Relatedness, Trait Mindfulness, and Character Strengths. Malaysian university students' Nature Relatedness with mindfulness experience (67.58 ± 7.87) >without mindfulness experience (64.98 ± 6.94), Malaysian university students Trait Mindfulness (84.86 ± 6.89) >without mindfulness experience (81.75 ± 6.65), Character Strengths of Malaysian university students with mindfulness experience (63.32 ± 9.1) >without mindfulness experience (57.76 ± 9.12).

4.3.4.8   Differences in Time in Nature One Week

Based on the results in Table 4.24, the Time in Nature of One Week had no significant impact on Chinese and Malaysian university students' Nature Relatedness, Trait Mindfulness, and Character Strengths.

4.3.4.9   Differences in Times in Nature One Week

In accordance with the results in Table 4.25, Times in Nature Per Week had no significant impact on Malaysian university students' Nature Relatedness, Trait Mindfulness, and Character Strengths. It has no significant impact on the Trait Mindfulness of Chinese university students. However, it has a significant impact on the Nature Relatedness and Character Strengths of Chinese university students. What is worth discussing is that multiple comparisons after using LSD are made. The pairwise comparison method does not find out which dimensions have significant differences.

Table 4.24   **The F-test of Nature Relatedness, Trait Mindfulness, and Character Strengths on Time in Nature One Week**

Variables	Time in Nature (T, hours)	Chinese University Students(N=386)				Malaysian University Students(N=247)			
		Number	Mean	SD	F	Number	Mean	SD	F
Nature Relatedness	① T≤0.5	43	61.49	8.73	1.55 p=0.14	14	67.64	8.03	0.54 p=0.83
	② 0.5<T≤1	45	64.71	9.14		16	65.31	8.21	
	③ 1<T≤2	55	65.64	7.92		51	65.31	6.88	
	④ 2<T≤3	63	65.05	7.96		46	65.76	6.22	
	⑤ 3<T≤4	61	65.46	7.53		52	65.33	8.12	
	⑥ 4<T≤5	26	65.35	10.54		27	66.96	7.35	
	⑦ 5<T≤6	15	68.27	6.9		10	67.6	8.91	
	⑧ 6<T≤7	15	66.93	5.16		11	64.82	6.26	
	⑨ >7	63	66.1	8.64		20	68	8.74	
Trait Mindfulness	① T≤0.5	43	62.05	7.36	0.99 p=0.44	14	83.5	9.65	0.65 p=0.74
	② 0.5<T≤1	45	61.98	6.37		16	81.06	6.76	
	③ 1<T≤2	55	64.35	5.98		51	82.47	6.99	
	④ 2<T≤3	63	63.68	6.35		46	84.09	6.31	
	⑤ 3<T≤4	61	63.05	5.96		52	82.67	7.15	
	⑥ 4<T≤5	26	63	6.93		27	82.48	6.04	
	⑦ 5<T≤6	15	63.53	6.83		10	86.2	9.48	
	⑧ 6<T≤7	15	63.33	5.51		11	82.64	3.8	
	⑨ >7	63	64.57	6.14		20	82.85	6.57	
Character Strengths	① T≤0.5	43	50.74	6.35	0.99 p=0.44	14	57.86	7.82	0.88 p=0.53
	② 0.5<T≤1	45	52.56	6.75		16	55.31	8.09	
	③ 1<T≤2	55	53.6	6.84		51	60.51	9.9	
	④ 2<T≤3	63	53	6.32		46	60.87	9.21	
	⑤ 3<T≤4	61	51.74	7.11		52	60.88	9.89	
	⑥ 4<T≤5	26	54.46	7.5		27	58.89	9.3	
	⑦ 5<T≤6	15	53.07	6.47		10	61.9	7.56	
	⑧ 6<T≤7	15	53.6	5.84		11	61.55	8.03	
	⑨ >7	63	54.13	6.72		20	58.65	11.74	

Note: $*p<0.05$, $**p<0.01$, $***p<0.001$

Table 4.25　The F-test of Nature Relatedness, Trait Mindfulness, and Character Strengths on Times in Nature One Week

Variables	Times in nature one week	Chinese University Students (N=386)				Malaysian University Students (N=247)			
		Number	Mean	SD	F	Number	Mean	SD	F
Nature Relatedness	① 0 time	28	60.82	8.92	2.20* p=0.03	13	66.38	9.02	1.07 p=0.38
	② 1 time	51	64.51	7.84		19	64.95	7.33	
	③ 2 times	67	65.78	7.89		59	65.22	6.72	
	④ 3 times	65	65.37	8.26		40	64.53	7.63	
	⑤ 4 times	39	66.79	8.33		42	66.57	7.25	
	⑥ 5 times	44	63.7	8.56		31	65.9	8.4	
	⑦ 6 times	29	64.17	7.94		10	65.8	8.26	
	⑧ 7 times	63	67.14	8.61		9	68.78	5.07	
	⑨ 8 times or more	0	0	0		24	69.17	7.03	
Trait Mindfulness	① 0 time	28	62.43	7.73	1.25 p=0.27	13	84.85	9.32	0.67 p=0.72
	② 1 time	51	61.29	6.78		19	81.68	7.56	
	③ 2 times	67	64.16	6.34		59	82.56	7.34	
	④ 3 times	65	63.54	5.24		40	81.85	6.24	
	⑤ 4 times	39	64.1	5.13		42	82.9	6.81	
	⑥ 5 times	44	63	6.41		31	83.87	6.6	
	⑦ 6 times	29	63.93	5.77		10	83	5.48	
	⑧ 7 times	63	64.03	7.16		9	86	7.35	
	⑨ 8 times or more	0	0	0		24	83.67	6.03	
Character Strengths	① 0 time	28	50.18	6.43	2.76** p=0.008	13	57	7.55	0.782 p=0.62
	② 1 time	51	51	6.14		19	57.58	8.92	
	③ 2 times	67	53.7	6.74		59	60	9.7	
	④ 3 times	65	52.37	5.94		40	59	9.23	
	⑤ 4 times	39	54.1	6.7		42	60.26	9.24	
	⑥ 5 times	44	54.36	6.62		31	62.19	9.26	
	⑦ 6 times	29	51	7.12		10	58.6	8.3	
	⑧ 7 times	63	54.4	7.38		9	63.67	10.45	
	⑨ 8 times or more	0	0	0		24	60.54	11.65	

Note: *p<0.05, **p<0.01, ***p<0.001

4.3.4.10   Differences in Activities in Nature

As indicated by the F-test results in Table 4.26, activities in nature have no significant impact on Chinese university students' Nature Relatedness, Trait Mindfulness, and Character Strengths. However, activities in nature have a significant impact on Malaysian university students' Nature Relatedness, and Trait Mindfulness, but there is no significant difference in Character Strengths. Multiple post-LSD comparisons was used and we can find that in terms of Nature Relatedness, ①>③, ①>⑤,①>⑥,①>⑧,②>③, ⑦>③,④>⑤, ④>⑥, ②>⑤,⑦>⑤,⑧>⑤, ②>⑥,⑦>⑥, ⑦>⑧. On the aspect of Trait Mindfulness, ⑦>①,⑦>③, ⑦>④,⑦>⑤, ⑦>⑥,⑦>⑧,②>③. The meanings of the above symbols are as follows: ① Walking, ② Running, ③ Cycling, ④ Hiking, ⑤ Gardening, ⑥ Meditation, ⑦ Sightseeing, ⑧ Jogging, ⑨ Others. The specific mean and variance are shown in Table 4.26.

4.3.4.11   Differences in Emotional Experience

Based on the F-test results in Table 4.27, Emotional Experience has a significant impact on the Nature Relatedness, Trait Mindfulness, and Character Strengths of Chinese and Malaysian university students. As revealed by the LSD post hoc multiple comparisons results, for the sample of Chinese university students, in terms of Nature Relatedness, ⑨>⑤, ⑨>⑥, ⑨>⑦; in terms of Trait Mindfulness, ⑥>⑨, and in terms of Character Strengths, ⑨>⑤, ⑨>⑥, ⑨>⑦. For the sample of Malaysian university students, in terms of Nature Relatedness, ⑧>④, ⑨>④, ⑨>⑤,⑥>⑤, ⑦>⑤, ⑧>⑤, ⑧>⑥, ⑨>⑥, ⑧>⑦, ⑨>⑦, ⑨>⑧; in terms of Trait Mindfulness, ⑧>⑤, ⑧>⑥, ⑧>⑦, ⑨>⑤, ⑨>⑥, ⑨>⑦; in terms of Character Strengths, ⑧>④, ⑧>⑤, ⑧>⑥, ⑧>⑦, ⑨>④, ⑨>⑤, ⑨>⑥, ⑨>⑦. The meanings of the above symbols are as follows: 1 = very negative, 9 = very positive. Table 4.27 displays the specific mean and variance values.

Table 4.26   The F-test of Nature Relatedness, Trait Mindfulness, and Character Strengths on Activities in Nature

Variables	Activities in Nature	Chinese University Students (N=386)				Malaysian University Students (N=247)			
		N	Mean	SD	F	N	Mean	SD	F
Nature Relatedness	① Walking	200	64.71	8.25	0.98 p=0.45	129	66.84	6.88	3.817*** p=0.000 (①>③, ①>⑤, ①>⑥, ①>⑧, ②>③, ⑦>③, ④>⑤, ④>⑥, ②>⑤, ⑦>⑤, ⑧>⑤, ②>⑥, ⑦>⑥, ⑦>⑧)
	② Running	49	65.78	9.04		13	68.31	10.01	
	③ Cycling	33	67.15	9.09		9	61.67	6.5	
	④ Hiking	10	66.3	6.58		19	65.79	8.2	
	⑤ Gardening	3	66.67	8.74		7	57.86	5.15	
	⑥ Meditation	7	62.71	4.72		9	59.78	4.99	
	⑦ Sightseeing	35	67	7.72		28	68.86	7.41	
	⑧ Jogging	0	0	0		31	63.81	6.54	
	⑨ Others	49	63.67	8.68		2	69	7.07	
Trait Mindfulness	① Walking	200	62.71	6.07	0.98 p=0.45	129	83.05	6.55	2.175* p=0.03 (⑦>①, ⑦>③, ⑦>④, ⑦>⑤, ⑦>⑥, ⑦>⑧, ②>③)
	② Running	49	64.73	6.77		13	84.77	9.38	
	③ Cycling	33	65.52	5.84		9	78.56	7.47	
	④ Hiking	10	64.6	6.52		19	81.11	6.14	
	⑤ Gardening	3	66.67	8.96		7	80.29	9.72	
	⑥ Meditation	7	58.29	6.82		9	79.56	3.91	
	⑦ Sightseeing	35	63.31	6.16		28	86.43	7.21	
	⑧ Jogging	0	0	0		31	82.58	6.17	
	⑨ Others	49	63.61	6.85		2	86	2.83	
Character Strengths	① Walking	200	52.41	6.64	1.44 p=0.19	129	60.88	9.15	1.392 p=0.2
	② Running	49	54.76	7.76		13	61.15	12.27	
	③ Cycling	33	54.48	7.12		9	58.89	12.23	
	④ Hiking	10	54.9	3.25		19	57.84	9.73	
	⑤ Gardening	3	48.67	10.07		7	52.43	6.43	
	⑥ Meditation	7	50.43	8.14		9	53.89	7.56	
	⑦ Sightseeing	35	52.34	6.94		28	60.82	8.6	
	⑧ Jogging	0	0	0		31	59.61	10.04	
	⑨ Others	49	52.53	5.41		2	62.5	0.71	

Note: * p<0.05, ** p<0.01, *** p<0.001

175

Table 4.27　The F-test of Nature Relatedness, Trait Mindfulness, and Character Strengths on Emotional Experience in Nature Differences

Variables	Emotional experience in nature (1=Very negative, 9=Very positive)	Chinese University Students (N=386)				Malaysian University Students (N=247)			
		N	Mean	SD	F	N	Mean	SD	F
Nature Relatedness	①	0	0	0		0	0	0	
	②	6	64.5	11.67		0	0	0	
	③	3	68.67	8.96		0	0	0	
	④	4	60.75	5.44	8.06*** p=0.000 (⑨>⑤, ⑨>⑥, ⑨>⑦)	4	58.5	3.32	16.30*** p=0.000 (⑧>④, ⑨>④, ⑨>⑤, ⑥>⑤, ⑦>⑤, ⑧>⑤, ⑧>⑥, ⑨>⑥, ⑥>⑧, ⑧>⑦, ⑨>⑦, ⑨>⑧)
	⑤	21	59.43	9.29		15	56.93	6.58	
	⑥	42	61.67	8.11		23	61.22	5.58	
	⑦	124	63.69	7.12		33	62.91	5.9	
	⑧	87	65.44	7.74		56	66.34	5.17	
	⑨	99	69.54	8.25		116	69.09	7.34	
Trait Mindfulness	①	0	0	0		0	0	0	
	②	6	66	4.98		0	0	0	
	③	3	62.33	5.69		0	0	0	
	④	4	58	9.83	3.61** p=0.001(⑥>⑨)	4	80.75	8.42	8.14*** p=0.000 (⑧>⑤, ⑧>⑥, ⑧>⑦, ⑨>⑤, ⑨>⑥, ⑨>⑦)
	⑤	21	61	6.61		15	77.73	5.95	
	⑥	42	60.07	5.91		23	79.39	4.23	
	⑦	124	63.64	5.85		33	79.24	5.69	
	⑧	87	63.55	6.66		56	84.36	7.63	
	⑨	99	64.89	6.21		116	84.83	6.38	
Character Strengths	①	0	0	0		0	0	0	
	②	6	55.17	6.27		0	0	0	
	③	3	56.33	11.85		0	0	0	
	④	4	44.75	5.62	7.30*** p=0.000(⑨>⑤, ⑨>⑥, ⑨>⑦)	4	51.75	7.89	13.18*** p=0.000 (⑧>④, ⑧>⑤, ⑧>⑥, ⑧>⑦, ⑨>④, ⑨>⑤, ⑨>⑥, ⑨>⑦)
	⑤	21	49.71	7.36		15	50.73	7.99	
	⑥	42	49.98	5.43		23	53.26	6.39	
	⑦	124	51.57	5.79		33	55.27	8.88	
	⑧	87	53.56	6.82		56	61.45	7.68	
	⑨	99	55.95	6.71		116	63.34	9.16	

Note：* p<0.05，**p<0.01，***p<0.001

176

4.3.5 Analysis of the Differences in Nature Relatedness, Trait Mindfulness, Character Strengths, and Other Variables Between Chinese and Malaysian University Students (Answering RQ2b)

RQ2b: Are there differences in Nature Relatedness, Trait Mindfulness, and Character Strengths among Chinese and Malaysian university students?

Using an independent sample t-test, the differences between Chinese and Malaysian university students in various variables were compared. University students from the two countries showed no significant difference in "time in nature per week", "times in nature per week", "activities in nature", and Nature Relatedness, but showed significant differences in mindfulness experience, emotional experience in nature, NR-self, NR-perspective, NR-experience, Trait Mindfulness, observing, describing, acting with awareness, non-judging, non-reactivity, Character Strengths, caring inquisitiveness, and self-control. Further analysis reveals that, apart from Chinese university students scoring higher than Malaysian university students in the dimensions of mindfulness experience and NR-perspective, Malaysian university students score higher than Chinese university students in the other 18 dimensions. The specific mean and variance are shown in the following Table 4.28.

Table 4.28 **Independent Sample t-test for Differences in Various Variables**

Between Chinese and Malaysian University Students

Number	Variables	Chinese or Malaysian University Students	M	SD	t	p
1	Mindfulness Experience	CUS	1.76	0.43	3.85 ***	0.00
		MUS	1.61	0.49		
2	Time in Nature	CUS	4.67	2.58	0.26	0.79
		MUS	4.62	2.09		

Continued

Number	Variables	Chinese or Malaysian University Students	M	SD	t	p
3	Times in Nature	CUS	4.55	2.22	−0.37	0.71
		MUS	4.62	2.17		
4	Activities in Nature	CUS	2.94	2.66	−1.56	0.12
		MUS	3.29	2.81		
5	Emotional Experience in Nature	CUS	7.42	1.34	−4.42 ***	0.00
		MUS	7.9	1.33		
6	Nature in the Self	CUS	4.18	1.49	−5.93 ***	0.00
		MUS	4.9	1.5		
7	NR-Self	CUS	31.36	4.34	−3.14 **	0.002
		MUS	32.46	4.29		
8	NR-Perspective	CUS	23.88	3.37	7.31 ***	0.00
		MUS	21.94	3.05		
9	NR-Experience	CUS	9.92	1.99	−10.90 ***	0.00
		MUS	11.61	1.75		
10	Nature Relatedness	CUS	65.15	8.36	−1.31	0.19
		MUS	66	7.43		
11	Observing	CUS	14.41	2.54	−6.48 ***	0.00
		MUS	15.78	2.68		
12	Describing	CUS	15.58	2.85	−9.97 ***	0.00
		MUS	17.78	2.46		
13	Acting with Awareness	CUS	14.97	3.06	−4.75 ***	0.00
		MUS	16.02	2.45		
14	Non-judging	CUS	8.32	1.83	−42.71 ***	0.00
		MUS	14.85	1.94		
15	Non-reactivity	CUS	10.09	1.93	−40.97 ***	0.00
		MUS	18.52	2.83		

Continued

Number	Variables	Chinese or Malaysian University Students	M	SD	t	p
16	Trait Mindfulness	CUS	63.38	6.36	−36.49 ***	0.00
		MUS	82.94	6.9		
17	Caring	CUS	19.83	2.71	−4.74 ***	0.00
		MUS	21.12	3.67		
18	Inquisitiveness	CUS	16.95	2.88	−8.84 ***	0.00
		MUS	19.33	3.55		
19	Self-control	CUS	16.11	3.02	−13.09 ***	0.00
		MUS	19.5	3.27		
20	Character Strengths	CUS	52.89	6.74	−10.14 ***	0.00
		MUS	59.95	9.51		

Note: * $p<0.05$, ** $p<0.01$, *** $p<0.001$; CUS = Chinese university students (N = 386); MUS = Malaysian university students (N = 247)

4.3.6 Correlation Matrix of Demographic Variables with Three Variables

To examine the relationships between variables and determine the suitability for further analysis, a linear correlation analysis is conducted between demographic variables and the total scores of the three main variables. This lays the foundation for subsequent mediation analysis and examination of whether demographic variables need to be controlled in this study. Specific results are presented in the covariance matrix table below.

4.3.6.1 Analysis of the Sample of Chinese University Students

For the sample of Chinese university students, as shown in Table 4.29, the three main variables, Nature Relatedness, Character Strengths, and Trait

Mindfulness, are all significantly correlated with each other. The demographic main variables, age, gender, academic year, only child, and family location, are not significantly correlated with the study variables. Therefore, there is no need to control these variables in subsequent analyses.

Table 4.29   **Correlation Matrix of Demographic Variables With Three Variables**

(Chinese University Students, N=386)

Variables	Age	Gender	Academic Year	Only Child	Family Location	Nature Relatedness	Trait Mindfulness	Character Strengths
Age	1							
Gender	0.16**	1						
Academic Year	0.73***	0.34***	1					
Only Child	0.13*	0.16**	0.13*	1				
Family Location	0.19***	−0.03	0.03	0.36***	1			
Nature Relatedness	−0.06	0.09	−0.09	−0.08	−0.04	1		
Trait Mindfulness	0.04	−0.01	0.03	−0.06	−0.06	0.24**	1	
Character Strengths	0.01	−0.05	−0.06	−0.06	−0.07	0.44**	0.47**	1

Note: * $p<0.05$, **$p<0.01$, ***$p<0.001$

4.3.6.2   Analysis of the Sample of Malaysian University Students

However, for the sample of Malaysian university students, as shown in Table 4.30, the three main variables, Nature Relatedness, Character Strengths, and Trait Mindfulness, are also significantly correlated with each other. The demographic main variable, age, is not significantly correlated with the study variables. However, other demographic variables, such as gender, academic year, only child, and family location, are significantly correlated with the study variable Nature Relatedness. Gender and family location are also significantly correlated with the study variable Character Strengths. Since these demographic variables are not the focus of the study, they will be treated as control variables in subsequent analyses.

Table 4.30 **Correlation Matrix of Demographic Variables With Three Variables**

(Malaysian University Students, N=247)

Variables	Age	Gender	Academic Year	Only Child	Family Location	Nature Relatedness	Trait Mindfulness	Character Strengths
Age	1							
Gender	−0.04	1						
Academic Year	0.82***	−0.07	1					
Only Child	0.11	0.15*	−0.03	1				
Family Location	0.16*	−0.10	0.20**	−0.04	1			
Nature Relatedness	−0.08	0.16*	−0.13*	0.17**	−0.02	1		
Trait Mindfulness	−0.01	0.1	−0.04	0.10	−0.01	0.60***	1	
Character Strengths	−0.04	0.13*	−0.09	0.09	0.13*	0.59***	0.58***	1

Note: *p<0.05, **p<0.01, ***p<0.001

4.4 Analysis of the Influence of Nature Relatedness on Character Strengths Among Chinese and Malaysian University Students (Answering RQ3a, RQ3b)

This part of the study is mainly to examine the relationship and causal relationship between Nature Relatedness and Character Strengths among Chinese and Malaysian university students, to demonstrate whether the influence of Nature Relatedness on Character Strengths is valid, and answer RQ3a and RQ3b, the answer is affirmative.

4.4.1 Analysis of the Relationship Between Nature Relatedness and Character Strengths Among Chinese and Malaysian University Students (Answering RQ3a)

RQ3a: Is there a significant correlation between Nature Relatedness and Character Strengths among Chinese and Malaysian university students?

As shown by the correlation matrix in Table 4.31, there is a significant correlation between Nature Relatedness and Character Strengths among Chinese and Malaysian university students, with significance levels of p<0.001.

Table 4.31 **Correlation Matrix of Nature Relatedness and Character Strengths**

Variables	Chinese University Students(N = 386)		Malaysian University Students(N = 247)	
	Nature Relatedness	Character Strengths	Nature Relatedness	Character Strengths
Nature Relatedness	1		1	
Character Strengths	0.44 ***	1	0.59 ***	1

Note: * p<0.05, **p<0.01, ***p<0.001

4.4.2 Analysis of the Causal Relationship Between Nature Relatedness and Character Strengths Among Chinese and Malaysian University Students (Answering RQ3b)

RQ3b: Does Nature Relatedness predict Character Strengths positively among Chinese and Malaysian university students?

This section of the study explores the three dimensions of Nature Relatedness, namely NR-self, NR-perspective, NR-experience, and their direct impact on the three dimensions of Character Strengths, namely caring, inquisitiveness, self-control. Use AMOS 28.0 to test the relationship between the independent and dependent variables.

4.4.2.1 The Direct Impact of Nature Relatedness on Character Strengths Among Chinese University Students

1. The Direct Impact of NR-self on Character Strengths Among Chinese University Students

First, examine the direct impact of the first dimension of Nature Relatedness among Chinese university students, NR-self, on the three dimensions of Character Strengths, namely Caring, Inquisitiveness, and Self-control. From the results in Table 4.32, overall, they are all significant. More specifically, the standardized path coefficient between NR-self and Character Strengths dimension Caring is 0.40, the standardized path coefficient between NR-self and Character Strengths dimension Inquisitiveness is 0.27, and the standardized path coefficient between NR-self and Character Strengths dimension Self-control is 0.32, all of which are significant at the 0.001 level. Based on the standardized coefficient values of each path, it can be seen that among the three dimensions of Character Strengths, NR-self had the highest impact on the Caring dimension of Character Strengths, the lowest impact on Inquisitiveness, and the impact on the Self-control dimension is in the middle of the two. Therefore, the effect diagram of the direct impact of NR-self and Character Strengths is shown in Figure 4.4.

Table 4.32 **The Specific Numerical Values of the Direct Impact of NR-Self on Character Strengths Among Chinese University Students**

Path	Relationship between variables	Estimate	SE	CR	P	Standardized estimate
1	NR-self→Caring	0.25	0.03	8.67	***	0.40
2	NR-self→Inquisitiveness	0.18	0.03	5.39	***	0.27
3	NR-self→Self-control	0.22	0.03	6.53	***	0.32

Note: *p<0.05, **p<0.01, ***p<0.001

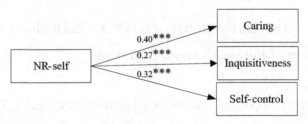

Note: *p<0.05, **p<0.01, ***p<0.001

Figure 4.4   Direct Effect Diagram of NR-self on Character Strengths Among Chinese University Students

2. The Direct Impact of NR-perspective on Character Strengths Among Chinese University Students

The following Table 4.33 lists the direct impact of NR-perspective on Character Strengths among Chinese university students. On the three dimensions of Character Strengths, namely Caring, Inquisitiveness, and Self-control. From the results in Table 4.33, overall, they are all significant. More specifically, the standardized path coefficient of NR-perspective and Caring is 0.43, the standardized path coefficient of NR-perspective and Inquisiteness is 0.18, and the standardized path coefficient of NR-perspective and Self-control is 0.18, all of which are significant at the 0.001 level. In line with the standardized coefficient values of each path, it can be seen that among NR-perspective on Character Strengths, it had the greatest impact on the Character Strengths dimension of Caring, the smallest impact on Inquisitiveness, and a moderate impact on the Self-control dimension. Therefore, the direct impact of NR-perspective and Character Strengths is shown in Figure 4.5.

Table 4.33   **The Specific Numerical Values of the Direct Impact of NR-Perspective on Character Strengths Among Chinese University Students**

Path	Relationship between variables	Estimate	SE	CR	p	Standardized estimate
1	NR-perspective→Caring	0.35	0.04	9.42	***	0.43

Continued

Path	Relationship between variables	Estimate	SE	CR	p	Standardized estimate
2	NR-perspective→Inquisitiveness	0.15	0.04	3.54	***	0.18
3	NR-perspective→Self-control	0.16	0.05	3.66	***	0.18

Note: *p<0.05, **p<0.01, ***p<0.001

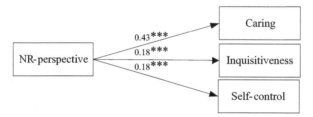

Note: *p<0.05, **p<0.01, ***p<0.001

Figure 4.5   Direct Effect Diagram of NR-perspective on Character Strengths Among Chinese University Students

3. The Direct Impact of NR-experience on Character Strengths Among Chinese University Students

The following Table 4.34 details the direct impact of Chinese university students' NR-experience on the three dimensions of Character Strengths. From the results in Table 4.34, overall, they are all significant. More specifically, the standardized path coefficients for NR-experience and Caring are 0.20, 0.33 for NR-experience and Inquisitiveness, and 0.35 for NR-experience and Self-control, all of which are significant at the 0.001 level. As shown by the standardized coefficient values of each path, it can be seen that among the three dimensions of Character Strengths affected by NR-experience, it has the greatest impact on Self-control, the smallest impact on Caring, and the impact on the Inquisitiveness dimension in the middle of the two. Therefore, the effect diagram of the direct impact of NR-experience and Character Strengths is shown in Figure 4.6.

185

Table 4.34   **The Specific Numerical Values of the Direct Impact of NR-Experience on Character Strengths Among Chinese University Students**

Path	Relationship between variables	Estimate	SE	CR	P	Standardized estimate
1	NR-experience→Caring	0.27	0.07	3.97	***	0.20
2	NR-experience→Inquisitiveness	0.48	0.07	6.87	***	0.33
3	NR-experience→Self-control	0.53	0.07	7.27	***	0.35

Note: * p<0.05, **p<0.01, ***p<0.001

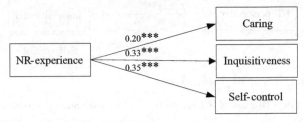

Note: * p<0.05, **p<0.01, ***p<0.001

Figure 4.6   Direct Effect Diagram of NR-Experience on Character Strengths Among Chinese University Students

4.4.2.2   The Direct Impact of Nature Relatedness on Character Strengths Among Malaysian University Students

1. The Direct Impact of NR-self on Character Strengths Among Malaysian University Students

First, examine the direct impact of the first dimension (NR-self) on the three dimensions of Character Strengths (Caring, Inquisitiveness, and Self-control). From the results in Table 4.35, overall, they were all significant. More specifically, the standardized path coefficient of NR-self and Caring was 0.56, the standardized path coefficient of NR-self and Inquisitiveness was 0.47, and the standardized path coefficient of NR-self and Self-control was 0.56, all of which were significant at the 0.001 level. As indicated by the standardized coefficient values of each path, it can be seen that among the three dimensions

186

of Character Strengths, NR-self has the greatest impact on the Caring dimension of Character Strengths, the least impact on Inquisitiveness, and the impact on the Self-control dimension was in the middle of the two. Therefore, the effect diagram of the direct impact of NR-self and Character Strengths is shown in Figure 4.7.

Table 4.35   **The Specific Numerical Values of the Direct Impact of NR-Self on Character Strengths Among Malaysian University Students**

Path	Relationship between variables	Estimate	SE	CR	p	Standardized estimate
1	NR-self→Caring	0.48	0.05	10.67	***	0.56
2	NR-self→Inquisitiveness	0.39	0.05	8.41	***	0.47
3	NR-self→Self-control	0.43	0.04	10.61	***	0.56

Note: * p<0.05, **p<0.01, ***p<0.001

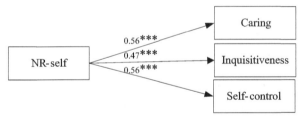

Note: * p<0.05, **p<0.01, ***p<0.001

Figure 4.7   Direct Effect Diagram of NR-self on Character Strengths Among Malaysian University Students

2. The Direct Impact of NR-perspective on Character Strengths Among Malaysian University Students

Table 4.36 describes the direct impact of the second dimension of Malaysian university students' Nature Relatedness, NR-perspective, on the three dimensions of Character Strengths (Caring, Inquisitiveness, and Self-control). As can be seen from the results of the table, they are all significant in general.

More specifically, the normalized path coefficient of NR-perspective and the dimension of Caring of Character Strengths is 0.42, the normalized path coefficient of NR-perspective and the dimension of inquisitiveness of Character Strengths is 0.18, and the normalized path coefficient of NR-perspective and the dimension of self-control of Character Strengths is 0.25.

Table 4.36   **The Specific Numerical Values of the Direct Impact of NR-Perspective on Character Strengths Among Malaysian University Students**

Path	Relationship between variables	Estimate	SE	CR	P	Standardized estimate
1	NR-perspective→Caring	0.50	0.07	7.23	***	0.42
2	NR-perspective→Inquisitiveness	0.21	0.07	2.83	**	0.18
3	NR-perspective→Self-control	0.27	0.07	4.04	***	0.25

Note: $*p<0.05$, $**p<0.01$, $***p<0.001$

As can be seen from the table, the path coefficients of NR-perspective on the Caring and Self-control dimensions of Character Strengths are significant at the level of 0.001, while the path coefficient of NR-perspective and the dimension of Inquisitiveness of Character Strengths is significant at the level of 0.01. As revealed by the standardized coefficient values of each path, among the impacts of NR-perspective on the three dimensions of Character Strengths, its impact on the dimension of Caring of Character Strengths is the largest, and its impact on the dimension of Inquisitiveness is the smallest, while its impact on the dimension of Self-control is in the middle. Therefore, the direct impact effect diagram of NR-perspective and Character Strengths is shown in Figure 4.8.

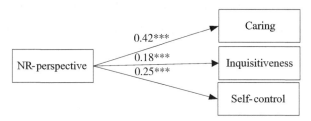

Note: *p<0.05, **p<0.01, ***p<0.001

Figure 4.8   Direct Effect Diagram of NR-perspective on Character Strengths Among Malaysian University Students

3. The Direct Impact of NR-experience on Character Strengths Among Malaysian University Students

Table 4. 37 illustrates the direct impact of NR-experience, the third dimension of Malaysian university students' Nature Relatedness, on the three dimensions of Character Strengths (Caring, Inquisitiveness, and Self-control). As can be seen from the results of the table, they are all significant in general. More specifically, the normalized path coefficient of NR-experience and the dimension of Caring of Character Strengths is 0. 40, the normalized path coefficient of NR-experience and the dimension of Inquisitiveness of Character Strengths is 0.50, and the normalized path coefficient of NR-experience and the dimension of Self-control of Character Strengths is 0. 49, all of which are significant at the level of 0.001. As shown by the standardized path coefficients of each path, among the impacts of NR-experience on the three dimensions of Character Strengths, its impact on the dimension of Inquisitiveness of Character Strengths is the largest, and its impact on Caring is the smallest, while its impact on the dimension of Self-control is in the middle. Therefore, the direct impact effect diagram of NR-experience and Character Strengths is shown in Figure 4.9.

189

Table 4.37   **The Specific Numerical Values of the Direct Impact of NR-Experience**

on Character Strengths Among Malaysian University Students

Path	Relationship between variables	Estimate	SE	CR	p	Standardized estimate
1	NR-experience→Caring	0.84	0.12	6.84	***	0.40
2	NR-experience→Inquisitiveness	1.01	0.11	9.02	***	0.50
3	NR-experience→Self-control	0.92	0.10	8.82	***	0.49

Note: *p<0.05, **p<0.01, ***p<0.001

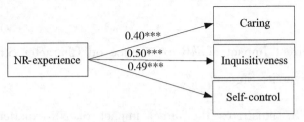

Note: *p<0.05, **p<0.01, ***p<0.001

Figure 4.9   Direct Effect Diagram of NR-experience on Character Strengths Among Malaysian
University Students

4.5   Analysis of the Mediating Effect of Trait Mindfulness on the Role of Nature Relatedness on Character Strengths Among Chinese and Malaysian University Students (Answering RQ4a, RQ4b)

This part of the study primarily aims at examining the relationship between
Nature Relatedness and Trait Mindfulness, as well as between Trait Mindfulness
and Character Strengths among Chinese and Malaysian university students, and
to answer RQ4a, the answer is yes. Then, to investigate the mediating effect of
Trait Mindfulness on the relationship between Nature Relatedness and Character
Strengths among Malaysian and Chinese university students, and to answer
RQ4b, the answer is partial mediation.

4.5.1 Analysis of the Relationship Between Nature Relatedness and Trait Mindfulness, Trait Mindfulness and Character Strengths Among Chinese and Malaysian University Students (Answering RQ4a)

RQ4a: Is there a significant correlation between Nature Relatedness and Trait Mindfulness, Trait Mindfulness and Character Strengths among Chinese and Malaysian university students?

As shown in the Correlation matrix in the following Table 4.38, the Nature Relatedness, Trait Mindfulness, and Character Strengths of Chinese and Malaysian university students are significantly correlated with each other, and the significance is extremely strong, with a significance level of $p<0.001$.

Table 4.38　**Correlation Matrix of Nature Relatedness, Trait Mindfulness, and Character Strengths**

Variables	Chinese University Students (N=386)			Malaysian University Students (N=247)		
	Nature Relatedness	Trait Mindfulness	Character Strengths	Nature Relatedness	Trait Mindfulness	Character Strengths
Nature Relatedness	1			1		
Trait Mindfulness	0.24***	1		0.60***	1	
Character Strengths	0.44***	0.47***	1	0.59***	0.58***	1

Note: * $p<0.05$, ** $p<0.01$, *** $p<0.001$

4.5.2 Analysis of the Mediating Effect of Trait Mindfulness on the Role of Nature Relatedness on Character Strengths Among Chinese and Malaysian University Students (Answering RQ4b)

RQ4b: Does Trait Mindfulness have a mediating effect on the relationship between Nature Relatedness and Character Strengths among Chinese and Malaysian university students?

In this study, two methods were used for conducting mediation analysis. The first method involved using Model 4 of the PROCESS macro provided by Hayes (2018) for manifesting variable mediation analysis. However, this analysis method can only provide preliminary mediation effects, and to some extent, may not be as detailed. To address this limitation, the second method involved using AMOS 28.0 to construct latent variable models to obtain more accurate results (Wen et al., 2004). It is hoped that by using these two mediation analysis methods, more comprehensive results can be obtained.

First, when conducting mediation analysis using Model 4 of the PROCESS macro, the path coefficients between three variables were primarily examined to determine if they reached significant levels. The total, indirect, and mediation effect values were also observed, and the effect size percentages for the indirect and mediation effects were calculated. Second, in the structural equation analysis, the fitting index values were utilized, which were the same as the confirmatory factors mentioned earlier. This includes the comprehensive use of absolute fit index and relative fit index. Three absolute fit indexes were selected: $x^2/$ df, which is generally acceptable if it is less than 5; the Root Mean Square Error of Approximation (RMSEA), which is generally acceptable if it is less than 0.08; and the Goodness of Fit Index (GFI), which is ideal if it is generally above 0.9. Additionally, three relative fitness indicators are selected, namely the Normed Fit Index (NFI) value, Relative Fit Index (RFI) value, and Comparative Fit Index (CFI) value, which are generally acceptable if they are above 0.90.

4.5.2.1 Analyzing the Mediating Effect Using Model 4 of the PROCESS Macro

1. Exploring the Mediating Role of Trait Mindfulness Between Nature Relatedness and Character Strengths Among Chinese University Students

In order to explore the underlying mechanism of the significant positive effect of Nature Relatedness on Character Strengths, Trait Mindfulness was introduced as a mediator in this study. The mediating effect was examined using Model 4 of the PROCESS macro in SPSS, and the Bootstrap method provided by Hayes (2018) was used to verify the mediating effect of Trait Mindfulness between Nature Relatedness and Character Strengths. The path coefficients of Trait Mindfulness between Nature Relatedness and Character Strengths are shown in Figure 4.10 below.

Note: *p<0.05, **p<0.01, ***p<0.001

Figure 4.10   Path Coefficient Diagram for Nature Relatedness, Trait Mindfulness, and Character Strengths Among Chinese University Students

For the sample of Chinese university students, demographic variables were not needed as control variables. Regression analysis revealed that Nature Relatedness significantly and positively predicted Character Strengths (Effect = 0.28, $p < 0.001$), as well as Trait Mindfulness (Effect = 0.18, $p < 0.001$). Additionally, Trait Mindfulness significantly and positively predicted Character Strengths (Effect = 0.41, p<0.001), as shown in Figure 4.10.

The path coefficient diagram in Table 4.39 shows that the bootstrap 95% confidence intervals for the upper and lower limits of the mediation effect of Nature Relatedness on Character Strengths and Trait Mindfulness, as indicated in the table, do not include 0. This indicates that Nature Relatedness not only has a direct effect on Character Strengths but also has a mediating effect through Trait Mindfulness. The direct effect (0.28) and the mediating effect (0.08) account for 77.78% and 22.22% of the total effect (0.36), respectively.

Table 4.39   **Decomposition Table of Total Effects, Direct Effects, and Mediating**
Effects Among Chinese University Students

	Effect	Boot SE	Boot LLCI	Boot ULCI	Relative mediation effect
Total effect	0.36	0.04	0.28	0.43	
Direct effect	0.28	0.03	0.21	0.35	77.78%
Mediation effect	0.08	0.02	0.04	0.11	22.22%

Abbreviations: Boot SE, Boot LLCI, and Boot ULCI represent the standard error, lower limit, and upper limit of the 95% confidence interval of the bias-corrected percentile Bootstrap method for estimating indirect effects.

2. Analyzing the Mediating Effect of Trait Mindfulness on the Role of Nature Relatedness on Character Strengths Among Malaysian University Students

For the sample of Malaysian university students, regression analysis revealed that, as shown in Figure 4.11, Nature Relatedness significantly and positively predicted Character Strengths (Effect=0.47, p<0.001); Trait Mindfulness (Effect=0.56, p < 0.001); Trait Mindfulness significantly and positively predicted Character Strengths (Effect=0.49, p<0.001).

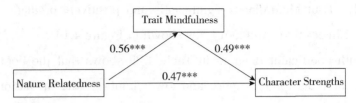

Note: *p<0.05, **p<0.01, ***p<0.001

Figure 4.11   Path Coefficient Diagram for Nature Relatedness, Trait Mindfulness, and Character Strengths Among Malaysian University Students

For the sample of Malaysian university students, the demographic variables gender, academic year, only child, and family location were included as control variables in the mediation model. Regression analysis revealed that Nature Relatedness significantly and positively predicted Character Strengths (Effect = 0.47, p < 0.001), as well as Trait Mindfulness (Effect = 0.56, p < 0.001). Additionally, Trait Mindfulness significantly and positively predicted Character Strengths (Effect = 0.49, p<0.001), refer to Table 4.40 for details.

Table 4.40 **Decomposition Table of Total Effects, Direct Effects, and Mediating Effects Among Malaysian University Students**

	Effect	Boot SE	Boot LLCI	Boot ULCI	Relative Mediation Effect
Total Effect	0.74	0.07	0.61	0.87	/
Direct Effect	0.47	0.08	0.31	0.62	63.51%
Mediation Effect	0.27	0.05	0.18	0.37	36.49%

Abbreviations: Boot SE, Boot LLCI, and Boot ULCI represent the standard error, lower limit, and upper limit of the 95% confidence interval of the bias-corrected percentile Bootstrap method for estimating indirect effects.

The path coefficient diagram in Table 4.40 shows that the bootstrap 95% confidence intervals for the upper and lower limits of the mediation effect of Nature Relatedness on Character Strengths and Trait Mindfulness, as depicted in the table, do not include 0. This indicates that Nature Relatedness not only has a direct effect on Character Strengths but also has a mediating effect through Trait Mindfulness. The direct effect (0.47) and the mediating effect (0.27) account for 63.51% and 36.49% of the total effect (0.74), respectively.

By examining the path coefficient diagrams and conducting mediation effect tests for Nature Relatedness, Trait Mindfulness, and Character Strengths among university students in China and Malaysia, it can be observed that Nature Relatedness not only has a direct positive impact on Character Strengths but also influences Character Strengths through the mediating effect of Trait Mindfulness in both samples.

4.5.2.2   Analyzing the Mediating Effect Using AMOS

First, a full model validation was conducted, and none of the indicators of the full mediation model for Chinese university students and Malaysian university students were able to meet (RMSEA>0.1). Therefore, the next step is to validate and revise the model based on the five dimensions of mindfulness, and finally obtain an acceptable model.

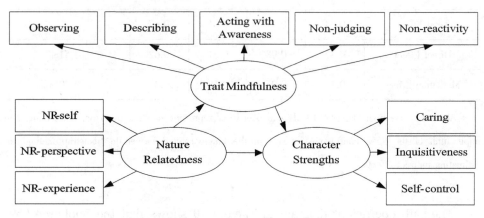

Figure 4.12   Theoretical Full Model of the Mediation Model

1. Exploring the Mediating Role of Trait Mindfulness Between Nature Relatedness and Character Strengths Among Chinese University Students

In the 386 samples of Chinese university students, each dimension of mindfulness was entered into the mediation model one by one for exploration. Finally, the two dimensions of mindfulness were entered into the mediation model, namely observing and describing, to obtain an acceptable mediation model, as shown in Figure 4.13.

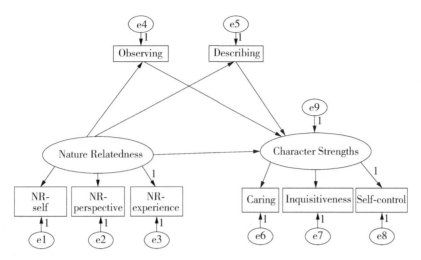

Figure 4.13   The Mediation Model Diagram Among Chinese University Students

By using AMOS 28.0 software, the construction validity of the mediation model was tested by calculating the 386 sample data of Chinese university students obtained from the survey. The specific calculation results are shown in Table 4.41.

Table 4.41   **Various Indices of Confirmatory Factor Analysis in the Mediation Model Among Chinese University Students**

Model	χ^2	df	χ^2/df	NFI	RFI	IFI	TLI	CFI	RMSEA
The Mediation Model	29.478	12	2.46<3	0.969	0.929	0.982	0.956	0.981	0.062

The calculated absolute fit index of the explored Chinese university students' mediation model is: $\chi^2/\text{df} = 2.46 < 3$, falls between 1 and 3, which is considered equivalent and ideal. $p = 0.003 < 0.01$, indicating that this model meets the required significance criteria. In addition, the calculation results of relative fitting indicators are NFI = 0.969, RFI = 0.929, IFI = 0.982, TLI = 0.956, CFI = 0.981, all of which exceed the ideal critical value standard of 0.9. RMSEA = 0.062, reaching the ideal critical value standard of less than 0.07. Based on the above absolute and relative fitting indicators, the explored Chinese university students' mediation model is acceptable.

2. Analyzing the Mediating Effect of Trait Mindfulness on the Role of Nature Relatedness on Character Strengths Among Malaysian University Students

In the 247 samples of Malaysian university students, the five dimensions of mindfulness were validated and corrected, and each dimension was entered into the mediation model for exploration. Finally, the three dimensions of mindfulness were entered into the mediation model, namely observing, describing, and non-reactivity, to obtain an acceptable mediation model, as shown in the following Figure 4.14.

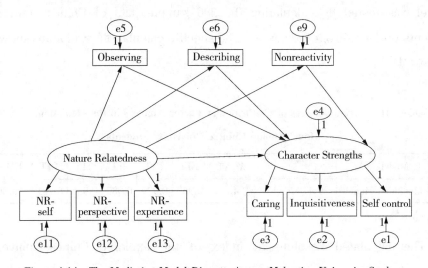

Figure 4.14 The Mediation Model Diagram Among Malaysian University Students

By using AMOS28. 0 software to calculate the construct validity of the mediation model on the sample data of 247 Malaysian university students obtained from the survey, the specific calculation results are shown in Table 4.42.

Table 4.42   **Various Indices of Confirmatory Factor Analysis in the Mediation**
Model Among Malaysian University Students

Model	χ^2	df	χ^2/df	NFI	RFI	IFI	TLI	CFI	RMSEA
The mediation model	23.896	13	1.838<3	0.982	0.950	0.992	0.976	0.991	0.058

As shown in Table 4.42, the absolute fit index calculation result of the explored Malaysian university students' mediation model is: $\chi^2/$ df $= 1.838 < 3$, falls between 1 and 3, which is considered equivalent and ideal. p$=0.032<0.05$, indicating that this model meets the required criteria. In addition, the calculation results of relative fitting indicators are NFI$=0.982$, RFI$=0.950$, IFI$=0.992$, TLI $= 0.976$, CFI $= 0.991$, all of which exceed the ideal critical value standard of 0.9. RMSEA$=0.058$, reaching the ideal critical value standard of less than 0.07. Based on the above absolute and relative fitting indicators, the explored Malaysian university students' mediation model is acceptable.

4.6   Conclusion

Based on the summary and comparison of the studies' results, the findings did not fully match the original research hypothesis, as shown in Table 4.43. First, the research hypothesis corresponding to RQ1 was accepted, namely that the Chinese Three-dimensional Nature Relatedness Scale had high validity and reliability. Second, for RQ2a and RQ2b, the hypothesis corresponding to RQ2a was mostly accepted, with an acceptance rate of 7 out of 11, indicating that there were some differences in Nature Relatedness, Trait Mindfulness, and Character Strengths among Chinese and Malaysian university students in different demographic and other variables. The hypothesis corresponding to RQ2b was also mostly accepted, with a ratio of 20 out of 16. Third, for research questions 3a and 3b, the hypothesis corresponding to RQ3a was accepted,

Table 4.43

Results of the Studies

Research questions	Research hypotheses	Accepted/ Rejected	Research answers
RQ1: Does the Three-dimensional Nature Relatedness Scale have high validity and reliability?	**H1:** The Chinese Three-dimensional Nature Relatedness Scale has high validity and reliability.	Accepted	1. The Chinese Three-dimensional Nature Relatedness Scale has high validity and reliability.
RQ2a: Are there differences in Nature Relatedness, Trait Mindfulness, and Character Strengths among Chinese and Malaysian university students in different demographic and other variables?	**H2a:** There are differences in Nature Relatedness, Trait Mindfulness, and Character Strengths among Chinese and Malaysian university students in different demographic and other variables.	Mostly accepted (7/11)	**2a:** There are some differences in Nature Relatedness, Trait Mindfulness, and Character Strengths among Chinese and Malaysian university students in different demographic and other variables.
RQ2b: Are there differences in Nature Relatedness, Trait Mindfulness, Character Strengths, and other variables among Chinese and Malaysian university students?	**H2b:** There are differences in Nature Relatedness, Trait Mindfulness, and Character Strengths among Chinese and Malaysian university students.	Mostly accepted (16/20)	**2b:** There are some differences in Nature Relatedness, Trait Mindfulness, Character Strengths, and other variables among Chinese and Malaysian university students.
RQ3a: Is there a significant correlation between Nature Relatedness and Character Strengths among Chinese and Malaysian university students?	**H3a:** There is a significant correlation between Nature Relatedness and Character Strengths among Chinese and Malaysian university students.	Accepted	**3a:** There is a significant correlation between Nature Relatedness and Character Strengths among Chinese and Malaysian university students.
RQ3b: Does Nature Relatedness predict Character Strengths positively among Chinese and Malaysian university students?	**H3b:** Nature Relatedness predicts Character Strengths positively among Chinese and Malaysian university students.	Accepted	**3b:** Nature Relatedness predicts Character Strengths positively among Chinese and Malaysian university students.
RQ4a: Is there a significant correlation between Nature Relatedness and Trait Mindfulness, Trait Mindfulness, and Character Strengths among Chinese and Malaysian university students?	**H4a:** There is a significant correlation between Nature Relatedness and Trait Mindfulness, Trait Mindfulness, and Character Strengths among Chinese and Malaysian university students.	Accepted	**4a:** There is a significant correlation between Nature Relatedness and Trait Mindfulness, Trait Mindfulness, and Character Strengths among Chinese and Malaysian university students.
RQ4b: Does Trait Mindfulness have a mediating effect on the relationship between Nature Relatedness and Character Strengths among Chinese and Malaysian university students?	**H4b:** Trait Mindfulness has a mediating effect on the relationship between Nature Relatedness and Character Strengths among Chinese and Malaysian university students.	Partially accepted (2/5, 3/5)	**4b:** Trait Mindfulness has a partially mediating effect on the relationship between Nature Relatedness and Character Strengths among Chinese and Malaysian university students.

indicating that there was a significant correlation between Nature Relatedness and Character Strengths among Chinese and Malaysian university students. The hypothesis corresponding to RQ3b was also accepted, indicating that Nature Relatedness positively predicts Character Strengths among Chinese and Malaysian university students. Fourth, for research questions 4a and 4b, the hypothesis corresponding to RQ4a was accepted, indicating that there was a significant correlation between Nature Relatedness and Trait Mindfulness, as well as between Trait Mindfulness and Character Strengths among Chinese and Malaysian university students. However, the hypothesis corresponding to RQ4b was partially accepted, indicating that Trait Mindfulness had a partially mediating effect on the relationship between Nature Relatedness and Character Strengths among Chinese and Malaysian university students. Specifically, for Chinese university students, the Observing and Describing dimensions of Trait Mindfulness play a mediating role, while for Malaysian university students, the observing, describing, and non-reactivity dimensions of Trait Mindfulness play a mediating role.

CHAPTER 5   DISCUSSION AND CONCLUSIONS

5.1   Introduction

This chapter discusses the results of the quantitative research in Chapter 4, the implications of research findings, and the limitations of the study. Based on these results, suggestions for future research are proposed, and a conclusion is drawn. The first part of this chapter discusses the validity and reliability of the Chinese version of the Nature Relatedness Scale. The results indicate that the revised Chinese Three-dimensional Nature Relatedness Scale has high validity and reliability, making it an effective research tool for studying the relationship between Chinese university students and nature. Hypothesis 1 is validated. This section compares the validity and reliability indicators of our study with the original scale and discusses the applicability of the scale.

The second part discusses the quantitative results, including respondents' demographics, descriptive results on the three main variables and their sub-dimensions, differences in Nature Relatedness, Trait Mindfulness, and Character Strengths across different demographic and other variables, and differences between Chinese and Malaysian university students in these variables. The results show some differences in Nature Relatedness, Trait Mindfulness, and Character Strengths among Chinese and Malaysian university students across different demographic and other variables, largely confirming Hypothesis 2a. Additionally, there are some differences in these variables between Chinese and Malaysian university students, largely confirming Hypothesis 2b.

The third part discusses the influence of Nature Relatedness on Character Strengths, by exploring the correlation and causal relationship between Nature Relatedness and Character Strengths. The results show a significant correlation between Nature Relatedness and Character Strengths among Chinese and Malaysian university students, validating Hypothesis 3a. Further discussion focuses on how Nature Relatedness positively predicts Character Strengths, validating Hypothesis 3b.

The fourth part discusses the mediating role of Trait Mindfulness in the relationship between Nature Relatedness and Character Strengths. This is achieved through discussing the correlation between Nature Relatedness Trait Mindfulness, and Trait Mindfulness and Character Strengths. The study confirms a significant correlation between Nature Relatedness and Trait Mindfulness, Trait Mindfulness and Character Strengths among Chinese and Malaysian university students, validating Hypothesis 4a. Furthermore, it discusses the mediating effect of Trait Mindfulness, showing that Trait Mindfulness partially mediates the relationship between Nature Relatedness and Character Strengths among Chinese and Malaysian university students. The analysis reveals that this mediolting effect opercltes through the sub-dimensions of Trait Mindfulness. These sub-dimensions exhibit slight variations between the two countries, which partially confirming Hypothesis 4b. Building on the discussion of the quantitative research results, this chapter also discusses the implications, limitations, and suggestions for future research, concluding with a brief conclusion.

5.2   Revision of Chinese Version of Nature Relatedness Scale

5.2.1   Revision Process of the Chinese Version of the Nature Relatedness Scale

In the revision process of the Chinese version of the Nature Relatedness Scale, translation and back-translation were essential steps to ensure both cultural adaptability and linguistic accuracy. This study further conducted a comprehensibility assessment among university students to refine the scale. The involvement of the original scale developers provided valuable professional guidance throughout the translation and back-translation process, ensuring the scientific rigor and precision of the procedure. The back-translation process, as a verification method, helped to mitigate potential translation biases, ensuring that the final Chinese version accurately reflected the meaning of the original scale. This process also offered important insights for the development of other language versions. The assistance and guidance from the original developers strengthened the credibility and authority of the scale, establishing a solid foundation for future cross-cultural comparative research. However, it is important to note that, despite the safeguards provided by the translation and back-translation process, some culture-specific terms and expressions were difficult to fully convey due to linguistic and cultural differences. Certain nature-related descriptions in the scale may lack direct equivalents in the Chinese cultural context, which could lead to potential misunderstandings among respondents. As a result, this study conducted a subsequent comprehensibility assessment among university students to further refine and revise the scale.

In the evaluation of the comprehensibility of the preliminary Chinese version of the NRS, items with comprehensibility rates between 60% and 90% were refined, with particular attention given to the low comprehensibility of the reverse-scored items. To address this issue, all reverse-scored items were converted to forward-scored items after random interviews and expert discussions. This change made the Chinese descriptions of the scale more aligned with the target population's understanding habits, significantly improving its comprehensibility. The revised Chinese NRS achieved a comprehensibility score of 95% to 100%, indicating that the scale can be effectively understood and used. This adjustment not only enhanced the scale's cross-cultural applicability but also aligned with existing research on the potential biases of reverse-scored items in cross-cultural measurements (Baumgartner & Weijters, 2015). However, the complete conversion of reverse-scored items may increase the risk of acquiescence bias, where respondents tend to mechanically give consistent answers, potentially affecting the measurement validity in specific research contexts.

In the item analysis of the revised Chinese NRS, the correlation coefficients between each item and the total score ranged from 0.38 to 0.77 (all $p<0.001$), confirming that each item contributed valuable information to the total score and effectively measured different dimensions of Nature Relatedness. Therefore, all items were retained in the scale at this stage, with no items removed. However, for items with correlation coefficients between 0.3 and 0.4, while they fall within an acceptable range, they may potentially affect the internal consistency coefficient of the scale or lead to less ideal results in subsequent EFA or CFA.

In the exploratory factor analysis (EFA) of the revised Chinese NRS, a hierarchical (three-subscale) factor analysis method was adopted. As Wu (2013) suggested, if the structural dimensions of the scale were determined through theoretical research and expert validity testing during the questionnaire development stage, the factor analysis can be performed separately for each sub-scale, rather than analyzing all items of the entire scale. This method allows for more precise verification of the structure of each sub-scale in the revised

Chinese NRS, enhancing the specificity and interpretability of the analysis. However, its disadvantage is that hierarchical analysis may overlook potential associations within the overall structure of the Chinese version of the scale. The results of the EFA showed that for the NR-self and NR-perspective dimensions, the factor analysis still maintained a unidimensional structure, while in the NR-experience dimension, two common factors were observed in the structure matrix. Since the first common factor covered more items, it was retained, and the second common factor (which included items 4 and 13) was removed. Furthermore, by comparing the original expressions of items 4 and 13 with their revised Chinese versions, potential cultural differences were identified. For example, item 4 "My ideal vacation spot would be a remote, wilderness area" and item 13 (reverse scored) "The thought of being deep in the woods, away from civilization, is frightening." In the Chinese cultural context, due to the emphasis on safety education, it is difficult for people to identify with the ideas of "ideal vacation spot being a wilderness" or "not being afraid of being deep in the woods, away from civilization." Therefore, considering both the EFA results and the cultural suitability of the items, it is reasonable to remove items 4 and 13. However, directly removing these two items without replacing them with culturally appropriate alternatives could somewhat affect the comprehensiveness of the scale.

At the initial stage of Confirmatory Factor Analysis (CFA), items 3 and 6 were removed due to their factor loadings being below 0.3. The revised 17-item version of the NRS-C demonstrated a good fit for the three-factor model, aligning with previous research findings (Nisbet et al., 2009). The removal of these items without adding or replacing them may have affected the overall comprehensiveness of the scale. Further comparisons revealed that the second-order model of the NRS-C exhibited a better fit than the first-order model, with $\chi^2/df = 2.508$, which was below the recommended threshold of 3, indicating a good model fit and strong alignment between the data and the theoretical model.

206

Additionally, IFI (0.934), TLI (0.918), and CFI (0.933), all exceeded 0.90, approaching the ideal level and demonstrating a high degree of model fit. The RMSEA value of 0.061, which was below 0.08 and close to the excellent benchmark of 0.06, further suggested that model errors were well controlled within a reasonable range, indicating a good model fit. Although NFI (0.888) and RFI (0.863) were slightly below 0.90, possibly due to sample size and other factors, the overall model fit remained acceptable. These findings suggested that the revised scale was robust while also providing potential directions for further refinement and optimization.

5.2.2 Validity of Chinese Version of Nature Relatedness Scale

Nisbet et al. (2009) pointed out that a unidimensional measurement tool may not fully capture the complexity of Nature Relatedness, as the relationship between humans and nature involves not only emotional or cognitive aspects but also physical contact and interaction. The Nature Relatedness Scale they developed includes three dimensions: NR-self (self dimension), NR-perspective (perspective dimension), and NR-experience (experience dimension), consisting of 21 items rated on a 5-point Likert scale. In terms of the scale's validity, the correlation between the Nature Relatedness Scale and the New Ecological Paradigm Scale ($r=0.54$, $p<0.01$), as well as with the New Ecological Consciousness Scale ($r=0.60$, $p<0.01$), supported the good validity of the instrument (Nisbet et al., 2009).

In the revision of the Chinese version of the scale, convergent validity and construct validity were used as standards for validity evaluation. First, regarding convergent validity, the Chinese version of the Nature Relatedness Scale showed significant correlations with both the Inclusion of Nature in the Self Scale (INS) and the Connectedness to Nature Scale (CNS) ($p<0.001$). The correlation with CNS reached as high as 0.71, while the correlation with INS was relatively lower at 0.35, yet still statistically significant. Given that these scales measure related but not identical constructs, such results are considered acceptable (Westen & Rosenthal, 2005). Overall, the sub-scales reflect different yet interconnected dimensions of Nature Relatedness. Second, for construct validity, the results of the confirmatory factor analysis (CFA) indicated a good model fit for the three-factor model. In the exploratory factor analysis, two items (Items 4 and 13) from the third dimension, NR-experience, were removed. During the CFA phase, one item (Item 3) from the second dimension, NR-perspective, and one item (Item 6) from the third dimension, NR-experience, were also removed. The final version of the Chinese Nature Relatedness Scale contained 17 items and was structured as a second-order model, with $X^2/\mathrm{df}<3$ and RMSEA = 0.061 < 0.08, indicating a good model fit and therefore strong construct validity.

5.2.3   Reliability of Chinese Version of Nature Relatedness Scale

In terms of internal consistency reliability, the Chinese version of the scale and its sub-scales demonstrated reliability comparable to that of the original English version. The original Nature Relatedness Scale consisted of three sub-scales with 21 items rated on a 5-point scale, and the Cronbach's alpha coefficients were as follows: NR-self, $\alpha = 0.84$; NR-perspective, $\alpha = 0.66$; and NR-experience, $\alpha = 0.80$. The overall internal consistency reliability of the total scale was 0.87, and the test-retest reliability over an interval of 6 to 8 weeks was 0.85, indicating good reliability (Nisbet et al., 2009). In contrast, the revised Chinese version of the Nature Relatedness Scale consisted of 17 items, four fewer than the original version, while retaining the 5-point rating format. The reliability analysis of the revised Chinese version of the scale showed the following alpha coefficients for each sub-scale: NR-self, $\alpha = 0.88$; NR-perspective, $\alpha = 0.75$; and NR-experience, $\alpha = 0.71$. The overall internal consistency reliability of the total scale was 0.91, indicating high reliability. According to Cicchetti (1994), a Cronbach's alpha between 0.70 and 0.80 was considered acceptable, while values above 0.80 were considered good. Compared to the original scale, the revised Chinese version of the scale showed slightly higher reliability for the NR-self subscale, NR-perspective subscale, and total scale, as well as slightly lower reliability for the NR-experience subscale.

In summary, the revised standardized Chinese version of the Three-dimensional Nature Relatedness Scale has strengths, weaknesses, opportunities, and threats. A notable strength is its adjustment to the Chinese cultural context, making it more suitable for Chinese-speaking populations worldwide. The scale demonstrates high reliability and validity, with strong cross-cultural adaptability, providing a reliable tool for assessing Nature Relatedness in both Chinese populations and Mandarin-speaking groups in other countries. However, the scale also has some weaknesses, primarily in its applicability to specific groups. For example, the scale may not fully capture the perception and engagement with nature in elderly individuals or younger children. Further adaptation and validation of the scale for specific age groups are necessary. Moreover, despite cultural adjustments, the scale may not fully address all potential cultural differences, which requires further refinement in future research. With the growing societal emphasis on environmental protection and ecological psychology, the standardized Chinese version of the Three-dimensional Nature Relatedness Scale is expected to find broader applications. The scale not only provides an effective tool for researchers but can also offer valuable support for policymakers, especially in the formulation of policies related to environmental protection, ecological development, and mental health by the Chinese government and educational departments. Policymakers can use the scale's results to better understand the public's relationship with nature and promote policies for green development, ecological conservation, and mental health education. Additionally, the scale's use can assist educational institutions in designing more targeted curricula and activities to encourage positive interactions between students and the natural environment. There are also potential threats to the application of the scale. Interest in environmental issues may fluctuate in society, or reductions in research funding could affect the widespread use of the scale. Furthermore, with the continuous development of new measurement tools and technologies, traditional scales may face the risk of being replaced by more advanced tools. Therefore, it is crucial to keep the scale updated and adaptable to ensure its continued relevance.

5.3 Differences in Nature Relatedness, Trait Mindfulness, and Character Strengths Among Chinese and Malaysian University Students Across Different Demographic Variables, and Comparative Analysis

5.3.1 Demographic Characteristics of the Participants

In the administration of the scale, demographic variables were first included as items, divided into primary demographic information and secondary demographic information. The primary demographic information obtained from the survey was used for reporting purposes regarding the background of the participants in this study. It primarily includes ① age, ② gender, ③ academic year, and ④ major. Secondary demographic information includes ⑤ only child status, ⑥ family location, ⑦ mindfulness experience, ⑧ time in nature one week, ⑨ times in nature one week, ⑩ activities in nature, and ⑪ emotional experiences in nature. The collected information enabled researchers to understand the background of the participants. It is worth mentioning that since Malaysia is a multi-racial country, a question is added to the questionnaire for Malaysian participants to indicate their race, indicating that the participants in this study are from the three main races in Malaysia: Malay, Malaysian Chinese, and Malaysian Indian. However, age, gender, academic year, and major are not the focus of this study, and therefore, the findings will not be affected by these four aspects. They are only included for background information. The secondary demographic information, such as only child status, family location, mindfulness experience, time in nature one week, times in nature one week, activities in nature, and emotional experiences in nature, as reported in Chapter 4 (see Table 4.15), are intended to provide further insight into the background of the respondents.

5.3.1.1 Discussion of the Primary Demographic Information

Gender Distribution: The statistical results regarding gender distribution among university participants in China show a total of 386 participants, with males accounting for 40.4% and females for 59.6%. In Malaysia, there are 247 university participants, with males accounting for 20.2% and females for 79.8%. The proportion of females is higher than males in both countries, aligning with the common trend of more female university students in real life. The gender ratio is relatively balanced among Chinese participants, while there is a significant difference in the gender ratio among Malaysian university students.

Age Distribution: Among university participants in China, there are 386 participants, with 18-year-olds accounting for 28.2%, 19-year-olds for 33.2%, 20-year-olds for 22.5%, 21-year-olds for 9.8%, 22-year-olds for 4.7%, and 23-year-olds for 1.6%. There are no university students over 23 years old, primarily because most Chinese universities require students to be at least 18 years old to enroll, and the survey did not include non-traditional students. Among Malaysian university participants, there are 247 participants, with 20-year-olds accounting for 10.5%, 21-year-olds for 22.3%, 22-year-olds for 19.8%, 23-year-olds for 23.1%, and those over 23 years old for 24.3%. There are no 18- and 19-year-old participants, mainly because Malaysian universities generally require students to be at least 20 years old to enroll. The age distribution highlights the differences in university enrollment ages and pre-higher education systems between the two countries.

Concerning the distribution of participants based on their current academic year, among university participants in China, the proportions for Year 1, Year 2, Year 3, and Year 4 are 46.1%, 33.2%, 10.6%, and 10.1%, respectively. In Malaysia, the proportions for the corresponding academic year are 34.4%, 21.9%, 20.2%, and 23.5%. Both countries have participants from all four academic years, with Year 1 having the highest proportion of participants, followed by Year 2.

Concerning the distribution of participants by their majors, among university participants in China, the proportions for Humanities and Social Sciences, Science and Engineering, and Arts and Sports are 13.7%, 75.6%, and 10.6%, respectively. This is because the Chinese sample is drawn from three universities with a mix of majors. In contrast, the Malaysian sample is only from one university, where all participants are from the Humanities and Social Sciences. This limitation should be noted in the study.

5.3.1.2   Discussion of the Secondary Demographic Information as Follows

Regarding whether participants are the only child in their family, among university participants in China, the proportions for Only Child Status and Not an Only Child are 29.3% and 70.7%, respectively. In Malaysia, the proportions for Only Child Status and Not an Only Child are 6.5% and 93.5%, respectively. This data also reflects the different family structures of university students in the two countries, with a higher proportion of Only Child in China.

Concerning the family location of participants, among university participants in China, the proportions for urban and rural locations are 42% and 58%, respectively. In Malaysia, the proportions for urban and rural locations are 45.3% and 54.7%, respectively. The proportions of urban and rural locations are very similar between the two countries, both approaching a 1 : 1 ratio.

Regarding participants' mindfulness experience, among university participants in China, the proportions for having mindfulness experience and not having mindfulness experience are 24. 4% and 75. 6%, respectively. In Malaysia, the proportions are 39.3% and 60.7%, respectively. The proportion of university students in Malaysia with mindfulness experience is higher than that in China, approximately 1.6 times higher. This difference may be related to the widespread religious practice of daily prayers in Malaysia, as prayer is also considered a form of mindfulness experience. This phenomenon is supported by previous research, as prayer, one of the most ancient forms of meditation, aligns and relaxes the mental state of the mind (Johnson, 2018). Similarly, another quantitative analysis showed that mindfulness was negatively correlated with mind-wandering during prayer and that religious salience predicted mindfulness, indicating the relationship between religion and mindfulness, especially during prayer (Syamila & Mansoer, 2023).

Regarding the time spent in nature per week, among university participants in China, the proportions for different time intervals (① Less than half an hour, ② 0.5-1 hour, ③ 1-2 hours, ④ 2-3 hours, ⑤ 3-4 hours, ⑥ 4-5 hours, ⑦ 5-6 hours, ⑧ 6-7 hours, ⑨ 8 hours or more) are 11.1%, 11.7%, 14.2%, 16.3%, 15.8%, 6.7%, 3.9%, 3.9%, 16.3%, respectively. For Malaysia, the proportions are 5.7%, 6.5%, 20.6%, 18.6%, 0%, 21.1%, 10.9%, 4%, 4.5%, respectively. Approximately 50% of students in both countries spend more than 3 hours per week in nature, indicating that half of the students in both countries spend more than 3 hours per week in nature. The proportion of Chinese university students spending 8 hours or more per week in nature is 16.3%, while for Malaysian university students, it is only 4.5%, which may be related to the consistently hot weather in Malaysia.

Regarding the frequency of visits to nature per week, 45.3% of Chinese university students and 46.9% of Malaysian university students go to nature four times or more per week. The proportions are very close. In China, no one goes to nature eight times or more per week, while in Malaysia, 9.7% of university students do so, indicating that Malaysian university students are more frequent in their deep immersion in nature per week compared to Chinese university students.

Concerning the types of activities in nature, the proportions among Chinese university students are: walking 51.8%, running 12.7%, cycling 8.5%, hiking 2.6%, gardening 0.3%, meditation 2.3%, sightseeing 9.1%, and others 12.7%. However, for Malaysian university students, the proportions are: walking 52.2%, running 5.3%, cycling 3.6%, hiking 7.7%, gardening 2.8%, meditation 3.6%, sightseeing 11.3%, and others 13.4%. The highest proportion of activities in nature for both countries' university students is walking, accounting for 51.8% and 52.2%, respectively, indicating that walking is the most popular way for them to immerse themselves in nature. The second most common activity type in nature for Chinese university students is running and others, while for Malaysian university students, it is others and sightseeing.

Regarding the emotional experience in nature, the researcher asked participants to evaluate their emotional experience in nature on a scale of 1 to 9, with 1 representing negative and 9 representing positive. Among Chinese university students, 25.6% chose 9, indicating an extremely positive emotional experience in nature. In contrast, among Malaysian university students, 47% chose 9. This proportion is nearly twice that of Chinese university students. This difference could be related to the timing of the survey, as China was experiencing winter with colder weather at the time.

5.3.2   Descriptive Results

The descriptive statistics focused on the results of the three main variables measured by the questionnaires, reflecting the total scores and subscale scores of the three questionnaires (see Table 4.16). In terms of total scores, the mean scores for Chinese university students were 65.15 for Nature Relatedness, 63.38 for Trait Mindfulness, and 52.89 for Character Strengths. For Malaysian university students, the mean scores were 66 for Nature Relatedness, 82.94 for Trait Mindfulness, and 59.95 for Character Strengths. The mean score of Trait Mindfulness for Malaysian university students was significantly higher than that of Chinese university students, while the differences in the other two main variables were not particularly large. Whether there are significant differences between university students in these aspects will be further discussed in the section on difference analysis. In future research, cross-cultural factors can also be considered as an entry point for the study of Trait Mindfulness.

In comparing with their respective means, the mean scores of all three main variables were higher than their respective means, indicating that university students in both countries had a good level of Nature Relatedness, Trait Mindfulness, and Character Strengths, all of which were above average. Regarding the sub-scales, except for Chinese university students scoring lower than the mean on the non-judging and non-reactivity sub-scales of Mindfulness, all other sub-scales were above average. This result is consistent with previous studies, indicating that among the five dimensions of Mindfulness in university students, the scores for non-judging and non-reactivity are relatively lower compared to the other three dimensions (Jiang, 2023; Huai, 2023). This may be related to the Chinese education system and the family education environment, where there is a tendency to judge students, leading to automatic reactivity.

5.3.3 Differences in Nature Relatedness, Trait Mindfulness, and Character Strengths Across Different Demographic

Among the eleven variables, there are partially significant differences in 7 out of 11 variables, namely ① Gender, ③ Academic Year, ⑤ Only Child Status, ⑥ Family Location, ⑦ Mindfulness Experience, ⑩ Activities in Nature, and ⑪ Emotional Experience. The other four variables show no significant differences, which are ② Age, ④ Major, ⑧ Time in Nature, and ⑨ Times in Nature. Regarding the lack of age difference, this can be attributed to the narrow age range of the participants, as they are all university students. However, another study has shown that Character Strengths are significantly and positively correlated with age (Merino et al., 2020). Next, the demographic and other variables with partially significant differences are discussed.

Gender did not have a significant impact on the Nature Relatedness, Trait Mindfulness, and Character Strengths of Chinese university students. Similarly, gender did not significantly influence the Nature Relatedness and Trait Mindfulness of Malaysian university students, but it did have a significant influence on their Character Strengths (see Table 4.17). The Character Strengths of Malaysian female university students (60.55 ± 9.23) were higher than those of males (57.54 ± 10.18), which was consistent with previous research findings in Malaysia regarding gender differences in Character Strengths. Similarly, previous studies did not find any significant relationship between age and gender in Nature Relatedness (Bashan et al., 2021).

The academic year had no significant effect on the Nature Relatedness, Trait Mindfulness, and Character Strengths of Chinese university students. It also did not significantly influence the Trait Mindfulness and Character Strengths of Malaysian university students. However, the academic year had a significant effect on the Nature Relatedness of Malaysian university students (see Table 4.19). After LSD post-hoc multiple comparisons, the scores of Year 1 (67.4 ± 7.29) were found to be higher than those of Year 2 (64.65±7.78); Year 1 (67.4±7.29) were higher than those of Year 4 (64.21 ± 7.61); Year 3 (67.16 ± 6.43) were higher than those of Year 4 (64.21±7.61). Malaysian university students in Year 1 had the highest Nature Relatedness scores, while those in Year 4 had the lowest. This could be due to Year 1 students being more proactive and having more time to engage in outdoor activities, while Year 4 students are busy with graduation and job hunting, with less time for nature connection.

Only Child Status did not significantly affect the Nature Relatedness, Trait Mindfulness, and Character Strengths of Chinese university students. Similarly, it did not significantly influence the Trait Mindfulness and Character Strengths of Malaysian university students. However, Only Child Status had a significant impact on the Nature Relatedness of Malaysian university students (see Table 4.20). The Nature Relatedness level of Malaysian university students who were not only child at home (66.32 ± 66.32) was higher than that of those who were only children at home (61.31 ± 61.31). This indicated that in Malaysian families, children who were not the only child tend to have a stronger connection with nature than those who were the only child.

Family Location Status did not have a significant impact on the Nature Relatedness, Trait Mindfulness, and Character Strengths of Chinese university students. Similarly, Family Location Status did not significantly influence the Nature Relatedness and Trait Mindfulness of Malaysian university students, but it had a significant impact on the Character Strengths of Malaysian university students (see Table 4.22). The data suggests that whether one's family lives in a rural or urban area does not significantly affect the level of Nature Relatedness among university students. While rural areas offer more opportunities for contact with nature, the study emphasizes that attention to nature is more important than mere proximity. This finding contradicts previous research, which found that urban dwellers and those who spent their childhood in urban areas reported significantly lower scores of Nature Relatedness compared to rural inhabitants (Bashan et al., 2021).

This study also suggests that in future research, to compare urban and rural dwellers, researchers can collect information regarding their family location using an urbanization scale following Shwartz et al. (2012). The scale presents five levels of urbanization, with a 5-point Likert scale recorded as urban/rural: ① Large city, ② Medium/small city, ③ Settlement, ④ Village, ⑤ Moshav or Kibbutz. Large cities and Medium/small cities can be recorded as urban areas, while Settlement, Village, Moshav, or Kibbutz can be coded as rural areas. Additionally, researchers can categorize respondents based on their current place of residence and childhood place of residence to further explore the impact of family location on Nature Relatedness.

The data analysis of this study also showed that Rural Malaysian university students had higher Character Strengths (61. 07 ± 9. 71) compared to Urban students (58. 58 ± 9. 07). This suggests that the Character Strengths of urban individuals also need to be considered. This is consistent with the viewpoint of Park and Peterson (2010), who argued that urban psychology should focus on strengths and assets contributing to a good life as much as on the problems of urbanization.

Mindfulness experience did not have a significant impact on Chinese university students' Nature Relatedness, Trait Mindfulness, and Character Strengths (see Table 4.23). This could be due to the study design, which only included a binary option for mindfulness experience (yes or no), without considering the frequency of mindfulness practice. Research has shown that the frequency of mindfulness practice can influence its effectiveness, and future studies could consider options such as monthly, bi-weekly, weekly, or almost daily practice, in contrast to less frequent practice (almost never or never) (Yang, 2022).

However, mindfulness experience had a significant influence on Malaysian university students' Nature Relatedness, Trait Mindfulness, and Character Strengths. Malaysian university students' Nature Relatedness with mindfulness experience (67.58±7.87) was higher than those without mindfulness experience (64.98±6.94), which was consistent with previous research findings (Schutte & Malouff, 2018). This study, which used a meta-analytic investigation across 12 samples totaling 2435 individuals, showed that Malaysian university students' Trait Mindfulness (84. 86 ± 6. 89) was higher among those with mindfulness experience compared to those without (81.75±6.65). Similarly, the Character Strengths of Malaysian university students with mindfulness experience (63.32± 9.1) were higher than those without mindfulness experience (57. 76 ± 9. 12).

Previous studies have also reached similar conclusions, although the sample for this study was collected from students at a medium-sized Spanish university.

The frequency of "activities in nature" did not have a significant impact on Chinese university students' Nature Relatedness, Trait Mindfulness, and Character Strengths. However, these activities had a significant impact on Malaysian university students' Nature Relatedness and Trait Mindfulness, with no significant difference in Character Strengths (see Table 4.26). Multiple post-LSD comparisons revealed that university students who frequently engaged in walking in nature had higher levels of Nature Relatedness. Conversely, those who frequently engaged in sightseeing activities in nature had higher levels of Trait Mindfulness. This phenomenon may be explained by the fact that engaging in walking in nature makes individuals more attentive to nature and more likely to form a connection with it. What's more, sightseeing activities may enhance observation and attention, thereby promoting higher levels of Trait Mindfulness. This result is consistent with previous research findings (Chou & Hung, 2021). Previous research has also shown that by taking at least 30-minute forest walks once a week continuously for eight weeks, individuals experience increased attention recovery, reflection, and re-established a relationship with nature.

Emotional experience has a significant impact on the Nature Relatedness, Trait Mindfulness, and Character Strengths of Chinese and Malaysian university students (see Table 4.27). This is the only variable that has an impact on all three main variables for both countries' university students. For Chinese university students, individuals who experience extremely positive emotions (rated 9, the highest score) in nature have higher levels of Nature Relatedness and Character Strengths. Those who experience moderately positive emotions (rated 6, between 1-9) in nature have higher levels of Trait Mindfulness. For Malaysian university students, those who experience highly positive emotions (rated 8 or 9) in nature have higher levels of Nature Relatedness, Trait Mindfulness, and Character Strengths. These results are similar to existing

219

research findings, although there is debate over causality. For example, some studies suggested that Trait Mindfulness can predict a reduction in negative emotional experiences (Fogarty et al., 2015), and mindfulness in nature can enhance positive emotions (Nisbet et al., 2019).

5. 3. 4   Differences in Nature Relatedness, Trait Mindfulness, Character Strengths, and Other Variables Between Chinese and Malaysian University Students

A comparison was made between Chinese and Malaysian university students in various variables. The two groups showed no significant difference in "time in nature one week," "times in nature one week," "activities in nature," and Nature Relatedness. This is different from the findings of a cross-cultural study on Nature Relatedness, where researchers surveyed university students from Hungary, India, Republic of Korea, and Canada (N = 798) and conducted cross-cultural difference analysis. The study found cross-cultural differences in many key components related to nature (Kövi et al., 2023).

University students from the two countries showed significant differences in mindfulness experience, emotional experience in nature, and all three dimensions of Nature Relatedness (NR-self, NR-perspective, NR-experience), as well as Trait Mindfulness and its five dimensions (observing, describing, acting with awareness, non-judging, non-reactivity), Character Strengths, and its three dimensions (Caring, Inquisitiveness, and Self-control) (see Table 4.28). McGrath's (2015) study also confirmed cross-cultural differences in Character Strengths.

In summary, this study reveals the current state of Nature Relatedness, Trait Mindfulness, and Character Strengths among university students in China and Malaysia, as well as the differences between the two groups. These findings provide valuable data for cross-cultural research. Specifically, the study compares various demographic variables and shows that significant differences exist in gender, academic year, only child status, family location, mindfulness experience, activities in nature, and emotional experience in nature, highlighting the unique aspects of students' natural experiences and psychological development and maturity. These insights offer valuable reference for educational authorities and policymakers, helping them design more targeted curricula and activities to promote students' psychological and emotional growth. Through this comparative analysis, educators and researchers in psychology can better understand the needs of university students from different cultural backgrounds and advance the implementation of mental health and environmental education. However, there are some limitations to the study, primarily in terms of sample selection and methodology. Although the study shows significant differences between the two countries across multiple dimensions, it remains to be seen whether these differences represent the general trends among all Chinese and Malaysian university students. Furthermore, the study does not fully consider other potential cultural and social factors, such as family educational background and regional differences, which may influence students' perceptions and emotional experiences with nature. Therefore, the external validity and generalizability of the findings may be somewhat limited.

From an opportunity perspective, the findings provide essential information for policymakers in both countries, which could inform the development of mental health and environmental education policies. Especially in China and Malaysia, where the importance of mental health and environmental education is growing, governments can incorporate more content related to the natural environment and psychological development into the education system, fostering positive emotional connections with nature among students. However, as social and cultural changes and educational policies evolve, students' perceptions of nature may change, which could affect the applicability of the study's results. Emerging cross-cultural psychological research and new measurement tools may offer more precise analytical methods, which could challenge the continued relevance of the current research conclusions.

5.4   Correlation and Predictive Effect Between Nature Relatedness and Character Strengths Among Chinese and Malaysian University Students

5.4.1   Correlation Between Nature Relatedness and Character Strengths Among Chinese and Malaysian University Students

Based on the correlation matrix in Table 4.31, there is a significant correlation between Nature Relatedness and Character Strengths among Chinese and Malaysian university students, with significance levels of $p < 0.001$. The correlation coefficients are $r = 0.44$ for Chinese university students and $r = 0.59$ for Malaysian university students. Additionally, the sub-dimensions within each construct are also significantly correlated. This result confirms previous research, such as Merino et al. (2020), who investigated the correlation between Nature Relatedness and Character Strengths. Their study revealed a significant empirical relationship between Character Strengths and Nature Relatedness, highlighting notable differences in aesthetic ability among individual Character Strengths. Furthermore, each character strength correlates positively and significantly with Nature Relatedness. For instance, Nisbet et al. (2009) discovered correlations between Nature Relatedness and personality traits such as agreeableness and openness to experience.

5.4.2   Predictive Effect Between Nature Relatedness and Character Strengths Among Chinese and Malaysian University Students

This study used AMOS 28.0 to test the relationship between the independent variable (Nature Relatedness) and the dependent variable (Character

Strengths). The direct effect diagram of Nature Relatedness's three dimensions (NR-self, NR-perspective, NR-experience) on Character Strengths shows a causal relationship between Nature Relatedness and Character Strengths (Caring, Inquisitiveness, Self-control) among Chinese and Malaysian university students (refer to section 4.4.2). All path coefficients are highly significant (p< 0.001). This result is supported by previous research, such as studies suggesting that the natural environment enhances self-control (Taylor et al., 2002). Additionally, several studies have found that connectedness to nature can improve some individual Character Strengths (Yang et al., 2017; Li et al., 2018).

In summary, Nature Relatedness among Chinese and Malaysian university students positively predicts overall Character Strengths, as well as the specific dimensions of Caring, Inquisitiveness, and Self-control. This indicates that fostering the relatedness with nature contributes to the development of positive psychological traits, offering valuable insights for personal growth and positive psychology. Additionally, this finding holds significant implications for individual well-being and societal progress by linking the bond with nature to the enhancement of character traits such as Caring, Inquisitiveness, and Self-regulation, which support prosocial behavior, curiosity, and self-control. However, the study's results may face limitations in terms of generalizability. For example, the sample may not adequately represent diverse populations, particularly across variations in age, educational background, and geographic location. This could affect the applicability of the observed relationship between Nature Relatedness and Character Strengths across different populations. Furthermore, although the study highlights correlations, further longitudinal experimental research is needed to establish causal links between nature exposure and the development of these traits. The findings offer multiple opportunities for policy development, especially in education and mental health. The research suggests that promoting Nature Relatedness could be an effective strategy to enhance Character Strengths such as Caring, Inquisitiveness, and Self-control. This insight can inform educational curricula and extracurricular activities by encouraging more time spent on nature-based activities. For government and educational departments in China and Malaysia, these findings support the integration of nature-based interventions into school programs, which not only aid students' mental health but also foster their social skills. Moreover, incorporating nature experiences into educational policies could align with broader initiatives for sustainable development, ecological education, and mental health promotion. One potential threat to these findings is the fluctuating public interest in environmental issues, which may impact the implementation of nature education programs. Economic factors and other policy priorities may also reduce focus on nature-based curricular content. Additionally, as technology and virtual learning environments continue to advance, motivating students to engage directly with nature in traditional ways may pose a challenge. This could limit the effectiveness of such interventions in fostering Character Strengths, highlighting the need for ongoing adaptation and innovation in how nature-related experiences are incorporated into educational settings.

5.5　Correlation and Mediating Effect of Trait Mindfulness on the Relationship Between Nature Relatedness and Character Strengths Among Chinese and Malaysian University Students

5.5.1　Correlation Between Nature Relatedness and Trait Mindfulness, Trait Mindfulness and Character Strengths Among Chinese and Malaysian University Students

The correlation matrix demonstrates a significant and extremely strong correlation (p < 0. 001) among Nature Relatedness, Trait Mindfulness, and

Character Strengths in Chinese and Malaysian university students (see Table 4.38). The natural environment has restorative properties that can restore attention, and attention is an important component of Trait Mindfulness. The improvement of attention can also enhance Trait Mindfulness. Those who love nature also connect with it in various ways, showing openness and acceptance of various natural elements. Nisbet et al. (2009) believed that Nature Relatedness included an appreciation for and interaction with all other organisms on Earth, involving emotions, cognition, and experiences. They also argued that Nature Relatedness was not just about loving nature or shallowly enjoying pleasant natural elements (such as sunsets and snowflakes); it involved an understanding of the importance of all aspects of nature, even including things that may not be aesthetically pleasing to humans (such as spiders and snakes). This involves non-judgmental awareness and attention to natural elements, and Trait Mindfulness focuses on open and accepting attention to one's internal states and the external world. Individuals with high Nature Relatedness have a clear awareness of nature, make non-conceptual judgments about the natural environment, are present-focused, and consciously switch their attention between focal points (e.g., between the internal self and external environment), all of which are characteristics of Trait Mindfulness.

In previous studies on the relationship between Nature Relatedness and Trait Mindfulness, several studies have indicated a positive relationship between Nature Relatedness and mindfulness levels (Li, 2016). Furthermore, research has shown that exposure to nature contributes to an enhancement in individual mindfulness levels (Kaplan, 2001; Brymer et al., 2010). Additionally, studies have found that mindfulness as a trait correlates with Nature Relatedness (Howell et al., 2011; Barbaro & Pickett, 2016).

Moreover, in previous research on the relationship between Trait Mindfulness and Character Strengths, Mindfulness as a trait has been found to correlate with Character Strengths (Niemiec, 2014; Baer, 2015). Additionally, empirical evidence suggests that Trait Mindfulness has a positive influence on the development of Character Strengths (Yang, 2022).

In the field of positive psychology, some scholars have also focused on the association between Mindfulness or meditation and specific Character Strengths. For example, researchers have shown that the non-reactivity and non-judgment aspects of Mindfulness significantly predict perseverance as a Character Strength (Evans et al., 2009), and authenticity is positively correlated with mindfulness (Lakey et al., 2008). Activities such as loving-kindness meditation in mindfulness interventions can effectively promote individuals' kindness, love, and gratitude as Character Strengths (Germer, 2009; Gilbert, 2010). A study proposed a mutual support model of Mindfulness and Character Strengths, indicating that an 8-week mindfulness training enhanced individuals' curiosity, courage, enthusiasm, love, appreciation of beauty, and gratitude as Character Strengths (Pang et al., 2019b). Another study reported that using the Brief Strength Scale (Ho et al., 2016) to measure Character Strengths, the two dimensions of Mindfulness (observation and non-judgment) were positively correlated with the overall level of individual Character Strengths (Duan, 2016).

5.5.2 Mediating Effect of Trait Mindfulness on the Relationship Between Nature Relatedness and Character Strengths Among Chinese and Malaysian University Students

Initially, the mediation effect was examined by using Model 4 of the PROCESS macro in SPSS. For the sample of 386 Chinese university students, demographic variables were not needed as control variables. Trait Mindfulness total score was used as the mediating variable to test its mediating effect on Nature Relatedness and Character Strengths. In the sample of 247 Malaysian university students, four demographic variables (gender, academic year, only child status, family location) were included as control variables in the mediation model, and again, the mediating effect was significant. Overall, it

was found through the exploration of manifest variable relationships that Nature
Relatedness not only directly influenced Character Strengths but also affected
them through the mediating effect of Trait Mindfulness. However, it was worth
noting the limitations of the PROCESS macro method, as its results were
somewhat limited to manifest variables. For more accurate results using latent
variable models, further exploration using AMOS software was required.

Subsequently, a full mediation model was constructed by using AMOS 28.0,
with each dimension of Trait Mindfulness individually included in the mediation
model for exploration. Next, after repeated attempts, it was found that for the
sample of Chinese university students, including the observing and describing
dimensions of Mindfulness in the mediation model further improved the model
fit (see Figure 4.13). Observing and describing, as dimensions of Trait
Mindfulness, entered the mediation model and showed good fit. Similarly, in
the sample of 247 Malaysian university students, the mediation model was
validated. However, the difference was that three dimensions of Trait
Mindfulness entered the mediation model: observing, describing, and non-
reactivity. There is one more dimension in the Chinese university student
mediation model, indicating a mediating role for non-reactivity. The mediating
role of Mindfulness has also been confirmed in the following studies: Li (2016)
found that Mindfulness mediated the impact of Nature Relatedness on college
students' happiness, and mindfulness mediated the reduction of materialism in
Nature Relatedness (Chen, 2018).

It is worth noting that this study has provided preliminary answers to two
questions: whether there is a close relationship between Nature Relatedness and
Character Strengths, and how Nature Relatedness affects individual Character
Strengths. The study found that Nature Relatedness affects Character Strengths
through Trait Mindfulness. Specifically, an increase in Nature Relatedness leads
to an increase in Trait Mindfulness, which in turn enhances individual Character
Strengths. Nature Relatedness achieves this effect by increasing individuals'

observing and describing or non-reactivity levels towards nature, shifting their focus to the present, and enhancing their level of Trait Mindfulness. This accumulation over time further enhances Character Strengths. However, these conclusions need to be further validated through longitudinal and interventional studies, which will be the focus of future research. Additionally, further exploration and research are needed to understand how Trait Mindfulness affects Character Strengths.

In conclusion, the study results indicate that Trait Mindfulness partially mediates the relationship between Nature Relatedness and Character Strengths. This finding is significant, as it offers a new perspective on how specific dimensions of Mindfulness influence the effect of Nature Relatedness on Character Strengths across different cultural contexts. Specifically, the observing and describing dimensions showed a notable mediating effect among Chinese students, while the observing, describing, and non-reactivity dimensions played a mediating role among Malaysian students. These findings highlight the unique impact of Trait Mindfulness across cultural backgrounds and further support the potential value of mindfulness interventions in enhancing Nature Relatedness and positive character traits. However, some limitations of the study must be acknowledged. First, the generalizability of the results may be influenced by cultural differences, especially as different mindfulness dimensions show varying effects in students from different countries. Additionally, the cross-sectional design limits causal interpretations, so future research should employ longitudinal or experimental methods to verify whether these relationships hold over a broader timeframe. This study opens new opportunities for applications in mental health and education. The role of specific mindfulness dimensions (such as observing, describing, and non-reactivity) in enhancing Nature Relatedness and Character Strengths suggests that mindfulness training may help students develop these positive psychological traits. For educational and mental health institutions in China and Malaysia, these findings provide a theoretical basis for designing mindfulness-based educational programs or mental health interventions, thus promoting students' overall mental and physical well-being. Policymakers could also use these insights to integrate mindfulness practices with environmental education, supporting social harmony and sustainable development. Potential challenges to implement these findings include variations in the understanding and application of mindfulness across cultures, posing challenges for intervention design, especially in cross-cultural promotion. Thus, maintaining cultural sensitivity and continuously adapting intervention content to meet the needs of different populations will be essential when applying these study results in the future.

5.6 Implications of Research Findings

First, this study fills the gap in the Chinese version of the Three-dimensional Nature Relatedness Scale and provids a research tool for future studies. There is currently limited research on the three dimensions of Nature Relatedness in China, and there is a lack of localized measurement tools. The revised Nature Relatedness Scale in this study has good validity and reliability, effectively measuring the relationship between individuals and nature. It provides an effective measurement tool for future research on Nature Relatedness in Chinese samples and other Mandarin-speaking populations, and contributes to the measurement techniques of ecological and environmental psychology in China. Research on Nature Relatedness in Malaysia is also relatively blank, and this study hopes to serve as a catalyst, reminding Malaysian researchers to pay attention to the field of Nature Relatedness.

Second, this study addresses the gap in comparative studies of the three variables across samples from both countries. This is the first study in a Chinese sample to explore the relationship between Nature Relatedness, Trait Mindfulness, and Character Strengths. It validates previous foreign research on

229

the relationships between Nature Relatedness and Character Strengths, Nature Relatedness and Trait Mindfulness, and Trait Mindfulness and Character Strengths. This study has important reference value for Chinese researchers to start and expand research in this area. The study in Malaysia on the combination of the three factors is also the first, and this study will stimulate more discussion on the relationship among Nature Relatedness, Trait Mindfulness, and Character Strengths, with the hope of obtaining more evidence on how Nature Relatedness affects Character Strengths.

Finally, this study establishes a foundation for Nature-Based Mindfulness Interventions to foster Character Strengths. The introduction of Trait Mindfulness as a mediator variable to explore its role between Nature Relatedness and Character Strengths. Previous studies have only discussed the possible relationship between Nature Relatedness and Character Strengths, without considering Trait Mindfulness as a mediator variable in the relationship between the two. Therefore, introducing Trait Mindfulness as a mediator variable in the relationship between Nature Relatedness and Character Strengths is the most important innovation in this study.

5.7   Limitations

The first limitation of this study concerns the Measurement instruments. Specifically, the participants in the revision of the Chinese version of the Nature Relatedness Scale (NRS-C) were university students, which limits the generalizability of the NRS-C to other populations. Due to cultural differences, some items may be easily understood by university students, but they may require further validation in other groups, especially regarding their applicability to students below the university level. Future research could explore the applicability of the NRS-C among middle and primary school students and other groups in China to expand its use across different participant populations.

Additionally, in the confirmatory factor analysis (CFA) of the scale revision, the RMSEA value for the second-order model was 0.061, which is close to the excellent threshold of 0.06. The NFI and RFI indices were slightly below 0.90. While the overall model fit remains within an acceptable range, there is still room for improvement. Future research could further investigate potential influencing factors or adjust the model structure to enhance model fit. Due to time and cost constraints, this study did not assess test-retest reliability. Future research should aim to evaluate test-retest reliability after a 6-8 week interval and compare it with the original scale's test-retest reliability of 0.85. Furthermore, while a standardized Chinese version of the questionnaire was used for the Chinese university student sample, for the Malaysian university student sample, the measurement was based on the English version of the NRS-C corresponding to the Chinese version. However, it was neither translated into Malay, nor was there a Malay version of the revised scale for Malaysian university students. Therefore, this introduces limitations for cross-cultural research involving these scales. Lastly, this study focused on the localized revision of the Three-dimensional NRS in its Chinese version and did not standardize the Two-dimensional six-item NR6 (Nisbet & Zelenski, 2013). Future research may develop a more streamlined, efficient NR6-C based on the intended use.

The second limitation of this study concerns the universality of the sample, sampling method, and results. Firstly, the participants were limited to university students from China and Malaysia. Research has shown that the development of Nature Relatedness may have critical periods, such as the lasting effects of nature-related interventions on children under 11 years old (Liefländer et al., 2013). Future research could track the development of Nature Relatedness across different age groups. Secondly, the study employed a convenience sampling method, which limits the generalizability of the conclusions. Although the study attempted to cover a diverse range of

231

participants, the distribution was uneven (e.g., more females than males, more Year 1 and Year 2 students compared to Year 3 and Year 4 students, more students from Science & Engineering fields compared to those from Humanities, Arts, and Sports, and more urban students than those from rural areas and small towns). Future studies could use stratified sampling methods to ensure a more balanced distribution. Finally, regarding the universality of the results, the questionnaire used in this study was designed for the specific purposes of the current research and may not be suitable for other groups, such as primary and secondary school students.

Lastly, regarding research methods, due to resource limitations, this study used only questionnaires for data collection. Future research could combine implicit and explicit measurements, integrate multiple research methods, design experiments, or conduct longitudinal designs to further validate causal relationships, thereby making the conclusions more scientific.

5.8   Suggestions for Future Research

First, regarding the limitations of the measurement tools, future research could combine the Nature Relatedness Scale with other scales related to Nature Relatedness to investigate different participant groups. This would help extend the application of the Nature Relatedness Scale to a broader population. For example, future research could apply the scale to groups of different age ranges and cultural backgrounds, particularly by exploring the impact of Nature Relatedness on adolescents, elderly individuals, or other special populations. Additionally, the scale could be combined with other psychological tools to investigate the long-term effects of Nature Relatedness on mental health, emotion regulation, and environmental behavior. This approach would provide a more comprehensive understanding of the role and significance of Nature Relatedness at both individual and group levels. Furthermore, to address the adaptability limitations of the scale in the Malaysian sample, future research could translate the scale into Malay, conduct back translation, and revise the scale to localize it. This would not only help reduce the limitations of the Nature Relatedness Scale in cross-cultural research but also improve the scale's comparability and applicability across different cultures. Moreover, future research in multicultural countries like Malaysia should consider the Nature Relatedness experiences across various cultural backgrounds and explore how cultural differences affect people's relationship with nature and its influence on Character Strengths.

Second, to address the limitations regarding the generalizability of the sample, sampling methods, and research results, future research could expand the sample range to include participants beyond university students, such as those from primary and secondary schools, as well as elderly individuals. Studying different groups would provide a more comprehensive understanding of the development patterns and impacts of Nature Relatedness. Future research could also employ more representative sampling methods, such as random sampling or stratified sampling, rather than solely relying on convenience sampling. This would help ensure that the sample is more representative, thereby increasing the external validity of the conclusions. Additionally, expanding the scope of data collection by involving more schools and regions could increase the sample size and balance the distribution. In cross-national comparative research, collaborating with more universities could help obtain a broader and more diverse sample, ensuring the data's diversity and generalizability.

Furthermore, regarding the methodological limitations of this study, future research could use longitudinal designs to better understand the long-term development of Nature Relatedness and intervention effects. Tracking changes in Nature Relatedness at different time and its long-term impact on Character Strengths would help reveal the causal relationships between Nature Relatedness

233

and other psychological variables. Concerning nature-based psychological interventions, some researchers have already begun exploring these directions. Studies suggest that nature-based positive psychological interventions encourage participants to engage in nature-related activities, such as spending at least 30 minutes outdoors or in natural environments each day, listening to natural sounds, meditating, and observing wildlife (Hamann & Ivtzan, 2017). Other studies encourage participants to capture natural beauty and share it in public spaces for mutual exchange (Passmore & Holder, 2017). Regarding interventions that integrate mindfulness with Character Strengths, the Mindfulness-Based Strengths Practice Program (MBSP) combines mindfulness interventions with Character Strengths development, offering an 8-week program to cultivate mindfulness-based Character Strengths (Niemiec, 2023). As for integrating nature into mindfulness interventions, recent studies by researchers like Vitagliano et al. (2023) have conducted preliminary research on Group Nature-Based Mindfulness Interventions, such as Nature-Based Mindfulness Training for College Students with Anxiety. These studies provide possibilities for future interventions that combine Nature Relatedness and Mindfulness to enhance Character Strengths.

Lastly, the results of this study can inspire the governments and educational departments of China and Malaysia to formulate relevant policies that promote the importance of Nature Relatedness and mindfulness within the education system and social environments. Future research could encourage governments to support and fund nature-based mental health programs, promote outdoor activities in schools, and create more opportunities for students to engage with nature to enhance their positive psychological traits and personal development. Educational departments could incorporate Nature Relatedness and Mindfulness into mental health curricula and extracurricular activities, fostering Character Strengths, resilience, and overall well-being in students. With the support of these policies and educational practices, a more favorable environment for psychological health development can be created for future generations.

5.9 Conclusion

Character Strengths, reflected as positive qualities in a person's thoughts, emotions, and behaviors, play a crucial role in the personal development and well-being of university students. Developing and enhancing these strengths have become a major focus for governments and positive psychology practitioners in both China and Malaysia. However, prior research has lacked a standardized Chinese version of the Three-Dimensional Nature Relatedness Scale, and has been limited in providing comparative studies on Nature Relatedness, Trait Mindfulness, and Character Strengths between Chinese university students and Malaysian university students. Additionally, studies on the relationship between Nature Relatedness and Character Strengths, as well as the mechanisms influencing this relationship, are scarce. This study addresses these research gaps and provides valuable empirical evidence for university students, thereby enhancing their positive psychological traits and overall well-being.

The results of this research indicate that the revised Chinese version of the Three-dimensional Nature Relatedness Scale demonstrates strong validity and reliability, confirming its effectiveness as a research instrument for exploring university students' Nature Relatedness. This not only provides a foundation for future assessments of Nature Relatedness among Chinese populations but also offers a reliable tool for Mandarin speakers around the world. Additionally, the study outlines some characteristics of Chinese and Malaysian university students regarding Nature Relatedness, Trait Mindfulness, and Character Strengths. Comparative analyses revealed demographic differences between students in the two countries, underscoring the importance of considering these variables when examining students' psychological traits across diverse cultural backgrounds and further affirming the influential role of cultural and contextual factors in shaping these constructs. This finding enhances researchers' understanding of the unique features and differences between Chinese and Malaysian students, promotes cross-cultural research, and offers practical insights for government and university policymakers. Then, this study confirms a significant correlation between Nature Relatedness and Character Strengths, and Nature Relatedness positively predicts Character Strengths, highlighting the potential benefits of fostering a bond with nature for individual growth. Finally, results indicats significant correlations between Nature Relatedness and Trait Mindfulness, as well as between Trait Mindfulness and Character Strengths. Trait Mindfulness also serves as a partial mediator in the relationship between Nature Relatedness and Character Strengths, and this lays a theoretical foundation for developing Nature-Based Mindfulness Interventions to strengthen Character Strengths among university students.

In summary, this study establishes a standardized Chinese version of Nature Relatedness Scale, advance cross-cultural comparisons between university students in China and Malaysia, and provides a theoretical foundation for governments and educational departments in both countries to design intervention programs aimed at enhancing Character Strengths among university students.

APPENDICES

Appendix A   Example of Comments on Translation and Back-translation of the Nature Relatedness Scale

Item Number	Order	Items	1 Disagree strongly	2 Disagree a little	3 Neither Agree or disagree	4 Agree a little	5 Agree strongly
1	original	I enjoy being outdoors, even in unpleasant weather.					
	translation	即使在糟糕的天气里，我也喜欢待在户外。					
	Backtranslation	I enjoy outdoor activities even in bad weather.					
		我喜欢待在户外，即使在令人不愉快的天气。					
	adjustment	I enjoy being outdoors, even in unpleasant weather.					
2	original	Some species are just meant to die out or become extinct.					
	translation	有些物种注定要消亡或逐渐灭绝。					
	backtranslation	Some species are destined to become extinct or gradually disappear.					
3	original	Humans have the right to use natural resources any way we want.					
	translation	人类有权利随心所欲地使用自然资源。					
	backtranslation	Humans have the right to use natural resources as we wish.					
4	original	My ideal vacation spot would be a remote, wilderness area.					
	translation	遥远的原生态区域是我理想的度假胜地。					
	backtranslation	The remote wilderness is my ideal vacation destination.					
5	original	I always think about how my actions affect the environment.					
	translation	我总是考虑自己的行为是如何影响环境的。					
	backtranslation	I always consider how my actions impact the environment.					
6	original	I enjoy digging in the earth and getting dirt on my hands.					
	translation	我喜欢挖掘泥土，并享受双手沾满泥土的感觉。					
	backtranslation	I enjoy digging in the soil and the feeling of getting my hands dirty.					

批注 [LN1]: there may be a subtle difference here, from the original in that activities means "doing" something, versus simply being outdoors. For example, one could be sitting which is not really an activity (or maybe some people would consider that to qualify as "activity" ?) I think the goal here is to capture how people may be willing to be outdoors or not, when the weather might be less than ideal, but it doesn't necessarily involve a specific 'activity'.   Does that make sense to you?

Appendix B   The Approval Letter From the Original Scale Developer for the Chinese Version of the Nature Relatedness Scale

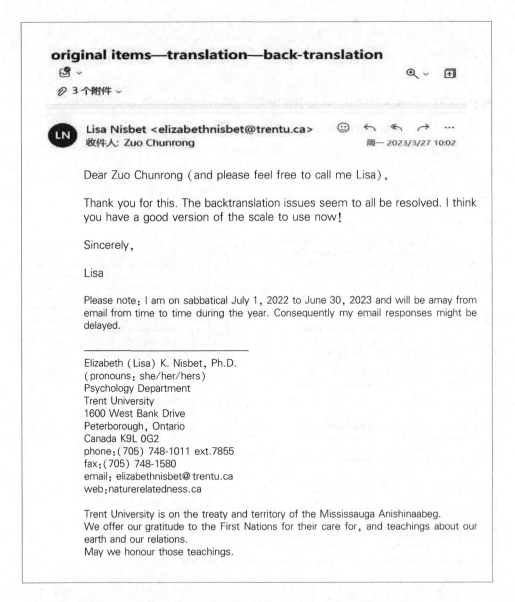

original items—translation—back-translation

3 个附件

Lisa Nisbet <elizabethnisbet@trentu.ca>
收件人: Zuo Chunrong   周一 2023/3/27 10:02

Dear Zuo Chunrong (and please feel free to call me Lisa),

Thank you for this. The backtranslation issues seem to all be resolved. I think you have a good version of the scale to use now!

Sincerely,

Lisa

Please note: I am on sabbatical July 1, 2022 to June 30, 2023 and will be amay from email from time to time during the year. Consequently my email responses might be delayed.

_____

Elizabeth (Lisa) K. Nisbet, Ph.D.
(pronouns: she/her/hers)
Psychology Department
Trent University
1600 West Bank Drive
Peterborough, Ontario
Canada K9L 0G2
phone: (705) 748-1011 ext.7855
fax: (705) 748-1580
email: elizabethnisbet@ trentu.ca
web: naturerelatedness.ca

Trent University is on the treaty and territory of the Mississauga Anishinaabeg.
We offer our gratitude to the First Nations for their care for, and teachings about our earth and our relations.
May we honour those teachings.

Appendix C　Participant Information Sheet and Consent Form (Chinese Version)

示例　　　　　　　　　　　　　　　　　　　　　　　　　　　　　　　附件 B

研 究 信 息

研 究 题 目: 自然关联性对中国和马来西亚大学生性格优势的影响
主要研究人员: 左春荣

介绍:

　　您被邀请自愿参与一项研究调查。本研究涉及中国和马来西亚大学生之间的自然相关性、性格优势和正念之间的关系。

　　在您同意参与之前,阅读和理解本研究信息非常重要。如果您同意参与,您将收到一份此表格的副本供您保留记录。

研究目的:

　　本研究的目的是确定自然关联性、性格优势和正念之间的关系,并分析这三个变量在中国和马来西亚大学生之间的差异。

参与者标准:

　　研究团队成员将讨论您是否有资格参与此研究。非常重要的是,您在与工作人员沟通时必须完全诚实。本研究将包括目前本科在读的学生,不包括已经毕业的学生。

研究程序:

　　在我们的基于问卷的研究中,问题的范围将集中在评估参与者的自然关联性、性格优势和正念。问卷将包含＿＿＿＿＿＿个问题,涵盖了该主题的各个方面。参与者预计需要花费大约＿＿＿＿＿＿分钟来完成问卷。

风险:

　　在这个基于问卷的研究中,参与的风险非常小。然而,我们承认以下潜在的保密风险:参与者在回答问题时可能泄露个人信息,存在轻微的保密风险。为了减轻这一风险,我们将确保所有收集的数据都经过匿名化处理并安全存储。机密信息不会与第三方分享。

　　重要的是要注意,参与这项研究是完全自愿的,参与者可以随时退出而不会受到任何处罚。我们已经获得了研究的伦理批准,所有数据将按照严格的保密和隐私准则处理,以确保参与者的福祉和数据安全。

报告健康经验:

　　如果您在与这项研究直接或间接相关的任何健康问题方面有任何困扰,请随时联系以下的研究人员。

参与研究：

您参与这项研究完全是自愿的。您可以拒绝参与研究，或者随时停止参与研究，而不会因此受到任何处罚或失去您本应享有的权益。如果您以任何方式违反了研究的资格标准，研究团队也可以在未经您同意的情况下终止您的参与。如果出现此类情况，研究团队成员将与您讨论。

可能的好处：

参与者参与这项研究可能获得以下好处：

个体的好处： 个体将有机会深入了解与自然关联性、性格优势和正念相关的研究。

社区的好处： 这项研究的结果可能对社区产生积极影响，提供关于自然关联性、性格优势和正念如何影响个体和社区的重要见解。这些发现可能有助于改善心理健康支持和教育项目。

大学的好处： 这项研究将有助于扩展关于中国和马来西亚大学生的自然关联性、性格优势和正念的研究领域。大学将能够利用这项研究的成果，包括数据分析和报告，来支持进一步的研究工作和社区合作项目。

您不会因参与这项研究而获得任何补偿。但您可以选择获取您的问卷结果。我们非常感谢您的参与，您的贡献对于我们的研究至关重要。

问题：

如果您对本研究有任何疑问或对您的权利有任何疑虑，请联系：

_____

_____

_____

_____

如果您对伦理审批或与本研究相关的任何问题/事项有任何疑问，请联系：

_____

_____

_____

_____

保密性：

您的信息将由研究人员保密，除非法律要求披露，否则不会公开。从这项研究中获得的不以个人身份识别的数据将出版供知识目的使用。

您的原始记录可能会被研究人员、本研究的伦理审查委员会以及监管机构审核，以验证研究程序和/或数据。您的信息可能会被存储和处理在计算机上。只有研究团队成员被授权访问您的信息。

通过签署这份同意书，您授权上述记录审核、信息存储和数据。

受试者信息和同意书
(签名页)

研 究 题 目: 自然关联性对中国和马来西亚大学生性格优势的影响
主要研究人员: 左春荣

要成为这项研究的一部分, 您必须签署这一页。签署这一页, 我确认以下内容:
- 我已阅读此受试者信息和同意书中的所有信息, 包括与本研究相关的任何风险信息, 并有时间考虑。
- 我的所有问题都已得到满意的答复。
- 我自愿同意成为这项研究的一部分, 遵循研究程序, 并按要求向研究人员提供必要的信息。
- 我可以自由选择随时停止参与这项研究。
- 我已收到一份此参与者信息和同意书的副本供自己保留。

_____

参与者姓名

_____

参与者身份证号

_____   _____

参与者签名   日期(年/月/日)

_____

个人姓名
进行同意讨论

_____   _____

个人签名   日期(年/月/日)
进行同意讨论

_____   _____

见证人姓名和签名   日期(年/月/日)

注意: i) 所有参与此研究的参与者不会被保险覆盖。

参与者材料发布同意书
签名页

研 究 题 目：自然关联性对中国和马来西亚大学生性格优势的影响
主要研究人员：左春荣

要成为这项研究的一部分，您必须签署这一页。

通过签署这一页，我确认以下内容：
- 我明白我的姓名不会出现在发布的材料上，并已经努力确保我的姓名的隐私性得到保密，尽管由于意外情况，隐私性不能完全得到保证。
- 我已阅读材料或材料所包含内容的一般描述，以及我可能被包括在其中的所有照片和图表，这些可能会被发布。
- 我已被提供机会阅读手稿并查看包括我的材料在内的所有材料，但已放弃了这样做的权利。
- 所有发布的材料将在全球研究人员之间共享。
- 这些材料还将用于本地出版物、图书出版物，并为众多本地和国际研究人员提供全球范围的访问。
- 我在此同意并允许这些材料在其他出版物中使用，前提是遵守以下条件：
- 这些材料不会用于广告宣传或包装材料。
- 这些材料不会在没有上下文的情况下使用，即：示例图片不会用于与图片无关的文章中。

参与者姓名＿＿＿＿＿＿＿＿＿＿＿＿＿＿＿＿＿＿＿＿＿＿＿

＿＿＿＿＿＿＿＿＿＿　＿＿＿＿＿＿＿＿＿＿　＿＿＿＿＿＿＿＿＿＿
参与者身份证号　　　参与者签名　　　　　日期(年/月/日)

＿＿＿＿＿＿＿＿＿＿＿＿＿＿＿＿＿＿＿＿　＿＿＿＿＿＿＿＿＿＿
个人签名　　　　　　　　　　　　　　　　日期(年/月/日)
进行同意讨论

注意：i)所有参与此研究的参与者不会被保险覆盖。

Appendix D   Participant Information Sheet and Consent Form (English Version)

RESEARCH INFORMATION

Research Title : The influence of nature relatedness on character strengths among Chinese and Malaysian university students

Name of main Researcher : Zuo Chunrong

INTRODUCTION
You are invited to take part voluntarily in a research survey. This research is about the relationship of nature relatedness, character strengths and mindfulness among Chinese and Malaysian university students.

It is important that you read and understand this research information before agreeing to participate in this study. You will receive a copy of this form to keep for your records if you agree to participate.

The questionnaire will consist of _____ items, covering various aspects of the topic. Participants are expected to spend approximately _____ minutes to complete the questionnaire.

PURPOSE OF THE STUDY
The purpose of this study are to determine the relationship of nature relatedness, character strengths and mindfulness, and analyze the differences in these three variables between Chinese and Malaysian university students.

PARTICIPANTS CRITERIA
The research team members will discuss your eligibility to participate in this study. It is important that you are completely truthful with the staff.

This study will include individuals who are currently enrolled as undergraduate students.

This study will not incude individuals who have already graduated.

STUDY PROCEDURES
For our questionnaire-based research, the scope of the questions will focus on assessing participants' nature relatedness, character strengths and mindfulness. The questionnaire will consist of _____ questions, covering various aspects of the topic. Participants are expected to spend approximately 10-15 minutes to complete the questionnaire.

RISKS
In this questionnaire-based study, there are minimal risks associated with participation. However, we acknowledge the following potential confidentiality risks: There is a slight risk of a breach of confidentiality, as participants may disclose personal information in their responses. To mitigate this risk, we will ensure that all date collected is anonymized and stored securely. Confidential information will not be shared with third parties.

It is important to note that participation in this study is entirely voluntary, and participants can withdraw at any time without penalty. We have also obtained ethical approval for this research, and all data will be handled in accordance with strict confidentiality and privacy guidelines to ensure participants' well-being and data security.

REPORTING HEALTH EXPERIENCES
Please contact, at any time, the following researcher if you experience any health problem either directly or indirectly related to this study.

PARTICIPATION IN THE STUDY

Your taking part in this study is entirely voluntary. You may refuse to take part in the study or you may stop your participation in the study at anytime, without any penalty or loss of benefits to which you are otherwise entitled. Your participation also may be stopped by the research team without your consent if in any form you have violated the study eligibility criteria. The research team member will discuss with you if the matter arises.

POSSIBLE BENEFITS [Benefit to Individual, Community, University]

Participants may obtain the following benefits from participating in this study:

1. Benefit to Individual: Individuals will have the opportunity to gain in-depth insights into research on nature relatedness, character strengths, and mindfulness.
2. Benefit to Community: The results of this study may have a positive impact on the community by offering crucial insights into how nature relatedness, character strengths, and mindfulness influence individuals and communities. These findings may help improve mental health support and educational programs.
3. Benefit to University: This study will contribute to expanding research in the areas of nature relatedness, character strengths, and mindfulness among Chinese and Malaysian University students. The university will be able to leverage the outcomes of this study, including data analysis and reports, to support further research efforts and community collaboration projects.

You will not receive any compensation for participating in this study. However you have the option to access your questionnaire results. Your participation is greatly appreciated, and your contribution is essential to our research.

QUESTIONS

If you have any question about this study or your rights, please contact:

_____
_____
_____
_____

If you have any questions regarding the Ethical Approval or any issue/problem related to this study, please contact:

_____
_____
_____
_____

CONFIDENTIALITY

Your information will be kept confidential by the researchers and will not be made publicly available unless disclosure is required by law.

Data obtained from this study that does not identify you individually will be published for knowledge purposes.

Your original records may be reviewed by the researcher, the Ethical Review Board for this study. and regulatory authorities for the purpose of verifying the study procedures and/or data. Your information may be held and processes on a computer. Only research team members are authorized to access your information.

By signing this consent form, you authorize the record review, information storage and data process described above.

ATTACHMENT S

Subject Information and Consent Form
(Signature Page)

Research Title :   The influence of nature relatedness on character strengths among
                            Chinese and Malaysian university students
Researcher's Name :   Zuo Chunrong

To become a part of this study, you must sign this page. By signing this page, I am confirming the following:

- I have read all of the information in this Subject Information and Consent Form including any information regarding the risk in this study and I have had time to think about it.
- All of my questions have been answered to my satisfaction.
- I voluntarily agree to be a part of this research study, to follow the study procedures, and to provide necessary information to the researchers, as requested.
- I may freely choose to stop being a part of this study at anytime.
- I have received a copy of this Participant Information and Consent Form to keep for myself.

_____

Participant Name

_____

Participant I. C No

_____   _____

Signature of Participant or Legal Representative   Date (dd/MM/yy)

_____

Name of Individual
Conducting Consent Discussion

_____   _____

Signature of Individual   Date (dd/MM/yy)
Conducting Consent Discussion

_____   _____

Name & Signature of Witness   Date (dd/MM/yy)

Note :

i) All participants who are involved in this study will not be covered by insurance.

ATTACHMENT P

Participant's Material Publication Consent Form
Signature Page

Research Title :   The influence of nature relatedness on character strengths among
Chinese and Malaysian university students

Researcher's Name :   Zuo Chunrong

To become a part this study, you must sign this page.

By signing this page, I am confirming the following:

- I understood that my name will not appear on the materials published and there have been efforts to make sure that the privacy of my name is kept confidential although the confidentiality is not completely guaranteed due to unexpected circumstances.

- I have read the materials or general description of what the material contains and reviewed all photographs and figures in which I am included that could be published.

- I have been offered the opportunity to read the manuscript and to see all materials in which I am included, but have waived my right to do so.

- All the published materials will be shared among the researchers world wide.

- The materials will also be used in local publications, book publications and accessed by many local and international researchers worldwide.

- I hereby agree and allow the materials to be used in other publications required by other publishers with these conditions.

- The materials will neither be used as advertisement purposes nor as packaging materials.

- The materials will not be used out of context—i.e. Sample pictures will not be used in an article which is unrelated subject to the picture.

Participant Name

Participant I.C No.   Participant's Signature   Date (dd/MM/yy)

Name and Signature of Individual   Date (dd/MM/yy)
Conducting Consent Discussion

Note:

i) All participants who are involved in this study will not be covered by insurance.

Appendix E   Example of Data Collection Permission Letters From A, B, and C Universities (Chinese Version)

数据收集申请书

姓名：_____

地址：_____

邮件地址：_____

电话：_____

申请时间：_____

数据收集地点：_____

地址：_____

尊敬的_____大学_____学院领导：

  我是_____，目前在_____研究机构工作。我正在进行一项关于"自然关联性对中国和马来西亚大学生性格优势的影响"的研究，研究对象是中国和马来西亚的本科生，探讨大学生自然关联性对性格优势的影响机制，以期对大学生积极心理品质提升提供新的理论视角。

  为了支持我的研究，我将使用问卷调查法进行数据收集，使用_____作为研究工具(见附件)，我希望能够在贵单位的协助下获取相关数据。这些数据将对我的研究产生重要影响，并且有助于我深入了解大学生自然关联性对性格优势的影响。

  我非常重视数据的保密性和合法性，将遵守任何相关的法律法规、学术伦理和贵单位的数据使用政策。我将确保数据仅用于研究目的，并不会泄露给任何未经授权的第三方。

  我诚恳地请求贵单位的支持，并请求数据收集许可，以确保我合法地进行数据收集。我深知这是一项重要的工作，我将非常感激贵单位的支持。如果您需要更多信息或有任何疑问，请随时与我联系。非常感谢您的时间和考虑。

  申请人签字：

审批单位盖章：

_____大学_____学院

时间：

Appendix F   Example of Data Collection Permission Letters From A, B, and C Universities (English Version)

Name: _____

Address: _____

Email: _____

Phone: _____

Application Date: _____

Data Collection Location: _____

Address: _____

Dear _____,

    I am _____. I am conducting a research "The influence of Nature Relatedness on Character Strengths among Chinese and Malaysian university students", focusing on undergraduate students from both China and Malaysia. The study aims at exploring the mechanism of the impact of Nature Relatedness on Character Strengths among university students, providing a new theoretical perspective for enhancing the positive psychological qualities of university students.

    To support my research, I will be conducting data collection through a questionnaire survey using the Nature Relatedness Scale, the Three-Dimensional Character Strengths Scale and the Five-Factor Mindfulness Scale as research tools. I hope to obtain relevant data with the assistance of your school. These data will have a significant impact on my research and contribute to a deeper understanding of the influence of Nature Relatedness on Character Strengths among university students.

    I highly value the confidentiality and legality of data and commit to adhering to all relevant laws, regulations, academic ethics, and the data usage policies of your school. I will ensure that the data is used exclusively for research purposes and will not be disclosed to any unauthorized third parties.

    I earnestly request the support of your school and seek permission for data collection to ensure that I conduct data collection in a legal manner. I understand the significance of this work and will be immensely grateful for your support. If you need any additional information or have any questions, please feel free to contact me. Thank you very much for your time and consideration.

    Applicant's Signature:

Stamped with the Seal of _____

_____ University

Date

CONSENT LETTER TO RESEARCH SITES

School of _____

University _____

Adress _____

Date: _____

Dear Sir/Madam.

CONSENT SEEKING LETTER

I am _____, from _____ in the above addressed university conducting a research titled "The influence of Nature Relatedness on Character Strengths among Chinese and Malaysian university students" in Quantitative mode using questionnaire as instruments. I humbly request from you permission and support to conduct the research in your school being one of my research sites.

I assure you total confidentiality as all information obtained will be used anonymously for this study only and remnants destroyed immediately after analysis to prevent eventual trace of participants' identity.

Attached is a copy of introduction letter from my institution and place of work for your consideration.

Yours faithfully

_____

Pusat Pengajian Ilmu Pendidikan
School of Educational Studies

Universiti Sains Malaysia
11800 USM Pulau Pinang

Our Ref.: P-PD0242/21(R)

Tel.　:　(6)04-653 3888 ext. 3231/3255
　　　　　(6)04-653 3956(Direct)

Date: 10/10/2023

Fax.　:　(6)04-657 2907
Email　: dean_edu@usm.my
Website: education.usm.my

TO WHOM IT MAY CONCERN

Please be advised that the person named below is a researcher at the School of Educational Studies, Universiti Sains Malaysia.

　　　Name　　　　: Zuo Chunrong

　　　Research Title　: The influence of nature reatedness on character strengths among Chinese and Malaysian university students.

2. We would very much appreciate any support or assistance that your kind department could extend her, in order to facilitate her efforts. We believe that the outcome of her study will be truly beneficial for the knowledge establishment on the whole.

3. For more information, please refer to me through email jayajohan@usm.my or +604-6532049.

Thank you kindly,

(**MOHD JAYA MOHD JOHAN**)
Senior Assistant Registrar

Appendix G   Documents Submitted to the Human Research Ethics Committee for Approval

Jawatankuasa Etika
Penyelidikan Manusia USM (JEPeM)

Human Research Ethics Committee USM (HREC)

Universiti Sains Malaysia
Kampus Kesihatan
16150 Kubang Kerian, Kelantan, Malaysia.
Tel.   :+609–767 3000/2354/2362
Fax. :+609–767 2351
Email: jepem@usm.my
Laman Web: www.jepem.kk.usm.my
                    www.usm.my

A. APPLICANT INFORMATION

Name: Zuo Chunrong

Email:

Institution: UNIVERSITI SAINS MALAYSIA

B. REGISTRATION AND APPLICATION INFORMATION

Study Title:	The influence of nature relatedness on character strengths among Chinese and Malaysian university students.
Type of Submission:	First Time Submission
Type of Study:	Non-Interventional Study
Duration:	6 months
Study Site(s):	Universiti Sains Malaysia, Beijing University of Aeronautics and Astronautics
Funding:	Grant Approved (University, Government or Private)

C. APPROVAL BY OTHER ETHICS COMMITTEE

Approval by other ethic committee:	Not Applicable
Name of Institutional Review Board or Ethics Review Committee:	
Approval Letter:	
Date of Ethics Approval:	0000-00-00
Date of expiration of ethics approval:	0000-00-00

251

D. TEAM MEMBER(s)

No.	Name	Role in study	CV

E. LIST OF UPLOADED DOCUMENT(s)

i. Protocol Medical & Health Sciences Document(s)

No.	Type of Document	Document
1	Introduction	
2	Problem statement & Study rationale	
3	Research Question(s)	
4	Objective	
5	Literature review	
6	Conceptual framework	
7	Research design	
8	Study area	
9	Study population	
10	Sample size estimation	
11	Research tool	
12	Operational definition	
13	Data collection method	
14	Study flowchart	
15	Data analysis	
16	Expected result(s)	
17	Full Research Proposal	
18	Gantt chart & milestone	
19	Subject criteria	
20	Sampling method & subject recruitment	

ii. Participant Information Sheet (PIS), Consent Form (CF) and OBB HUSM
* Only for project requires written informed consent

No.	Type of Document	Document
1	Endorsement Form	
2	Participant Information Sheet (PIS) & Consent Form (CF)	

iii. Endorsement Form
* All project require endorsement form EXCEPT for Industry Sponsored Research (ISR)

No.	Type of Document	Document
1	Endorsement Form	

End of Details

This PDF was created on 2023-09-08 16:34:50

This is a computer-generated document. No signature is required.

(For Secretary/Secretariat of JEPeM-USM Purposes Only)

1. **Allocation for JEPeM-USM application:**

[   ] Exempted from review

[   ] Expedited Review   [   ] Full Board Review

Primary Reviewers: Primary Reviewers:

1.   1.

2.   2.

3.   3.

2. **This application will be discussed in the Panel Meeting:**

[   ] Panel A   [   ] Panel D

[   ] Panel B   [   ] Panel E

[   ] Panel C   [   ] Panel F

_____

(Signature of Chairperson/ Advisor/Deputy Chairperson)   DATE:

RESEARCH PROPOSAL TEMPLATE FOR SOCIAL SCIENCES & OTHERS

Research title:

The influence of nature relatedness on character strengths among Chinese and Malaysian university students

Principal investigator: Zuo Chunrong

1 Introduction

Character strengths are a significant area of study within the field of positive psychology. They encompass a range of positive qualities that manifest in an individual's cognition, emotion, and behavior, contributing to personal well-being and benefiting others. Understanding character strengths is crucial for individuals to lead fulfilling lives. Existing research has predominantly focused on the positive outcomes associated with character strengths, yet there remains a limited exploration of the factors influencing their development.

Both the Chinese and Malaysian government place great emphasis on cultivating character strengths in university students, the research on the relationship between character strengths and other variables among Chinese and Malaysian university students primarily focuses on the effects of character strengths, with little attention given to factors that promote changes in character strengths. There is a lack of research on the mechanisms of character strengths (Yang, 2022).

In recent years, nature relatedness has become one of the hot topics in environmental psychology research. Based on a synthesis of previous research, some Chinese researchers have found a close correlation between nature connectedness and certain individuals' character strengths, such as fairness, kindness, vitality, creativity, teamwork and self-regulation (Yang et al., 2017). Nature relatedness intervention (NRI) has also become a positive psychological intervention strategy (Duan & Bu, 2018). All of these studies provide a new perspective for cultivating character strengths. In Malaysia, Jin (2018) discussed the influence of Nature Relatedness on Pro-Environmental Behaviors among Malaysian Chinese university students. In University of Technology Malaysia, the implementation of a green campus has already shown a positive impact in reducing climate change on their campus through the promotion of cycling, paper-saving, energy-saving, and water-saving initiatives (Najad et al., 2018). Mohamad (2017), using the case of Peninsular Malaysians, examined the differences in nature-related experiences during childhood between urban and rural areas. The study found that individuals who grew up in rural areas had more nature-related experiences compared to those who grew up in urban areas, providing a basis for environmental education.

ENDORSEMENT

This section should be signed by the administrative authority legally empowered to sign on behalf of the School/Department/Institution. This section is required only for initial submission.

STUDY PROTOCOL TITLE:	The influence of nature relatedness on character strengths among Chinese and Malaysian university students
Principal Investigator:	Zuo Chunrong

∗ Please tick[/] in the following boxes.

[/] I confirm that this application has been peer reviewed.

[/]I have checked and confirmed that all the comments made during the peer review have been addressed by the researchers.

[/]I have read this Application and agree that this research will be implemented under the supervision of this School/Department/Institution in accordance with the conditions of approval by the JEPeM – USM. I also confirm that the Principal Investigator is a student or staff in this institution.

Issuing School/Department/Institution:	SCHOOL OF EDUCATIONAL STUDIES UNIVERSITI SAINS MALAYSIA
Name of Endorsing Official School/Department/Institution:	ASSOCIATE PROFESSOR DR AZIAH ISMAIL DEPUTY DEAN OF RESEARCH INNOVATION AND INDUSTRY– COMMUNITY ENGAGEMENT
Signature and Stamp:	Date of Signature:

Appendix H   Approval Letter from Human Research Ethics Committee

Jawatankuasa Etika
Penyelidikan Manusia USM (JEPeM)

Human Research Ethics Committee USM (HREC)

12th January 2024
Miss Zuo Chunrong

Universiti Sains Malaysia
Kampus Kesihatan
16150 Kubang Kerian, Kelantan, Malaysia.
Tel.   :+609-767 3000/2354/2362
Fax. :+609-767 2351
Email: jepem@usm.my
Laman Web: www.jepem.kk.usm.my
www.usm.my

JEPeM Code: USM/JEPeM/PP/23100795
Protocol Title: The Influence of Nature Relatedness on Character Strengths among Chinese and Malaysian University Students

Dear Miss Zuo,
We wish to inform you that your study protocol has been reviewed and is hereby granted approval for implementation by the Jawatankuasa Etika Penyelidikan Manusia Universiti Sains Malaysia (JEPeM-USM). Your study has been assigned study protocol code USM/JEPeM/PP/23100795, which should be used for all communications to JEPeM-USM in relation to this study. This ethical approval is valid from 12th January 2024 until 11th January 2025.
Study Site: Malaysia and China

The following document has been approved for use in the study
1. Research Proposal
In addition to the above mentioned document, the following technical documents were included in the review on which this approval was based:
1. Participant Information Sheet and Consent Form(English version)
2. Participant Information Sheet and Consent Form(Chinese version)
3. Questionnaire (English version)
4. Questionnaire (Chinese version)
While the study is in progress, we request that you submit to us the following documents:
1. Application for renewal of ethical approval 45 days before the expiration date of this approval through submission of **JEPeM-USM FORM 3（B）2022: Continuing Review Application Form**.

256

2. Any changes in the protocol, especially those that may adversely affect the safety of the participants during the conduct of the trial including changes in personnel, must be submitted or reported using **JEPeM-USM FORM 3 (A) 2022: Study Protocol Amendment Submission Form**.

3. Revisions in the informed consent form using the **JEPeM-USM FORM 3(A) 2022: Study Protocol Amendment Submission Form**.

4. Reports of adverse events including from other study sites (national, international) using the **JEPeM-USM FORM 3(G) 2022: Adverse Events Report**.

5. Notice of early termination of the study and reasons for such using **JEPeM-usM FORM 3 (E) 2022**.

6. Any event which may have ethical significance.

7. Any information which is needed by the JEPeM-USM to do ongoing review.

8. Notice of time of completion of the study using **JEPeM-USM FORM 3(C) 2022: Final Report Form**.

Please note that forms may be downloaded from the JEPeM-USM website:
https: //jepem. kk. usm. my/

JEPeM-USM is in compliance with the Declaration of Helsinki, International Conference on Harmonization (ICH) Guidelines, Good Clinical Practice (GCP) Standards, Council for International Organizations of Medical Sciences (CIOMS) Guidelines, World Health Organization (WHO) Standards and Operational Guidance for Ethics Review of Health-Related Research and Surveying and Evaluating Ethical Review Practices, EC/IRB Standard Operating Procedures (SOPs), and Local Regulations and Standards in Ethical Review.

Thank you.
" MALAYSIA MADANI"
" BERKHIDMAT UNTUK NEGARA"

Sincerely,

ASSOC. PROF. DR. HASLINA HAROON
Deputy Chairperson
Jawatankuasa Etika Penyelidikan (Manusia) JEPeM
Universiti Sains Malaysia

Appendix I   Questionnaire (Chinese Version)

大学生自然关联性与性格优势问卷调查

您好！欢迎您参加我们的研究。对于您的参加，我们表示衷心的感谢。对于您的所有数据我们会严格保密，且所有数据将仅供研究之用。在开始做每一个调查问卷之前，请仔细阅读问卷前的作答要求。对于每一个问题，请看清后再回答。特别要注意的是：所有问题的答案都没有正确和错误之分，请您根据自己的直觉回答，不要想太多。尽量不选择中立选项。

★ 你是否愿意自愿参加本次问卷调查？　①是　②否

1. 您的年龄：

　　①18　②19　③20　④21　⑤22　⑥23　⑦其他_____

2. 您的性别：

　　①男　　②女

3. 您就读的年级：

　　①大一　②大二　③大三　④大四

4. 是否为独生子女：

　　①是　　②否

5. 在儿童时期，你是否是一个留守儿童：

　　①是　　②否

6. 您家庭所在地属于：

　　①城镇　②乡村

7. 您所学的专业属于：

　　①文史类　②理工类　③艺体类

8. 您是否为贫困生？若是，在贫困生库中的等级为：

258

①特困　　②贫困　　③一般贫困　　④非贫困生

9. 您是否有过正念的经历？（如果没听过这个词就选"否"）

①是　　②否

10. 最近一周，您在自然环境中度过多长时间？

①半小时以内　　②0.5~1 小时　　③1~2 小时　　④2~3 小时

⑤3~4 小时　　⑥4~5 小时　　⑦5~6 小时　　⑧6~7 小时

⑨8 小时及以上

11. 最近一周，您几次身处自然环境中？

①0 次　　②1 次　　③2 次　　④3 次　　⑤4 次

⑥5 次　　⑦6 次　　⑧7 次　　⑨8 次及以上

12. 最近一周，您在自然环境中进行的活动类型有：

①散步　　②跑步　　③骑自行车　　④徒步旅行

⑤园艺　　⑥静坐　　⑦看风景　　⑧其他

13. 请您简要描述一下在自然环境中的情绪体验。

_____

14. 请选择合适的数字代表您在自然环境中时的情绪体验：

1＝非常消极，9＝非常积极。①1 ②2 ③3 ④4 ⑤5 ⑥6 ⑦7 ⑧8 ⑨9

自然关联性量表

指导语：对于以下每一个陈述，请点击按钮评价您对描述的认可程度。

序号	题　　项	非常不同意	有点不同意	中立	有点同意	非常同意
1	我喜欢待在户外，即使天气不好。	1	2	3	4	5
2	一些物种有望继续存续或逐渐繁衍。	1	2	3	4	5
3	我常常思考自己的行为如何对环境产生影响。	1	2	3	4	5
4	我与自然和环境的联系，是我精神世界的一部分。	1	2	3	4	5

续表

序号	题 项	非常不同意	有点不同意	中立	有点同意	非常同意
5	我很清楚环境问题。	1	2	3	4	5
6	无论身处何地，我都会留意野生动物。	1	2	3	4	5
7	我经常到大自然中去。	1	2	3	4	5
8	哪怕我只做一点环保的事，都有可能对地球上的环境产生作用。	1	2	3	4	5
9	我不是与自然分离的，而是自然的一部分。	1	2	3	4	5
10	我对大自然的感受会对我的生活产生影响。	1	2	3	4	5
11	动物、鸟类和植物不应该比人类拥有更少的权利。	1	2	3	4	5
12	即使在城市中心，我也会留意身边的自然环境。	1	2	3	4	5
13	我与自然的关系是"我是谁"的重要组成部分。	1	2	3	4	5
14	保护自然是必要的，因为它没有强大到能从每一次人类的影响中恢复。	1	2	3	4	5
15	"非人类物种"的状况是人类未来发展的一个指标。	1	2	3	4	5
16	我会较多地关注动物所承受的痛苦。	1	2	3	4	5
17	我感觉与所有生物和地球都有着密切的联系。	1	2	3	4	5

自我包含自然量表

在下图每对圆圈中，一个标注"我"，另一个标注"自然"，代表"自我"与"自然"的圆圈从第一对到第七对圆圈，重叠程度逐渐提高，从 1 分到 7 分，请选择最能代表你自己与自然关系的图形。

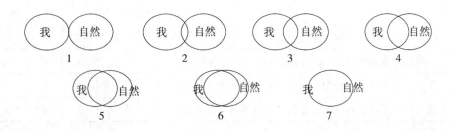

自然联结量表

指导语：以下列出了一些你与自然关系的句子，请认真阅读每一句，选择一个数字去代表你同意或者不同意的程度。

序号	题　项	非常不同意	比较不同意	不确定	比较同意	非常同意
1	我常感觉与大自然融为一体。	1	2	3	4	5
2	自然界是我归属的家园。	1	2	3	4	5
3	我承认并欣赏地球上其他生物的智慧。	1	2	3	4	5
4	我常感到与自然界是分离的。	1	2	3	4	5
5	当我思考生命意义的时候，我想自己是在大自然生命循环过程中。	1	2	3	4	5
6	动植物常让我有一种亲切感。	1	2	3	4	5
7	地球属于我，我也属于地球。	1	2	3	4	5
8	我非常清楚自己的行为会对自然界产生怎样的影响。	1	2	3	4	5
9	我常感觉自己是自然界生命之网的一部分。	1	2	3	4	5
10	无论人类还是其他生命体，都拥有同样的"生生不息之道"。	1	2	3	4	5
11	树木是森林的一部分，我自己也是自然界一部分。	1	2	3	4	5
12	我认为自己在自然金字塔的顶端。	1	2	3	4	5
13	在大自然中，我感觉自己很渺小，和花草树木一样微不足道。	1	2	3	4	5
14	我个人的幸福与大自然的好坏无关。	1	2	3	4	5

性格优势问卷

指导语：对于以下每一个陈述，请使用数字 1 到 5 来评价您对描述的认可程度。

序号	题　项	非常不像我	不像我	中立	像我	非常像我
1	我是一个高度自律的人。	1	2	3	4	5
2	我总是思考以后再讲话。	1	2	3	4	5
3	我有能力令其他人对一些事物产生兴趣。	1	2	3	4	5
4	我是个真正的终生学习者。	1	2	3	4	5
5	我总能想出新方法去做事情。	1	2	3	4	5
6	我不言放弃。	1	2	3	4	5
7	我从不让沮丧的境遇带走我的幽默感。	1	2	3	4	5
8	我精力充沛。	1	2	3	4	5
9	在任何情形下，我都能找到乐趣。	1	2	3	4	5
10	深思熟虑是我的性格特点之一。	1	2	3	4	5
11	我享受善待他人的感觉。	1	2	3	4	5
12	尊重团体的决定对我来说很重要。	1	2	3	4	5
13	我认为每个人都应该有发言权。	1	2	3	4	5
14	作为团队领导者，我认为每个成员都有对团体所做的事发表意见的权力。	1	2	3	4	5
15	别人相信我能帮他们保守秘密。	1	2	3	4	5

五因素正念量表

指导语：下面是一系列关于您日常生活的描述，请您根据每一个陈述事件在您最近一周(包括今天)的生活中发生的情况，选择最适合您的选项。

序号	题　项	从不或极少	很少	有时	经常	非常频繁或总是
1	我擅长于用言语描述我的情感。	1	2	3	4	5
2	我能清晰表达自己的信念、观点以及期望。	1	2	3	4	5
3	我观察自己的情绪，而不迷失其中。	1	2	3	4	5
4	我告诉自己，我不应该以我现在的这种方式来感受此时的情感。	1	2	3	4	5
5	我难以找到词语来表达我的所思所想。	1	2	3	4	5
6	我会注意我的一些感觉，比如：微风吹拂我的头发、阳光照在我的脸上的感觉。	1	2	3	4	5
7	我会评判自己的想法是好的或是坏的。	1	2	3	4	5
8	我难以把注意力集中在当前发生的事情上。	1	2	3	4	5
9	当我有悲伤的想法或景象时，我会"退一步"，并去觉知那些想法或景象的存在而不被其所控制。	1	2	3	4	5
10	我会注意一些声音，比如：时钟的嘀嗒声、小鸟的叽喳声、或者汽车穿梭的声音。	1	2	3	4	5
11	当我身体有种感觉时，我很难找到合适的词语来描述它。	1	2	3	4	5
12	我好像是自动地在做一些事情，并没有完全意识到它。	1	2	3	4	5
13	通常，当我有令人伤感的想法或者景象时，我能很快恢复平静。	1	2	3	4	5
14	我告诉我自己，我不应该思考我此刻正思考的东西。	1	2	3	4	5

续表

序号	题　项	从不或极少	很少	有时	经常	非常频繁或总是
15	我闻到了周围一些东西的气味或者芳香。	1	2	3	4	5
16	即便是我感到非常的不安时，我也能找到词语来表达它。	1	2	3	4	5
17	我草草地做完一些事情，而没有真正地集中注意力在其上。	1	2	3	4	5
18	当陷入令人烦恼的情绪或情境中，我能做到只是去注意它们，而不做出相应反应。	1	2	3	4	5
19	我想有些情绪是不对的或者是不合时宜的，我不应该体验到它们。	1	2	3	4	5
20	我注意到了艺术品和自然界中事物的一些视觉元素，如：颜色、形状、纹理还有光和影子。	1	2	3	4	5
21	当我有令人痛苦的想法或景象时，我通常只是去在注意它们，顺其自然。	1	2	3	4	5
22	我总是自动地工作或完成某项任务，而没有意识到我在做什么。	1	2	3	4	5
23	我发现自己做事情的时候，不专心在所做的事情上。	1	2	3	4	5
24	当不理智的想法出现时，我会自我否决。	1	2	3	4	5

问卷结束，请从头到尾检查一下有没有漏题，再次感谢您的参与和配合！

Appendix J   Questionnaire (English Version)

Survey on the Influence of Nature Relatedness
on Character Strengths Among University Students

Dear participant,

Welcome to our research.

We sincerely thank you for your participation.

You have the right to decide whether you are willing to participate in this survey. We assure you that all of your data will be kept strictly confidential and will only be used for research purposes. Before starting each survey questionnaire, please read the answering requirements carefully. Please read each question carefully before answering. It is important to note that there are no right or wrong answers to any of the questions. Please answer based on your intuition without overthinking. Try to avoid selecting neutral options as much as possible.

★ Are you willingly participating in this survey? ①Yes   ②No

1. Your age: ①19   ②20   ③21   ④22   ⑤23   ⑥Others

2. Your gender: ①Male   ②Female

3. Your current academic year: ①Year 1   ②Year 2   ③Year 3   ④Year 4

4. Are you the only child in your family? ①Yes   ②No

5. The location of your family is: ①Urban   ②Rural

6. Your major belongs to:

   ①Humanities and Social Sciences   ②Science and Engineering

   ③Arts and Sports

7. Have you had any experience with mindfulness? (If you haven't heard of this

term, choose "No")

①Yes ②No

8. How much time have you spent in a natural environment in the past week?

①Less than half an hour ②0. 5 ~ 1 hour ③1 ~ 2 hours ④2 ~ 3 hours

⑤3 ~ 4 hours ⑥4 ~ 5 hours ⑦5 ~ 6 hours ⑧6 ~ 7 hours ⑨8 hours or more

9. How many times have you been in a natural environment in the past week?

①0 times ②1 time ③2 times ④3 times ⑤4 times

⑥5 times ⑦6 times ⑧7 times ⑨8 times or more

10. [Multiple choice] What types of activities have you engaged in within the natural environment in the past week?

①Walking ②Running ③Cycling ④Hiking ⑤Gardening ⑥Meditation

⑦Sightseeing ⑧Others

11. Please briefly describe your emotional experience in the natural environment.

---

12. Please select the appropriate number to represent your emotional experience in the natural environment: 1 = Very negative, 9 = Very positive.

①1 ②2 ③3 ④4 ⑤5 ⑥6 ⑦7 ⑧8 ⑨9

Nature Relatedness Scale

Instructions: For each of the following, please rate the extent to which you agree with each statement, using the scale from 1 to 5 as shown below. Please respond as you really feel, rather than how you think "most people" feel.

1 = Disagree strongly

2 = Disagree a little

3 = Neither agree or disagree

4 = Agree a little

5 = Agree strongly

1	I enjoy being outdoors, even in unpleasant weather.	1	2	3	4	5
2	Some species are just meant to die out or become extinct.	1	2	3	4	5
3	I always think about how my actions affect the environment.	1	2	3	4	5
4	My connection to nature and the environment is a part of my spirituality.	1	2	3	4	5
5	I am very aware of environmental issues.	1	2	3	4	5
6	I take notice of wildlife wherever I am.	1	2	3	4	5
7	I don't often go out in nature.	1	2	3	4	5
8	Nothing I do will change problems in other places on the planet.	1	2	3	4	5
9	I am not separate from nature, but a part of nature.	1	2	3	4	5
10	My feelings about nature do not affect how I live my life.	1	2	3	4	5
11	Animals, birds and plants should have fewer rights than humans.	1	2	3	4	5
12	Even in the middle of the city, I notice nature around me.	1	2	3	4	5
13	My relationship to nature is an important part of who I am.	1	2	3	4	5
14	Conservation is unnecessary because nature is strong enough to recover from any human impact.	1	2	3	4	5
15	The state of non-human species is an indicator of the future for humans.	1	2	3	4	5
16	I think a lot about the suffering of animals.	1	2	3	4	5
17	I feel very connected to all living things and the earth.	1	2	3	4	5

Inclusion of Nature in the Self Scale

In the following diagram, there are pairs of circles labeled "Self" and "Nature", representing the relationship between "Self" and "Nature." The overlapping degree of the circles increases from the first pair to the seventh pair, ranging from 1 to 7. Please choose the graphic that best represents your relationship with nature.

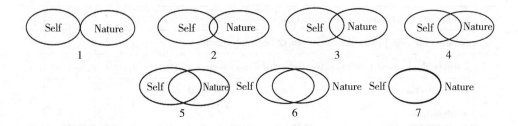

Three-dimensional Inventory of Character Strengths

Instructions: Please select the most suitable answer for each of the following descriptions. Please respond honestly and accurately.

1 = Very much unlike me

2 = Unlike me

3 = Neutral

4 = Like me

5 = Very much like me

1	I am a highly disciplined person.	1	2	3	4	5
2	I always think before I speak.	1	2	3	4	5
3	I have the ability to make other people feel interesting.	1	2	3	4	5
4	I am a true life-long learner.	1	2	3	4	5
5	I am always coming up with new ways to do things.	1	2	3	4	5
6	I do not give up.	1	2	3	4	5
7	I never allow a gloomy situation to take away my sense of humor.	1	2	3	4	5
8	I have lots of energy.	1	2	3	4	5
9	I can find something of interest in any situation.	1	2	3	4	5
10	Thinking things through is part of who I am.	1	2	3	4	5
11	I enjoy being kind to others.	1	2	3	4	5
12	It is important to me to respect decisions made by my group.	1	2	3	4	5
13	I believe that everyone should have a say.	1	2	3	4	5

Continued

| 14 | As a leader, I believe that everyone in the group should have a say in what the group does. | 1 | 2 | 3 | 4 | 5 |
| 15 | Others trust me to keep their secrets. | 1 | 2 | 3 | 4 | 5 |

Five Facet Mindfulness Questionnaire—Short Form

Instructions: Here is a series of descriptions about your daily life. Please choose the option that best fits your recent experiences in the past week (including today).

1 = Never or very rarely true

2 = Rarely true

3 = Sometimes true

4 = Often true

5 = Very often or always true

1	I'm good at finding words to describe my feelings.	1	2	3	4	5
2	I can easily put my beliefs, opinions, and expectations into words.	1	2	3	4	5
3	I watch my feelings without getting carried away by them.	1	2	3	4	5
4	I tell myself I shouldn't be feeling the way I'm feeling.	1	2	3	4	5
5	It's hard for me to find the words to describe what I'm thinking.	1	2	3	4	5
6	I pay attention to physical experiences, such as the wind in my hair or sun on my face.	1	2	3	4	5
7	I make judgments about whether my thoughts are good or bad.	1	2	3	4	5
8	I find it difficult to stay focused on what's happening in the present moment.	1	2	3	4	5
9	When I have distressing thoughts or images, I don't let myself be carried away by them.	1	2	3	4	5

Continued

10	Generally, I pay attention to sounds, such as clocks ticking, birds chirping, or cars passing.	1	2	3	4	5
11	When I feel something in my body, it's hard for me to find the right words to describe it.	1	2	3	4	5
12	It seems I am "running on automatic" without much awareness of what I'm doing.	1	2	3	4	5
13	When I have distressing thoughts or images, I feel calm soon after.	1	2	3	4	5
14	I tell myself that I shouldn't be thinking the way I'm thinking.	1	2	3	4	5
15	I notice the smells and aromas of things.	1	2	3	4	5
16	Even when I'm feeling terribly upset, I can find a way to put it into words.	1	2	3	4	5
17	I rush through activities without being really attentive to them.	1	2	3	4	5
18	Usually when I have distressing thoughts or images, I can just notice them without reacting.	1	2	3	4	5
19	I think some of my emotions are bad or inappropriate and I shouldn't feel them.	1	2	3	4	5
20	I notice visual elements in art or nature, such as colors, shapes, textures, or patterns of light and shadow.	1	2	3	4	5
21	When I have distressing thoughts or images, I just notice them and let them go.	1	2	3	4	5
22	I do jobs or tasks automatically without being aware of what I'm doing.	1	2	3	4	5
23	I find myself doing things without paying attention.	1	2	3	4	5
24	I disapprove of myself when I have illogical ideas.	1	2	3	4	5

The questionnaire is complete. **Please review from beginning to end to ensure no questions were missed.** Thank you for your participation and cooperation!

THE END

Appendix K   Examples of Campus Natural Elements for Nature-Based Mindfulness Intervention

The following are examples of campus natural elements that can be used to enhance nature connectedness, with the aim of being incorporated into future Nature-Based Mindfulness Interventions. Universiti Sains Malaysia (USM), known as the "Garden University of Asia," boasts beautiful landscapes and rich natural resources. The campus is home to a wide variety of plants and animals, which can foster students' sense of connection to nature, curiosity, and spirituality.

The expansive greenery allows students to focus their attention on towering trees when feeling fatigued, while healing elements such as red seeds, the rich fragrance of mangoes, vibrant flowers, and aromatic fruits provide a soothing experience. Especially after the rain, students may notice small mushrooms sprouting from the soil, frangipani flowers carpeting the ground, and smooth, symbolic red seeds scattered across the path—all of which serve as ideal, readily accessible focal points for mindfulness practice and offer strong therapeutic value.

The author has included these natural elements as an appendix in this monograph, in hopes of contributing to future efforts to cultivate Character Strengths through Nature-Based Mindfulness Interventions.

The woods in front of the library   The woods behind the mosque

Swimming Pool   Football Field

Fragrant Mango Inside South Gate   Small Mushrooms Outside the Window of E45 Lounge

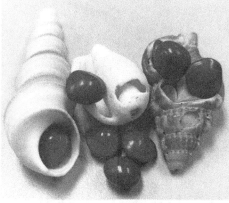
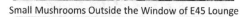

Tento Muido Near Building E45   Frangipani Near Building E45

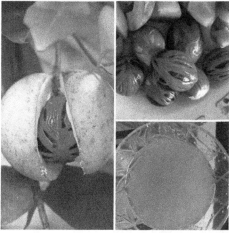

Healing Nutmeg Fruit   Fragrant Jasmine Flowers

BIBLIOGRAPHY

Abdollahi, A., Ahmed, A. A. A., Suksatan, W., Kumar, T., Majeed, M. S., Zainal, A. G., & Allen, K. A. (2022). Courage: a potential mediator of the relationship between personality and social anxiety. *Psychological Studies*, 67(1), 53-62. https://doi.org/10.1007/s12646-022-00641-2.

Adawiyah, R. (2023). Management of Religious Character Education in the Digital Era: The Role of Schools and Parents' Collaboration. *KnE Social Sciences*, 330-344. https://doi.org/10.18502/kss.v8i16.14052.

Ahmadi, A. (2016). *Mindfulness among students: The impact of faculty and demography in Malaysia*. Springer.

Ahmadi, A., Mustaffa, M. S., Haghdoost, A. A., & Alavi, M. (2014). Mindfulness and related factors among undergraduate students. *Procedia-Social and Behavioral Sciences*, 159, 20-24. https://doi.org/10.1016/j.sbspro.2014.12.321.

Allen, M. J., & Yen, W. M. (2001). *Introduction to measurement theory*. Waveland Press.

Alvarsson, J. J., Wiens, S., & Nilsson, M. E. (2010). Stress recovery during exposure to nature sound and environmental noise. *International Journal of Environmental Research and Public Health*, 7(3), 1036-1046. https://doi.org/10.3390/ ijerph7031036.

Arkkelin, D. (2014). Using SPSS to understand research and data analysis.

Aron, A., Aron, E. N., Tudor, M., & Nelson, G. (1991). Close relationships as including other in the self. *Journal of Personality and Social Psychology*,

60(2), 241.

Atchley, R. A., Strayer, D. L., & Atchley, P. (2012). Creativity in the wild: Improving creative reasoning through immersion in natural settings. *PloS One*, 7(12), e51474. https://doi.org/10.1371/journal.pone.0051474.

Bach, P., & Hayes, S. C. (2002). The use of Acceptance and Commitment Therapy to prevent the rehospitalization of psychotic patients: A randomized controlled trial. *Journal of Consulting and Clinical Psychology*, 70, 1129-1139. https://doi.org/10.1037/0022-006X.70.5.1129.

Baer, R. A. (Ed.). (2015). *Mindfulness-based treatment approaches: Clinician's guide to evidence base and applications*. Elsevier.

Baer, R. A., & Lykins, E. L. M. (2011). Mindfulness and positive psychological functioning. Designing positive psychology: Taking stock and moving forward, 335-348.

Baer, R. A., Smith, G. T., Hopkins, J., Krietemeyer, J., & Toney, L. (2006). Using self-report assessment methods to explore facets of mindfulness. *Assessment*, 13(1), 27-45. https://doi.org/10.1177/1073191105283504.

Baer, R. A., Smith, G. T., Lykins, E., Button, D., Krietemeyer, J., Sauer, S., & Walsh, E. (2008). Construct validity of the Five Facet Mindfulness Questionnaire in meditating and nonmeditating samples. *Assessment*, 15(3), 329-342. https://doi.org/10.1177/1073191107313003.

Baer, R. (2003). Mindfulness training as a clinical intervention: A conceptual and empirical review. *Clinical Psychology: Science and Practice*, 10(2), 125-142.

Barbaro, N., & Pickett, S. M. (2016). Mindfully green: Examining the effect of connectedness to nature on the relationship between mindfulness and engagement in pro-environmental behavior. *Personality and Individual Differences*, 93, 137-142. https://doi.org/10.1016/j.paid.2015.05.026.

Bashan, D., Colléony, A., & Shwartz, A. (2021). Urban versus rural? The effects of residential status on species identification skills and connection to nature. *People and Nature*, 3(2), 347-358. https://doi.org/10.1002/pan3. 10176.

Baumgartner, H., & Weijters, B. (2015). Response biases in cross-cultural measurement. In *Handbook of culture and consumer behavior* (Vol. 150). New York: Oxford University Press.

Bazkiaei, H. A., Heng, L. H., Khan, N. U., Saufi, R. B. A., & Kasim, R. S. R. (2020). Do entrepreneurial education and big-five personality traits predict entrepreneurial intention among universities students?. *Cogent Business & Management*, 7(1), 1801217. https://doi. org/10. 1080/23311975. 2020. 1801217.

Benfield, J. A., Rainbolt, G. N., Bell, P. A., & Donovan, G. H. (2015). Classrooms with nature views: Evidence of differing student perceptions and behaviors. *Environment and Behavior*, 47(2), 140-157. https://doi. org/10.1177/ 00139165134995.

Benfield, J. A., Taff, B. D., Newman, P., & Smyth, J. (2014). Natural sound facilitates mood recovery. *Ecopsychology*, 6(3), 183-188.

Berman, M. G., Jonides, J., & Kaplan, S. (2008). The cognitive benefits of interacting with nature. *Psychological Science*, 19(12), 1207-1212. https://doi.org/10.1111/j.1467-9280.2008.02225.x.

Berry, M. S., Sweeney, M. M., Morath, J., Odum, A. L., & Jordan, K. E. (2014). The nature of impulsivity: Visual exposure to natural environments decreases impulsive decision-making in a delay discounting task. *PloS One*, 9(5), e97915. https://doi.org/10.1371/journal.pone.0097915.

Berto, R. (2005). Exposure to restorative environments helps restore attentional capacity. *Journal of Environmental Psychology*, 25(3), 249-259. https://doi.org/10.1016/j.jenvp.2005.07.001.

Bishop, S. R., Lau, M., Shapiro, S., Carlson, L., Anderson, N. D., Carmody, J., & Devins, G. (2004). Mindfulness: A proposed operational definition. *Clinical Psychology: Science and Practice*, 11(3), 230. https://doi. org/

10.1093/ clipsy.bph077.

Blackie, L. E., Roepke, A. M., Forgeard, M. J., Jayawickreme, E., & Fleeson, W. (2014). Act well to be well: The promise of changing personality states to promote well-being. In *The Wiley Blackwell handbook of positive psychological interventions*, 462-474. https://doi.org/10.1002/9781118315927.ch27.

Blanca Mena, M. J., Alarcón Postigo, R., Arnau Gras, J., Bono Cabré, R., & Bendayan, R. (2017). Non-normal data: Is ANOVA still a valid option? *Psicothema*, 29 (4), 552-557. https://doi. org/10. 7334/psicothema2016. 383.

Boe, O. (2016). Building resilience: The role of Character Strengths in the selection and education of military leaders. *International Journal of Emergency Mental Health and Human Resilience*, 17(4), 714-716.

Boekhorst, M. G., & Duijndam, S. (2023). The association between facets of mindfulness and COVID-19 related distress: A cross-sectional study. *Acta Psychologica*, 233, 103826. https://doi.org/10.1016/j.actpsy.2023.103826.

Bohlmeijer, E., Ten Klooster, P. M., Fledderus, M., Veehof, M., & Baer, R. (2011). Psychometric properties of the five facet mindfulness questionnaire in depressed adults and development of a short form. *Assessment*, 18(3), 308-320. https://doi.org/10.1177/1073191111408231.

Boniface, N., Schenk, V., & Appel, P. (2012). Paleoproterozoic eclogites of MORB-type chemistry and three Proterozoic orogenic cycles in the Ubendian Belt (Tanzania): Evidence from monazite and zircon geochronology, and geochemistry. *Precambrian Research*, 192, 16-33. https://doi.org/10.1016/ j.precamres.2011.10.007.

Bowen, D. J., Neill, J. T., & Crisp, S. J. (2016). Wilderness adventure therapy effects on the mental health of youth participants. *Evaluation and Program Planning*, 58, 49-59.https://doi.org/10.1016/j.evalprogplan.2016.05.005.

Bratman, G. N., Daily, G. C., Levy, B. J., & Gross, J. J. (2015). The benefits of nature experience: Improved affect and cognition. *Landscape and Urban Planning*, 138, 41-50. https://doi.org/10.1016/j.landurbplan.2015.02.005.

Bratman, G. N., Hamilton, J. P., & Daily, G. C. (2012). The impacts of nature experience on human cognitive function and mental health. *Annals of the New York Academy of Sciences*, 1249(1), 118-136. https://doi.org/10.1111/j.1749-6632.2011.06400.x.

Bratman, G. N., Hamilton, J. P., Hahn, K. S., Daily, G. C., & Gross, J. J. (2015). Nature experience reduces rumination and subgenual prefrontal cortex activation. *Proceedings of the National Academy of Sciences*, 112(28), 8567-8572. https://doi.org/10.1073/pnas.1510459112.

Bressoud, N., Shankland, R., Ruch, W., & Gay, P. (2018). Character Strengths and children with special needs: A way to promote well-being all together! *Well-being in Education Systems*, 255.

Bright, D. S., Winn, B. A., & Kanov, J. (2014). Reconsidering virtue: Differences of perspective in virtue ethics and the positive social sciences. *Journal of Business Ethics*, 119, 445-460. https://doi.org/10.1007/s10551-013-1832-x.

Brislin, R. W. (1970). Back-translation for cross-cultural research. *Journal of Cross-cultural Psychology*, 1(3), 185-216. https://doi.org/10.1177/135910457000100301.

Brislin, R. W., & Baumgardner, S. R. (1971). Non-random sampling of individualsin cross-cultural research. *Journal of Cross-Cultural Psychology*, 2(4), 397-400. https://doi.org/10.1177/002202217100200410.

Brown, K. W., & Ryan, R. M. (2003). The benefits of being present: mindfulness and its role in psychological well-being. *Journal of Personality and Social Psychology*, 84(4), 822.

Brown, T. A. (2015). *Confirmatory factor analysis for applied research*. Guilford publications.

Brymer, E., Cuddihy, T. F., & Sharma-Brymer, V. (2010). The role of nature-based experiences in the development and maintenance of wellness. *Asia-Pacific Journal of Health, Sport and Physical Education*, 1(2), 21-27. https://doi.org/10.1080/18377122.2010.9730328.

Burns, G. W. (1999). Nature-guided therapy: A case example of ecopsychology in clinical practice. *Australian Journal of Outdoor Education*, 3(2), 9-14.

Campbell, D. T. (1969). Reforms as experiments. *American Psychologist*, 24(4), 409.

Capaldi, C. A., Dopko, R. L., & Zelenski, J. M. (2014). The relationship between nature connectedness and happiness: A meta-analysis. *Frontiers in Psychology*, 5, 92737. https://doi.org/10.3389/fpsyg.2014.00976.

Capaldi, C. A., Passmore, H. A., Nisbet, E. K., Zelenski, J. M., & Dopko, R. L. (2015). Flourishing in nature: A review of the benefits of connecting with nature and its application as a wellbeing intervention. *International Journal of Wellbeing*, 5(4). https://doi.org/10.5502/ijw.v5i4.449

Carleton, E. L., Barling, J., & Trivisonno, M. (2018). Leaders' Trait Mindfulness and transformational leadership: The mediating roles of leaders' positive affect and leadership self-efficacy. *Canadian Journal of Behavioural Science/Revue canadienne des sciences du comportement*, 50(3), 185.

Carpenter, J. K., Conroy, K., Gomez, A. F., Curren, L. C., & Hofmann, S. G. (2019). The relationship between Trait Mindfulness and affective symptoms: A meta-analysis of the Five Facet Mindfulness Questionnaire (FFMQ). *Clinical Psychology Review*, 74, 101785. https://doi.org/10.1016/j.cpr.2019.101785.

Centeno, R. P. R., & Fernandez, K. T. G. (2020). Effect of mindfulness on empathy and self-compassion: An adapted MBCT program on Filipino college students. *Behavioral Sciences*, 10(3), 61. https://doi.org/10.3390/bs10030061.

Chapman, M. J., Hare, D. J., Caton, S., Donalds, D., McInnis, E., &

Mitchell, D. (2013). The use of mindfulness with people with intellectual disabilities: a systematic review and narrative analysis. *Mindfulness*, 4, 179-189. https://doi.org/10.1007/s12671-013-0197-7.

Charoensukmongkol, P., & Suthatorn, P. (2018). Salespeople's Trait Mindfulness and emotional exhaustion: the mediating roles of optimism, resilience, and self-efficacy. *International Journal of Services, Economics and Management*, 9(2), 125-142. https://doi.org/10.1504/IJSEM.2018. 096075.

Chou, C. C., Keegan, J., Ditchman, N., Chan, F., Iwanaga, K., Kaya, C., ... & Tan, S. Y. (2021). Development and psychometric validation of a semantic differential measure of Character Strengths in a sample of Singaporean University students. *Journal of Asia Pacific Counseling*, 11 (1), 93-110.

Chou, W. Y., & Hung, S. H. (2021). Cumulative frequency of nature dose: How continuous and regular forest walking improves Nature Relatedness, restorativeness, and learning engagement in college students. *Sustainability*, 13(20), 11370. https://doi.org/10.3390/su132011370.

Christensen, H. S., & Bengtsson, A. (2011). The political competence of Internet participants: Evidence from Finland. *Information, Communication & Society*, 14 (6), 896-916. https://doi.org/10.1080/ 1369118X.2011.566931.

Chui, C. C. (2017). Character Strengths and positive outcomes. In social sciences postgraduate international seminar (SSPIS).

Cicchetti, D. V. (1994). Guidelines, criteria, and rules of thumb for evaluating normed and standardized assessment instruments in psychology. *Psychological Assessment*, 6(4), 284-290. https://doi.org/10.1037/1040- 3590.6.4.284.

Cimprich, B., & Ronis, D. L. (2001). Attention and symptom distress in women with and without breast cancer. *Nursing Research*, 50(2), 86-94.

Clatworthy, J., Hinds, J., & Camic, P. M. (2013). Gardening as a mental health intervention: A review. *Mental Health Review Journal*, 18(4), 214-225.

Clayton, S., & Opotow, S. (2003). Introduction: Identity and the Natural Environment. In S. Clayton & S. Opotow (Eds.), *Identity and the natural environment: The psychological significance of nature*, MIT Press, 1-24.

Cohen, J. (1992). Statistical power analysis. *Current directions in Psychological Science*, 1(3), 98-101. https://doi.org/10.1111/1467-8721. ep10768783.

Cornet A. (2019). A first exploration into psychological distress and Character Strengths in Cambodian students. *Singapore Conference of Applied Psychology*.

Creswell, J. W. (2013). *Educational research: Planning, conducting, and evaluating*. W. Ross MacDonald School Resource Services Library.

Creswell, J. W., & Creswell, J. D. (2017). *Research design: Qualitative, quantitative, and mixed methods approaches*. Sage publications.

Creswell, J. W., & Poth, C. N. (2016). *Qualitative inquiry and research design: Choosing among five approaches*. Sage publications.

Davis, J. L., Green, J. D., & Reed, A. (2009). Interdependence with the environment: Commitment, interconnectedness, and environmental behavior. *Journal of Environmental Psychology*, 29(2), 173-180. https://doi.org/10.1016/j.jenvp. 2008.11.001.

DeVellis, R. F., & Thorpe, C. T. (2021). Scale development: Theory and applications. *Sage publications*.

Doob, J. L. (1960). Relative limit theorems in analysis. *Journal D'analyse Mathématique*, 8(1), 289-306.

Duan, W. (2016). Mediation role of individual strengths in dispositional mindfulness and mental health. *Personality and Individual Differences*, 99, 7-10. https://doi.ore/10.1016/j.paid.2016.04.078.

Duan, W., & Bu, H. (2017). Development and initial validation of a short three-dimensional inventory of Character Strengths. *Quality of Life Research*, 26 (9), 2519-2531. https://doi.org/10.1007/s11136-017-1579-4.

Duan, W., Ho, S. M. Y., Yu, B., Tang, X., Zhang, Y., Li, T., & Yuen, T. (2012). Factor Structure of the Chinese Virtues Questionnaire. *Research on Social Work Practice*, 22 (6), 680-688. https://doi. org/10. 1177/10497 31512450074.

Duan, Y., Wang, L., Sun, Q., Liu, X., Ding, S., Cheng, Q.,& Cheng, A. S. (2021). Prevalence and determinants of psychological distress in adolescent and young adult patients with cancer: a multicenter survey. *Asia-Pacific Journal of Oncology Nursing*, 8 (3), 314-321. https://doi. org/10.4103/2347-5625.311005.

Dunlap, R. E., Van Liere, K. D., Mertig, A. G., & Jones, R. E. (2000). New trends in measuring environmental attitudes: measuring endorsement of the new ecological paradigm: a revised NEP scale. *Journal of Social Issues*, 56 (3), 425-442. https://doi.org/10.1111/0022-4537.00176.

Dutcher, D. D., Finley, J. C., Luloff, A. E., & Johnson, J. B. (2007). Connectivity with nature as a measure of environmental values. *Environment and Behavior*, 39 (4), 474-493. https://doi. org/10. 1177/ 0013916506298794.

Edunov, S., Ott, M., Auli, M., & Grangier, D. (2018). Understanding back-translation at scale. *arXiv preprint arXiv*: 1808. 09381. https://doi.org/10. 48550/ arXiv.1808.09381.

Erdfelder, E., Faul, F., & Buchner, A. (1996). GPOWER: A general power analysis program. *Behavior Research Methods, Instruments, & Computers*, 28, 1-11. https://doi.org/10.3758/BF03203630.

Erdogan, M. (2015). The Effect of Summer Environmental Education Program (SEEP) on Elementary School Students' Environmental Literacy. *International Journal of Environmental and Science Education*, 10 (2),

165-181.

Evans, D. R., Baer, R. A., & Segerstrom, S. C. (2009). The effects of mindfulness and self-consciousness on persistence. *Personality and Individual Differences*, 47(4), 379-382. https://doi. org/10. 1016/j. paid. 2009.03.026.

Faul, F., Erdfelder, E., Buchner, A., & Lang, A. G. (2009). Statistical power analyses using G * Power 3. 1: Tests for correlation and regression analyses. *Behavior Research Methods*, 41(4), 1149-1160. https://doi.org/ 10.3758/BRM.41.4.1149.

Festinger, L. E., & Katz, D. E. (1953). Research methods in the behavioral sciences.

Fleeson, W. (2001). Toward a structure-and process-integrated view of personality: Traits as density distributions of states. *Journal of Personality and Social Psychology*, 80(6), 1011.

Fleeson, W. (2004). Moving personality beyond the person-situation debate: The challenge and the opportunity of within-person variability. *Current Directions in Psychological Science*, 13(2), 83-87. https://doi. org/10. 1111/j.0963-7214.2004.00280.x.

Fogarty, F. A., Lu, L. M., Sollers, J. J., Krivoschekov, S. G., Booth, R. J., & Consedine, N. S. (2015). Why it pays to be mindful: Trait mindfulness predicts physiological recovery from emotional stress and greater differentiation among negative emotions. *Mindfulness*, 6, 175-185.

Frumkin, H. (2001). Beyond toxicity: human health and the natural environment. *American Journal of Preventive Medicine*, 20(3), 234-240. https://doi.org/10.1016/S0749-3797(00)00317-2.

Gan, R., Xue, J., & Chen, S. (2023). Mindfulness and burnout among Chinese college students: mediation through sleep quality and perceived stress. *Psychology, Health & Medicine*, 28(7), 1755-1766. https://doi. org/10. 1080/13548506. 2023.2177686.

Gärtner, C. (2013). Enhancing readiness for change by enhancing mindfulness. *Journal of Change Management*, 13(1), 52-68. https://doi.org/10.1080/14697017.2013.768433.

Gaskin, C. J., & Happell, B. (2014). On exploratory factor analysis: A review of recent evidence, an assessment of current practice, and recommendations for future use. *International Journal of Nursing Studies*, 51(3), 511-521. https://doi.org/10.1016/j.ijnurstu.2013.10.005.

Gay, J., & Cole, M. (1967). The new mathematics and an old culture: A study of learning among the Kpelle of Liberia.

Gay, L. R., Miles, G. E. and Airasian, P. (2011) Educational Research: Competencies for Analysis and Applications. 10th Edition, *Pearson Education International*, Boston.

Gay, L. R., Mills, G. E., & Airasian, P. W. (2012). *Educational research: Competencies for analysis and applications*. Pearson.

Geng, L., Xu, J., Ye, L., Zhou, W., & Zhou, K. (2015). Connections with nature and environmental behaviors. *PloS One*, 10(5), e0127247. https://doi.org/10.1371/journal.pone.0127247.

Germer, C. (2009). *The mindful path to self-compassion: Freeing yourself from destructive thoughts and emotions*. Guilford Press.

Germer, C. K. (2005). Teaching mindfulness in therapy. *Mindfulness and psychotherapy*, 1(2), 113-129.

Gilbert, P. (2010). An introduction to compassion focused therapy in cognitive behavior therapy. *International Journal of Cognitive Therapy*, 3(2), 97-112. https://doi.org/10.1521/ijct.2010.3.2.97.

Giluk, T. L. (2009). Mindfulness, Big Five personality, and affect: A meta-analysis. *Personality and Individual Differences*, 47(8), 805-811. https://doi.org/10.1016/j.paid.2009.06.026.

Guan, Y., Chen, S. X., Levin, N., Bond, M. H., Luo, N., Xu, J., ... & Han, X. (2015). Differences in career decision-making profiles between American and Chinese university students: The relative strength of mediating mechanisms across cultures. *Journal of Cross-Cultural Psychology*, 46 (6), 856-872. https://doi.org/10.1177/0022022115585874.

Hair, J. F., Ringle, C. M., & Sarstedt, M. (2011). PLS-SEM: indeed a silver bullet. *Journal of Marketing Theory and Practice*, 19 (2), 139-151. https://doi.org/10.2753/MTP1069-6679190202.

Hamann, G. A., & Ivtzan, I. (2017). 30 minutes in nature a day can increase mood, well-being, meaning in life, and mindfulness: Effects of a pilot programme. *Social inquiry into well-being*, 2016, Vol. 2, No. 2. https://cris.mruni.eu/cris/handle/007/14584.

Hanley, A. W. (2016). The mindful personality: Associations between dispositional mindfulness and the Five Factor Model of personality. *Personality and Individual Differences*, 91, 154-158. https://doi.org/10.1016/j.paid.2015. 11.054.

Hartig, T., Evans, G. W., Jamner, L. D., Davis, D. S., & Gärling, T. (2003). Tracking restoration in natural and urban field settings. *Journal of Environmental Psychology*, 23 (2), 109-123. https://doi. org/10. 1016/S0272-4944 (02) 00109-3.

Harzer, C. (2016). *The eudaimonics of human strengths: The relations between Character Strengths and well-being.* Handbook of eudaimonic well-being, 307-322.

Harzer, C., & Ruch, W. (2015). The relationships of Character Strengths with coping, work-related stress, and job satisfaction. *Frontiers in Psychology*, 6, 165. https://doi.org/10.3389/fpsyg.2015.00165.

Hashmi, S. I., Din, A., & NAWI, N. H. M. (2015). Big-Five personality traits and its effect on emotional intelligence among public school personnel in Malaysia. *Southeast Asia Psychology Journal*, 3. https://doi.org/10.51200/sapj. v3i1.5661.

Hatfield, E., & Sprecher, S. (1995). Men's and women's preferences in marital partners in the United States, Russia, and Japan. *Journal of Cross-cultural Psychology*, 26(6), 728-750. https://doi.org/10.1177/002202219502600613.

Hayes, A. F. (2018). Partial, conditional, and moderated moderated mediation: Quantification, inference, and interpretation. *Communication Monographs*, 85 (1), 4-40. https://doi.org/10.1080/03637751.2017.1352100.

Henrich, J., Heine, S. J., & Norenzayan, A. (2010). Most people are not WEIRD. Nature, 466(7302), 29-29. https://doi.org/10.1038/466029a.

Hj Ramli, N. H., Alavi, M., Mehrinezhad, S. A., & Ahmadi, A. (2018). Academic stress and self-regulation among university students in Malaysia: Mediator role of mindfulness. *Behavioral Sciences*, 8(1), 12. https://doi.org/10.3390/ bs8010012.

Ho, S. M., Li, W. L., Duan, W., Siu, B. P., Yau, S., Yeung, G., & Wong, K. (2016). A Brief Strengths Scale for individuals with mental health issues. *Psychological Assessment*, 28 (2), 147. https://doi. org/10. 1037/ pas0000164.

Holden, L. J., & Mercer, T. (2014). Nature in the learning environment: Exploring the relationship between nature, memory, and mood. *Ecopsychology*, 6(4), 234-240. https://doi.org/10.1089/eco.2014.0034.

Howell, A. J., Dopko, R. L., Passmore, H. A., & Buro, K. (2011). Nature connectedness: Associations with well-being and mindfulness. *Personality and Individual Differences*, 51(2), 166-171. https://doi. org/10. 1016/j. paid. 2011.03.037.

Howell, R. T., Chong, W. T., Howell, C. J., & Schwabe, K. (2012). Happiness and life satisfaction in Malaysia. *Happiness Across Cultures: Views of Happiness and Quality of Life in Non-Western Cultures*, 43-55.

Hudson, N. W., & Fraley, R. C. (2015). Volitional personality trait change: Can people choose to change their personality traits?. *Journal of personality and social psychology*, 109 (3), 490. https://doi. org/10. 1037/ pspp0000021.

Ivtzan, I., & Lomas, T. (Eds.). (2016). *Mindfulness in positive psychology: The science of meditation and well being.* Routledge.

Jayaraja, A. R., Tan, S. A., & Ramasamy, P. N. (2017). Predicting role of mindfulness and procrastination on psychological well-being among university students in Malaysia. *Jurnal Psikologi Malaysia*, 31(2).

Jing X. Z. (2018). Exploring Higher Educated Youth on Nature Relatedness' Experiences, Perception, Affective, and Pro-Environmental Behaviors of Malaysian Chinese, Master's thesis, Taiwan Normal University.

John, O. P., Naumann, L. P., & Soto, C. J. (2008). Paradigm shift to the integrative big five trait taxonomy. *Handbook of personality: Theory and research*, 3(2), 114-158. OneTouch 4.0 Scanned Documents (elaborer. org).

Johnson, A. M., Vernon, P. A., Harris, J. A., & Jang, K. L. (2004). A behavior genetic investigation of the relationship between leadership and personality. *Twin Research and Human Genetics*, 7(1), 27-32. https://doi.org/10. 1375/ twin.7.1.27.

Johnson, K. A. (2018). Prayer: A helpful aid in recovery from depression. *Journal of Religion and Health*, 57(6), 2290-2300.

Joye, Y., & Bolderdijk, J. W. (2015). An exploratory study into the effects of extraordinary nature on emotions, mood, and prosociality. *Frontiers in Psychology*, 5, 1577. https://doi.org/10.3389/fpsyg.2014.01577.

Kabat-Zinn, J. (2003). Mindfulness-based interventions in context: past, present, and future. https://doi.org/10.1093/clipsy.bpg016.

Kaiser, H. (1970). A second generation Little Jiffy. *Psychometrika*, 35, 401-415.

Kaiser, H. (1974). An index of factorial simplicity. *Psychometrika*, 39, 31-36.

Kals, E., Schumacher, D., & Montada, L. (1999). Emotional affinity toward nature as a motivational basis to protect nature. *Environment and Behavior*, 31(2), 178-202. https://doi.org/10.1177/00139169921972056.

Kalyar, M. N., & Kalyar, H. (2018). Provocateurs of creative performance:

examining the roles of wisdom Character Strengths and stress. *Personnel Review*, 47(2), 334-352. https://doi.org/10.1108/PR-10-2016-0286.

Kaplan, R. (2001). The nature of the view from home: Psychological benefits. *Environment and Behavior*, 33(4), 507-542. https://doi.org/10.1177/00139160121973115.

Kaplan, S. (1995). The restorative benefits of nature: Toward an integrative framework. *Journal of Environmental Psychology*, 15(3), 169-182. https://doi.org/10.1016/0272-4944(95)90001-2.

Karim, N. S. A., Zamzuri, N. H. A., & Nor, Y. M. (2009). Exploring the relationship between Internet ethics in university students and the big five model of personality. *Computers &Education*, 53(1), 86-93. https://doi.org/10.1016/j. compedu.2009.01.001.

Keller, M. C., Fredrickson, B. L., Ybarra, O., Côté, S., Johnson, K., Mikels, J., ... & Wager, T. (2005). A warm heart and a clear head: The contingent effects of weather on mood and cognition. *Psychological Science*, 16(9), 724-731. https://doi.org/10.1111/j.1467-9280.2005.01602.x

Kellert, S. R., & Wilson, E. O. (Eds.). (1, & Pearson-Mims, C. 993). *The biophilia hypothesis*. Island Press.

Keng, S. L., Phang, C. K., & Oei, T. P. (2015). Effects of a brief mindfulness-based intervention program on psychological symptoms and well-being among medical students in Malaysia: a controlled study. *International Journal of Cognitive Therapy*, 8(4), 335-350. https://doi.org/10.1521/ijct.2015.8.4.335.

Keng, S. L., Smoski, M. J., & Robins, C. J. (2011). Effects of mindfulness on psychological health: A review of empirical studies. *Clinical Psychology Review*, 31(6), 1041-1056. https://doi.org/10.1016/j.cpr.2011.04.006.

Kiken, L. G., Garland, E. L., Bluth, K., Palsson, O. S., & Gaylord, S. A. (2015). From a state to a trait: Trajectories of state mindfulness in meditation during intervention predict changes in Trait Mindfulness.

Personality and Individual Differences, 81, 41-46. https://doi.org/10. 1016/j.paid.2014.12.044.

Kleespies, M. W., & Dierkes, P. W. (2023). Connection to nature of university students in the environmental field—An empirical study in 41 countries. *Biological Conservation*, 283, 110093. https://doi.org/10.1016/j. biocon. 2023.110093.

Kline, P. (2015). *A handbook of test construction (psychology revivals): Introduction to psychometric design*. Routledge. https://doi.org/10.4324/ 9781315695990.

Kline, R. B. (2023). *Principles and practice of structural equation modeling*. Guilford publications.

Koe Hwee Nga, J., & Shamuganathan, G. (2010). The influence of personality traits and demographic factors on social entrepreneurship start up intentions. *Journal of Business Ethics*, 95, 259-282.

Kövi, Z., Kim, H., Kamble, S., Mészáros, V., Lachance, D., & Nisbet, E. (2023). Cross-cultural validity of the Nature Relatedness Scale (NR-6) and links with wellbeing. *International Journal of Wellbeing*, 13(2). https:// doi.org/10.5502/ ijw. v13i2.2841.

Krejcie, R. V., & Morgan, D. W. (1970). Sample size determination table. *Educational and Psychological Measurement*, 30, 607-610.

Kristeller, J. L. (2003). Mindfulness, wisdom and eating: applying a multi-domain model of meditation effects. *Journal of Constructivism in the Human Sciences*, 8(2), 107-118.

Kühnen, U., Hannover, B., Roeder, U., Shah, A. A., Schubert, B., Upmeyer, A., & Zakaria, S. (2001). Cross-cultural variations in identifying embedded figures: Comparisons from the United States, Germany, Russia, and Malaysia. *Journal of Cross-Cultural Psychology*, 32(3), 366-372. https:// doi.org/10.1177/ 0022022101032003007.

Kuo, F. E., & Faber Taylor, A. (2004). A potential natural treatment for attention-deficit/hyperactivity disorder: evidence from a national study. *American Journal of Public Health*, 94(9), 1580-1586. https://doi.org/10. 2105/AJPH.94.9.1580.

Kuo, F. E., & Sullivan, W. C. (2001). Environment and crime in the inner city: Does vegetation reduce crime?. *Environment and Behavior*, 33(3), 343-367. https://doi.org/10.1177/0013916501333002.

Kyriazos, T. A. (2018). Applied psychometrics: sample size and sample power considerations in factor analysis (EFA, CFA) and SEM in general. *Psychology*, 9(08), 2207. https://doi.org/10.4236/psych.2018.98126.

Lakey, C. E., Kernis, M. H., Heppner, W. L., & Lance, C. E. (2008). Individual differences in authenticity and mindfulness as predictors of verbal defensiveness. *Journal of Research in Personality*, 42(1), 230-238. https://doi.org/10.1016/j.jrp.2007.05.002.

Lau, M. A., Bishop, S. R., Segal, Z. V., Buis, T., Anderson, N. D., Carlson, L., ... & Devins, G. (2006). The Toronto mindfulness scale: Development and validation. *Journal of Clinical Psychology*, 62 (12), 1445-1467. https://doi.org/10.1002/jclp.20326.

Lavy, S., Littman-Ovadia, H., & Bareli, Y. (2014). Strengths deployment as a mood-repair mechanism: Evidence from a diary study with a relationship exercise group. *The Journal of Positive Psychology*, 9 (6), 547-558. https://doi.org/10.1080/17439760.2014.936963.

Leary, M. R., Tipsord, J. M., & Tate, E. B. (2008). Allo-inclusive identity: Incorporating the social and natural worlds into one's sense of self. https://doi.org/10.1037/11771-013.

Leong, L. Y. C., Fischer, R., & McClure, J. (2014). Are nature lovers more innovative? The relationship between connectedness with nature and cognitive styles. *Journal of Environmental Psychology*, 40, 57-63. https://doi.org/10.1016/ j.jenvp.2014.03.007.

Liefländer, A. K., Fröhlich, G., Bogner, F. X., & Schultz, P. W. (2013).

Promoting connectedness with nature through environmental education. *Environmental Education Research*, 19(3), 370-384. https://doi.org/10. 1080/13504622. 2012.697545.

Linehan, M. M., (1993). *Cognitive-behavioral treatment of borderline personality disorder.* New York: Guilford.

Listiyandini, R. A., & Akmal, S. Z. (2017). Resilience and character strength among Indonesian university students. *In ASIA International Multidisciplinary Conference, Johor Bahru, Malaysia.*

Littman-Ovadia, H., & Lavy, S. (2016). Going the extra mile: Perseverance as a key character strength at work. *Journal of Career Assessment*, 24(2), 240-252. https://doi.org/10.1177/1069072715580322.

Littman-Ovadia, H., & Steger, M. (2010). Character Strengths and well-being among volunteers and employees: Toward an integrative model. *The Journal of Positive Psychology*, 5(6), 419-430. https://doi.org/10.1080/ 17439760. 2010.516765.

Littman-Ovadia, H., Potok, Y., & Ruch, W. (2013). The relationship between vocational personalities and Character Strengths in adults. *Psychology*, 4 (12), 985-993. https://doi.org/10.5167/uzh-88989.

Loeffler, T. A. (2004). A photo elicitation study of the meanings of outdoor adventure experiences. *Journal of Leisure Research*, 36 (4), 536-556. https://doi.org/ 10.1080/ 00222216.2004.11950035.

Lohr, V. I., & Pearson-Mims, C. H. (2000). Physical discomfort may be reduced in the presence of interior plants. *HortTechnology*, 10(1), 53-58.

Lopez D. S. Jr. (2012). The scientific Buddha: His short and happy life. New Haven, CT: Yale University Press.

Lounsbury, J. W., Hutchens, T., & Loveland, J. M. (2005). An investigation of big five personality traits and career decidedness among early and middle adolescents. *Journal of Career Assessment*, 13(1), 25-39. https://doi. org/10.1177/ 1069072704270272.

Malaysian Psychological Association, More about Malaysian Psychological Association (PSIMA). (2024). Malaysia-https://www.psima.org.my/-.

Malhotra, N. K., Kim, S. S., & Patil, A. (2006). Common method variance in IS research: A comparison of alternative approaches and a reanalysis of past research. *Management Science*, 52(12), 1865-1883. https://doi.org/10.1287/mnsc.1060.0597.

Malinowski, P. (2013). Neural mechanisms of attentional control in mindfulness meditation. *Frontiers in Neuroscience*, 7, 35772. https://doi.org/10.3389/fnins.2013.00008.

Marsh, H. W., Ellis, L. A., Parada, R. H., Richards, G., & Heubeck, B. G. (2005). A Short Version of the Self Description Questionnaire II: Operationalizing Criteria for Short-Form Evaluation With New Applications of Confirmatory Factor Analyses. *Psychological Assessment*, 17(1), 81-102. https://doi.org/10.1037/1040-3590.17.1.81.

Martyn, P., & Brymer, E. (2016). The relationship between Nature Relatedness and anxiety. *Journal of Health Psychology*, 21(7), 1436-1445. https://doi.org/10.1177/1359105314555169.

Mayer, B., Polak, M. G., & Remmerswaal, D. (2019). Mindfulness, interpretation bias, and levels of anxiety and depression: Two mediation studies. *Mindfulness*, 10, 55-65.

Mayer, F. S., & Frantz, C. M. (2004). The connectedness to nature scale: A measure of individuals' feeling in community with nature. *Journal of Environmental Psychology*, 24(4), 503-515. https://doi.org/10.1016/j.jenvp.2004.10.001.

Mayer, F. S., Frantz, C. M., Bruehlman-Senecal, E., & Dolliver, K. (2009). Why is nature beneficial? The role of connectedness to nature. *Environment and Behavior*, 41(5), 607-643. https://doi.org/10.1177/001391650831974.

McCrae, R. R., & Costa, P. T. (1987). Validation of the five-factor model of personality across instruments and observers. *Journal of Personality and Social Psychology*, 52(1), 81. https://doi.org/10.1037/0022-3514.52.1.81.

McCrae, R. R., & Terracciano, A. (2005). Universal features of personality traits from the observer's perspective: data from 50 cultures. *Journal of Personality and Social Psychology*, 88(3), 547. https://doi.org/10.1037/0022-3514.88.3.547.

McGrath, R. E. (2015). Character Strengths in 75 nations: An update. *The Journal of Positive Psychology*, 10(1), 41-52. https://doi.org/10.1080/17439760.2014.888580.

Mcsweeney, J., Rainham, D., Johnson, S. A., Sherry, S. B., & Singleton, J. (2014). Indoor nature exposure (INE): A health-promotion framework. *Health Promotion International*, 30(1), 126-139. https://doi.org/10.1093/heapro/dau081.

Medvedev, O. N., Krägeloh, C. U., Narayanan, A., & Siegert, R. J. (2017). Measuring mindfulness: Applying generalizability theory to distinguish between state and trait. *Mindfulness*, 8, 1036-1046.

Merino, A., Valor, C., & Redondo, R. (2020). Connectedness is in my character: the relationship between Nature Relatedness and Character Strengths. *Environmental Education Research*, 26(12), 1707-1728. https://doi.org/10.1080/13504622.2020.1825630.

Mesmer-Magnus, J., Manapragada, A., Viswesvaran, C., & Allen, J. W. (2017). Trait mindfulness at work: A meta-analysis of the personal and professional correlates of Trait Mindfulness. *Human Performance*, 30(2-3), 79-98. https://doi.org/10.1080/08959285.2017.1307842.

Mey, S. C., Abdullah, M. N. L. Y., & Yin, C. J. (2014). Profiling the Personality Traits of University Undergraduate and Postgraduate Students at a Research University in Malaysia. *Professional Counselor*, 4(4), 378-389.

Mills, G. E., & Gay, L. R. (2019). *Educational research: Competencies for analysis and applications*. Pearson. One Lake Street, Upper Saddle River,

New Jersey 07458.

Ministry of Education Malaysia, Malaysia Education Blueprint 2013-2025. (2013). Retrieved from https://www. pmo. gov. my/wp-content/uploads/ 2019/07/Malay sia-Education-Blueprint-2013-2025.pdf.

Mohamad Muslim, H. F., Hosaka, T., Numata, S., & Yahya, N. A. (2017). Nature-Related Experience during Childhood in Urban and Rural Areas: The Case of Peninsular Malaysians. *Urban Studies Research*, 2017(1), 7349219. https://doi.org/10.1155/2017/7349219.

Mumford, M. D., & Gustafson, S. B. (1988). Creativity syndrome: Integration, application, and innovation. *Psychological Bulletin*, 103(1), 27.

Mustapa, N. D., Maliki, N. Z., Aziz, N. F., & Hamzah, A. (2016). A review of the underlying constructs of connectedness to capture among children. In *1st International Conference on Humanities, Social Sciences and Environment*, 1-9.

Mustapha, M., & Hyland, M. E. (2017). Relationship of Values and Personality Traits in Malaysian College Students. *Sains Humanika*, 9(3-2). https:// doi.org/ 10.11113/sh.v9n3-2.1282.

Najad, P. G., Ahmad, A., & Zen, I. S. (2018). Approach to environmental sustainability and green campus at Universiti Teknologi Malaysia: A Review. *Environment and Ecology Research*, 6(3), 203-209.

Naroll, R., Alnot, W., Caplan, J., Hansen, J. F., Maxant, J., & Schmidt, N. (1970). A standard ethnographic sample: preliminary edition. *Current Anthropology*, 11(2), 235-248.

Nawi, N. H. M., Redzuan, M., Hashmi, S. I., & Din, A. (2015). Big-Five personality traits and its effect on emotional intelligence among public school personnel in Malaysia. *Journal of Southeast Asia Psychology* (*SAPJ*), 3(1), 14-14. https://doi.org/10.51200/sapj.v3i1.5661.

Niemiec, R. M. (2013). *Mindfulness and Character Strengths*. Boston, MA: Hogrefe Publishing.

Niemiec, R. M. (2023). Mindfulness and Character Strengths: *A Practitioner's Guide to MBSP*. Hogrefe Publishing GmbH.

Niemiec, R. M., & Wedding, D. (2014). Accentuate the Positive, Eliminate the Negative, Don't Mess With Mister In-Between. http://dx.doi.org/ 10.1032/ a0036802.

Niemiec, R., Rashid, T., & Spinella, M. (2012). Strong mindfulness: Integrating mindfulness and Character Strengths. *Journal of Mental Health Counseling*, 34 (3), 240-253. https://doi. org/10. 17744/mehc. 34. 3. 34p6328x2v204v21.

Nisbet, E. K., & Zelenski, J. M. (2013). The NR-6: A new brief measure of Nature Relatedness. *Frontiers in Psychology*, 4, 813. https://doi.org/10. 3389/fpsyg. 2013.00813.

Nisbet, E. K., & Zelenski, J. M. (2023). Nature Relatedness and subjective well-being. In *Encyclopedia of quality of life and well-being research*, Cham: Springer International Publishing, 1-9. https://doi.org/10.1007/978-3-031-17299-1_3909.

Nisbet, E. K., Zelenski, J. M., & Grandpierre, Z. (2019). Mindfulness in nature enhances connectedness and mood. *Ecopsychology*, 11(2), 81-91. https:// doi. org/10. 1089/eco. 2018. 0061.

Nisbet, E. K., Zelenski, J. M., & Murphy, S. A. (2009). The Nature Relatedness scale: Linking individuals' connection with nature to environmental concern and behavior. *Environment and Behavior*, 41(5), 715-740. https://doi.org/10.1177/ 0013916508318748.

Ohtsuka, Y., Yabunaka, N., & Takayama, S. (1998). Shinrin-yoku (forest-air bathing and walking) effectively decreases blood glucose levels in diabetic patients. *International Journal of Biometeorology*, 41, 125-127.

Osgood, C. E. (1960). The cross-cultural generality of visual-verbal synesthetic tendencies. *Behavioral Science*, 5(2), 146-169.

Oyserman, D., Coon, H. M., & Kemmelmeier, M. (2002). Rethinking individualism and collectivism: evaluation of theoretical assumptions and meta-analyses. *Psychological Bulletin*, 128 (1) , 3. https://doi. org/10. 1037/ 0033-2909.128.1.3.

Pang, D. , & Ruch, W. (2019a). Fusing Character Strengths and mindfulness interventions: Benefits for job satisfaction and performance. *Journal of Occupational Health Psychology*, 24 (1) , 150. https://doi. org/10. 1037/ ocp0000144.

Pang, D. , & Ruch, W. (2019b). The mutual support model of mindfulness and Character Strengths. *Mindfulness*, 10, 1545-1559. https://doi.org/10.1007/ s12671-019-01103-z.

Park, C. W. , MacInnis, D. J. , Priester, J. , Eisingerich, A. B. , & Iacobucci, D. (2010). Brand attachment and brand attitude strength: Conceptual and empirical differentiation of two critical brand equity drivers. *Journal of Marketing*, 74(6) , 1-17. https://doi.org/10.1509/jmkg.74.6.1.

Park, N. , & Peterson, C. (2006). Character Strengths and happiness among young children: Content analysis of parental descriptions. *Journal of Happiness Studies*, 7, 323-341. https://doi. org/10. 1007/s10902-005-3648- 6.

Park, N. , & Peterson, C. (2010). Does it matter where we live?: The urban psychology of Character Strengths. *American Psychologist*, 65 (6) , 535- 547. https://doi.org/10.1037/a0019621.

Park, N. , Peterson, C. , & Seligman, M. E. (2004). Strengths of character and well-being. *Journal of Social and Clinical Psychology*, 23 (5) , 603-619. https://doi.org/10.1521/jscp.23.5.603.50748.

Park, N. , Peterson, C. , & Seligman, M. E. (2006). Character Strengths in fifty-four nations and the fifty US states. *The Journal of Positive Psychology*, 1 (3) , 118-129. https://doi.org/10.1080/17439760600619567.

Park, T. , Reilly-Spong, M. , & Gross, C. R. (2013). Mindfulness: a systematic review of instruments to measure an emergent patient-reported outcome

(PRO). *Quality of Life Research*, 22, 2639-2659. https://doi.org/10.1007/s11136-013-0395-8.

Parker, S. K., & Collins, C. G. (2010). Taking stock: Integrating and differentiating multiple proactive behaviors. *Journal of Management*, 36 (3), 633-662. https://doi.org/10.1177/0149206308321554.

Passmore, H. A., & Holder, M. D. (2017). Noticing nature: Individual and social benefits of a two-week intervention. *The Journal of Positive Psychology*, 12 (6), 537-546. https://doi. org/10. 1080/17439760. 2016. 1221126.

Passmore, H. A., Yang, Y., & Sabine, S. (2022). An extended replication study of the well-being intervention, the noticing nature intervention (NNI). *Journal of Happiness Studies*, 23 (6), 2663-2683. https://doi. org/10. 1007/s10902-022-00516-3.

Pei-Lee, T., Chen, C. Y., Chin, W. C., & Siew, Y. Y. (2011). Do the big five personality factors affect knowledge sharing behaviour? A study of Malaysian universities. *Malaysian Journal of Library & Information Science*, 16(1), 47-62.

Perkins, H. E. (2010). Measuring love and care for nature. *Journal of Environmental Psychology*, 30 (4), 455-463. https://doi. org/10. 1016/j. jenvp.2010.05.004.

Peterson, C., & Seligman, M. E. (2006). The values in action (VIA) classification of strengths. *A life worth living: Contributions to positive psychology*, 29-48.

Peterson, C., Park, N., & Seligman, M. E. (2006). Greater strengths of character and recovery from illness. *The Journal of Positive Psychology*, 1 (1), 17-26. https://doi.org/10.1080/17439760600619567.

Peterson, C., Ruch, W., Beermann, U., Park, N., & Seligman, M. E. (2007). Strengths of character, orientations to happiness, and life satisfaction. *The Journal of Positive Psychology*, 2(3), 149-156. https://doi. org/10.1080/

17439760701 228938.

Phang, C. K., Mukhtar, F., Ibrahim, N., & Mohd. Sidik, S. (2016). Mindful Attention Awareness Scale (MAAS): factorial validity and psychometric properties in a sample of medical students in Malaysia. *The Journal of Mental Health Training, Education and Practice*, 11(5), 305-316.

Pimthong, S. (2015). Psychosocial factors correlated with sufficient consumption behavior of students in Thailand and Malaysia. *Asian Social Science*, 11(4), 169. http://dx.doi.org/10.5539/ass.v11n4p169.

Poon, L. L., Song, T., Rosenfeld, R., Lin, X., Rogers, M. B., Zhou, B., ... & Ghedin, E. (2016). Quantifying influenza virus diversity and transmission in humans. *Nature Genetics*, 48(2), 195-200. https://doi. org/10. 1038/ ng. 3479.

Prajapati, B., Dunne, M., & Armstrong, R. (2010). Sample size estimation and statistical power analyses. *Optometry Today*, 16(7), 10-18.

Prasetyo, D. T., Djuwita, R., & Ariyanto, A. (2018). Who is more related to the nature? A study from Indonesia. In E3S Web of Conferences (Vol. 74, p. 08009). *EDP Sciences*. https://doi. org/10. 1051/e3sconf/20187408009.

Price-Williams, D. R. (1961). A study concerning concepts of conservation of quantities among primitive children. *Acta Psychologica*, 18, 297-305.

Proyer, R. T., Gander, F., Wellenzohn, S., & Ruch, W. (2013). What good are Character Strengths beyond subjective well-being? The contribution of the good character on self-reported health-oriented behavior, physical fitness, and the subjective health status. *The Journal of Positive Psychology*, 8(3), 222-232. https://doi.org/10.1080/17439760.2013.777767.

Proyer, R. T., Gander, F., Wellenzohn, S., & Ruch, W. (2015). Strengths-based positive psychology interventions: A randomized placebo-controlled online trial on long-term effects for a signature strengths-vs. a lesser strengths-intervention. *Frontiers in Psychology*, 6, 456. https://doi. org/ 10.3389/fpsyg.2015.00456.

Proyer, R. T., Ruch, W., & Buschor, C. (2013). Testing strengths-based interventions: A preliminary study on the effectiveness of a program targeting curiosity, gratitude, hope, humor, and zest for enhancing life satisfaction. *Journal of Happiness Studies*, 14, 275-292. https://doi.org/ 10.1007/s10902-012-9331-9.

Randal, C., Pratt, D., & Bucci, S. (2015). Mindfulness and self-esteem: a systematic review. *Mindfulness*, 6, 1366-1378.

Roberts, B. W., Kuncel, N. R., Shiner, R., Caspi, A., & Goldberg, L. R. (2007). The power of personality: The comparative validity of personality traits, socioeconomic status, and cognitive ability for predicting important life outcomes. *Perspectives on Psychological Science*, 2(4), 313-345. https://doi.org/10.1111/j.1745-6916.2007.00047.x.

Rofa, N. (2022). A study of entrepreneurial potential and entrepreneurial personality traits among vocational colleges students in Malaysia: moderating effects of entrepreneurial mentoring (*Doctoral dissertation*, *Universiti Teknologi MARA (UiTM)*).

Rosenstreich, E., & Margalit, M. (2015). Loneliness, mindfulness, and academic achievements: A moderation effect among first-year college students. *The Open Psychology Journal*, 8(1). https://doi.org/10.2174/ 1874350101508 010138.

Roslan, S., Ismail, M., Zaremohzzabieh, Z., Ahmad, N., Mohamad, Z., Der Jiun Ooi, N. A. I., & Qamaruzzaman, F. (2022). The ecopsychological, spiritual, physiological health and mood benefits of zikr meditation and nature for Muslim university students. *International Journal of Academic Research in Business &Social Sciences*, 12(9), 1929-1949. http://hrmars. com/index.php/ pages/ detail/IJARBSS.

Ryan, C., Russell, S. T., Huebner, D., Diaz, R., & Sanchez, J. (2010). Family acceptance in adolescence and the health of LGBT young adults. *Journal of Child and Adolescent Psychiatric Nursing*, 23(4), 205-213.

https://doi.org/10.1111/j.1744-6171.2010.00246.x

Sahak, S. N. B. M. (2018). Spirituality as mediator for relationships between nature exposure, connectedness to nature and psychological well-being of school students in Johor Bahru, Malaysia.

Schultz, P. W. (2001). The structure of environmental concern: Concern for self, other people, and the biosphere. *Journal of Environmental Psychology*, 21(4), 327-339. https://doi.org/10.1006/jevp.2001.0227.

Schultz, P. W. (2002). Inclusion with nature: The psychology of human-nature relations. In *Psychology of Sustainable Development*, Boston, MA: Springer US, 61-78. https://doi.org/10.1007/978-1-4615-0995-0_4.

Schultz, P. W., Shriver, C., Tabanico, J. J., & Khazian, A. M. (2004). Implicit connections with nature. *Journal of Environmental Psychology*, 24(1), 31-42. https://doi.org/10.1016/S0272-4944(03)00022-7.

Schutte, N. S., & Malouff, J. M. (2018). Mindfulness and connectedness to nature: A meta-analytic investigation. *Personality and Individual Differences*, 127, 10-14. https://doi.org/10.1016/j.paid.2018.01.034.

Segal, Z. V., Teasdale, J. D., Williams, J. M., & Gemar, M. C. (2002). The mindfulness-based cognitive therapy adherence scale: Inter-rater reliability, adherence to protocol and treatment distinctiveness. *Clinical Psychology & Psychotherapy*, 9(2), 131-138. https://doi.org/10.1002/cpp.320.

Segal, Z., Williams, M., & Teasdale, J. (2018). *Mindfulness-based cognitive therapy for depression*. Guilford publications.

Sekaran, U. and Bougie, R. 2009. *Research Methods for Business: A Skill Building Approach*, 5th ed. Wiley.

Seligman, M. E., Ernst, R. M., Gillham, J., Reivich, K., & Linkins, M. (2009). Positive education: Positive psychology and classroom interventions. *Oxford Review of Education*, 35(3), 293-311. https://doi.org/10.1080/0305498 0902934563.

Seligman, M. E., Steen, T. A., Park, N., & Peterson, C. (2005). Positive psychology progress: empirical validation of interventions. *American Psychologist*, 60(5), 410.

Sheldon, K. M., & King, L. (2001). Why positive psychology is necessary. *American Psychologist*, 56(3), 216. https://doi.org/10.1037/0003-066X. 56.3.216.

Shwartz, A., Cosquer, A., Jaillon, A., Piron, A., Julliard, R., Raymond, R., Simon, L., & Prévot-Julliard, A.-C. (2012). Urban biodiversity, CityDwellers, and conservation: How does an outdoor activity day affect the human-nature relationship? *PLoS ONE*, 7(6), e38642. https://doi.org/ 10.1371/journal.pone. 0038642.

Silvas, D. V. (2013). Measuring an emotional connection to nature among children. Unpublished doctoral dissertation. Colorado State University.

Singleton, R. A., & Straits, B. C. (2012). *Survey interviewing. The SAGE handbook of interview research: The complexity of the craft*, 77-98.

Soliemanifar, O., Nikoubakht, A., & Shaabani, F. (2022). The relationship between Trait Mindfulness and critical thinking: the mediating effect of metacognitive awareness. *Psychological Studies*, 67(2), 139-149. https:// doi.org/10.1007/ s12646-021-00633-8.

Steger, M. F., & Kashdan, T. B. (2007). Stability and specificity of meaning in life and life satisfaction over one year. *Journal of Happiness Studies*, 8, 161-179. https://doi.org/10.1007/s10902-006-9011-8.

Stern, P. C., & Dietz, T. (1994). The value basis of environmental concern. *Journal of Social Issues*, 50(3), 65-84. https://doi.org/10.1111/j.1540-4560.1994.tb02420.x.

Syamila, M., & Mansoer, W. W. D. (2023). Mindfulness and Mind-Wandering in Prayer: a Mixed Methods Study of the Role of Spirituality and Religiosity in Islamic Preachers. *Psikis: Jurnal Psikologi Islami*, 9 (1), 122-136. https://doi.org/10.19109/psikis.v9i1.11314.

Talib, N. Z., Ang, S. Q., Shamsudin, J., & Nor, Z. M. (2023). Associations between body mass index and physical activity level with mindful eating behaviour among undergraduate medical students of Universiti Sains Malaysia. *Malaysian Journal of Nutrition*, 29(3). https://doi.org/10.31246/mjn-2022-0040.

Tam, K. P. (2013a). Concepts and measures related to connection to nature: Similarities and differences. *Journal of Environmental Psychology*, 34, 64-78. https://doi.org/10.1016/j.jenvp.2013.01.004.

Tam, K. P. (2013b). Dispositional empathy with nature. *Journal of Environmental Psychology*, 35, 92-104. https://doi.org/10.1016/j.jenvp.2013.05.004.

Tan, C. S., Hashim, I. H. M., Pheh, K. S., Pratt, C., Chung, M. H., & Setyowati, A. (2021). The mediating role of openness to experience and curiosity in the relationship between mindfulness and meaning in life: Evidence from four countries. *Current Psychology*, 1-11. https://doi.org/10.1007/s12144-021-01430-2.

Taylor, A. F., Kuo, F. E., & Sullivan, W. C. (2002). Views of nature and self-discipline: Evidence from inner city children. *Journal of Environmental Psychology*, 22(1-2), 49-63. https://doi.org/10.1006/jevp.2001.0241.

Taylor, C. A., Liang, B., Tracy, A. J., Williams, L. M., & Seigle, P. (2002). Gender differences in middle school adjustment, physical fighting, and social skills: Evaluation of a social competency program. *Journal of Primary Prevention*, 23, 259-272. https://doi.org/10.1023/A:1019976617776.

Teper, R., Segal, Z. V., & Inzlicht, M. (2013). Inside the mindful mind: How mindfulness enhances emotion regulation through improvements in executive control. *Current Directions in Psychological Science*, 22(6), 449-454. https://doi.org/10.1177/0963721413495869.

Thompson, R. (2012). *Environmental magnetism*. Springer Science & Business Media.

Truong, Q. C., Krägeloh, C. U., Siegert, R. J., Landon, J., & Medvedev, O. N. (2020). Applying generalizability theory to differentiate between trait and state in the Five Facet Mindfulness Questionnaire (FFMQ). *Mindfulness*, 11, 953-963. https://doi.org/10.1007/s12671-020-01324-7.

Ulrich, R. S. (1983). Aesthetic and affective response to natural environment. In *Behavior and the Natural Environment*. Boston, MA: Springer US, 85-125.

Ulrich, R. S., Simons, R. F., Losito, B. D., Fiorito, E., Miles, M. A., & Zelson, M. (1991). Stress recovery during exposure to natural and urban environments. *Journal of Environmental Psychology*, 11(3), 201-230. https://doi.org/10.1016/ S0272-4944(05)80184-7.

Van Den Berg, A. E., & Custers, M. H. (2011). Gardening promotes neuroendocrine and affective restoration from stress. *Journal of Health Psychology*, 16(1), 3-11. https://doi.org/10.1177/1359105310365577.

Van Den Berg, A. E., Maas, J., Verheij, R. A., & Groenewegen, P. P. (2010). Green space as a buffer between stressful life events and health. *Social Science & Medicine*, 70(8), 1203-1210. https://doi. org/10. 1016/j. socscimed.2010.01.002.

Van Den Hurk, P. A., Wingens, T., Giommi, F., Barendregt, H. P., Speckens, A. E., & van Schie, H. T. (2011). On the relationship between the practice of mindfulness meditation and personality—an exploratory analysis of the mediating role of mindfulness skills. *Mindfulness*, 2, 194-200. https://doi. org/10.1007/s12671-011-0060-7.

Vitagliano, L. A., Wester, K. L., Jones, C. T., Wyrick, D. L., & Vermeesch, A. L. (2023). Group nature-based mindfulness interventions: nature-based mindfulness training for college students with anxiety. *International Journal of Environmental Research and Public Health*, 20(2), 1451. https://doi.org/10.3390/ijerph20021451.

Wakefield, S., Yeudall, F., Taron, C., Reynolds, J., & Skinner, A. (2007).

Growing urban health: community gardening in South-East Toronto. *Health Promotion International*, 22(2), 92-101. https://doi.org/10.1093/heapro/dam001.

Waller, N. G., & Zavala, J. D. (1993). Evaluating the big five. *Psychological Inquiry*, 4(2), 131-134. https://doi.org/10.1207/s15327965pli0402_13.

Walton, T. N., & Jones, R. E. (2018). Ecological identity: The development and assessment of a measurement scale. *Environment and Behavior*, 50 (6), 657-689. https://doi.org/10.1177/0013916517710310.

Waters, L. (2011). A review of school-based positive psychology interventions. *The Australian Educational and Developmental Psychologist*, 28(2), 75-90. https://doi.org/10.1375/aedp.28.2.75.

Weber, M., Wagner, L., & Ruch, W. (2016). Positive feelings at school: On the relationships between students' Character Strengths, school-related affect, and school functioning. *Journal of Happiness Studies*, 17, 341-355. https://doi.org/10.1007/s10902-014-9597-1.

Weinstein, N., Brown, K. W., & Ryan, R. M. (2009). A multi-method examination of the effects of mindfulness on stress attribution, coping, and emotional well-being. *Journal of Research in Personality*, 43(3), 374-385. https://doi.org/10.1016/j.jrp.2008.12.008.

Wellenzohn, S., Proyer, R. T., & Ruch, W. (2016). Humor-based online positive psychology interventions: A randomized placebo-controlled long-term trial. *The Journal of Positive Psychology*, 11(6), 584-594. https://doi.org/10.1080/17439760.2015.1137624.

Westen, D., & Rosenthal, R. (2005). Improving construct validity: Cronbach, Meehl, and Neurath's ship: Comment. *Psychological Assessment*, 17(4), 409-412. https://doi.org/10.1037/1040-3590.17.4.409.

White, M. P., Alcock, I., Wheeler, B. W., & Depledge, M. H. (2013). Would you be happier living in a greener urban area? A fixed-effects analysis of panel data. *Psychological Science*, 24(6), 920-928. https://doi.org/10.

1177/09567976 12464659.

Wichrowski, M., Whiteson, J., Haas, F., Mola, A., & Rey, M. J. (2005). Effects of horticultural therapy on mood and heart rate in patients participating in an inpatient cardiopulmonary rehabilitation program. *Journal of Cardiopulmonary Rehabilitation and Prevention*, 25(5), 270-274.

Wilson, E. O. (Ed.). (1993). *The biophilia hypothesis*. Island Press.

Wu, J., & Lanier, L. L. (2003). Natural killer cells and cancer. *Advances in Cancer Research*, 90(1), 127-156.

Yeager, D. S., & Dweck, C. S. (2012). Mindsets that promote resilience: When students believe that personal characteristics can be developed. *Educational Psychologist*, 47 (4), 302-314. https://doi. org/10. 1080/ 00461520.2012.722805.

Yin, L. C., & Majid, R. A. (2018). The goodness of Character Strengths in education. *International Journal of Academic Research in Business and Social Sciences*, 8(6), 1237-1251. http://dx.doi.org/10.6007/IJARBSS/v8-i6/4512.

Yong, C., Zainudin, Z. N., Anuar, M. A. M., & Othman, W. N. W. (2022). Happiness and its Predictors among Undergraduate Students in Malaysia: A Systematic Review. *International Journal of Academic Research in Business and Social Sciences*, 12(8), 1223-1239. http://dx. doi. org/10. 6007/IJARBSS/v12-i8/14507.

Zelenski, J. M., Dopko, R. L., & Capaldi, C. A. (2015). Cooperation is in our nature: Nature exposure may promote cooperative and environmentally sustainable behavior. *Journal of Environmental Psychology*, 42, 24-31. https://doi.org/10.1016/j.jenvp.2015.01.005.

Zhou, Y., & Liu, X. P. (2011). Character Strengths of college students: the relationship between Character Strengths and subjective well-being. *Psychol. Dev. Educ*, 27, 536-542.

Zikmund, W. G., D'Alessandro, S., Winzar, H., Lowe, B., & Babin, B. (2014). *Marketing Research*. Sydney：Cengage Learning.

艾春燕, 王玲莉, 杨钰立 & 张宛筑. (2020). 少数民族大学生性格优势在家庭关怀与生活满意度间的中介作用. 中国健康心理学杂志, 28(05)：788-792. https://doi.org/10.13342/j.cnki.cjhp.2020.05.036.

曹娇. (2015). 大学生未来自我连续性、性格优势与健康行为的关系研究(硕士学位论文, 西南大学).

陈吉. (2018). 自然联结降低物质主义：正念与自我觉察的中介作用(硕士学位论文, 武汉大学).

陈丽萍 & 黄明明. (2022). 敬畏情绪对大学生亲环境行为的影响：自然联结的中介与环境价值观的调节作用. 乐山师范学院学报, 37(09),108-113.doi：10.16069/j.cnki.51-1610/g4.2022.09.014.

陈氏宇(TRAN THI TU). (2017). 中越当代大学生的良心特征以及影响因素的跨文化研究(博士学位论文, 湖南师范大学).

程小红. (2024). 正念团体训练对大学生睡眠质量的干预研究. 河南工学院学报, 32(04), 63-67.

邓玉琴. (2009). 心智觉知训练对大学生心理健康水平的干预效果(硕士学位论文, 首都师范大学).

丁媛慧. (2012). 正念练习对正念水平及主观幸福感的影响(硕士学位论文, 首都师范大学).

干瑜璐. (2023). 正念对大学生生活满意度的影响：自然联结感的中介作用. 浙江海洋大学学报(人文科学版), 40(03), 88-94.

郭浩. (2018). 大学生希望感状况与影响因素分析——基于武汉市四所高校的实证研究. 开封教育学院学报, 38(10), 158-159.

何元庆 & 连榕. (2018). 正念训练干预职业倦怠的回顾与展望. 福建师范大学学报(哲学社会科学版), (06), 79-87, 170.

怀艺伟. (2023). 大学生正念对无手机恐惧的影响：述情障碍与孤独感的中介作用(硕士学位论文, 哈尔滨工程大学).

贾诗杰. (2019). 正念训练对大学生学业压力的干预研究(硕士学位论文, 华中师范大学）.

江彬．（2022）．不同形式的正念认知课程对大学生抑郁情绪的调节（硕士学位论文，西南大学）．https：//doi.org/10.27684/d.cnki.gxndx.2022.001319．

李娜．（2016）．自然联结对大学生幸福感的影响：正念的中介作用（硕士学位论文，北京林业大学）．

李姝．（2015）．大学生性格优势状况调查及与心理健康的关系研究（硕士学位论文，华中师范大学）．

李永慧．（2019）．希望特质团体心理辅导对大学生考试焦虑干预效果研究．中国临床心理学杂志，27（01），206-209，142．https：//doi：10.16128/j.cnki.1005-3611.2019.01.043．

李一茗，黎坚 & 伍芳辉．（2018）．自然联结的概念、功能与促进．心理发展与教育，34（01），120-127．https：//doi：10.16187/j.cnki.issn1001-4918.2018.01.15．

廖军和，欧阳儒阳，左春荣，等．（2015）．贫困大学生感戴与主观幸福感的关系：链式中介效应分析．中国临床心理学杂志，23（04）：722-724，728．https：//doi：10.16128/j.cnki.1005-3611.2015.04.036．

刘斯漫，刘柯廷，李田田 & 卢莉．（2015）．大学生正念对主观幸福感的影响：情绪调节及心理弹性的中介作用．心理科学，38（04），889-895．https：//doi：10.16719/j.cnki.1671-6981.2015.04.017．

刘万伦 & 汤静静．（2019）．大学生正念水平与主观幸福感关系研究．牡丹江师范学院学报（社会科学版），（05），105-113．https：//doi：10.13815/j.cnki.jmtc（pss）.2019.05.013．

鲁俊华，李珊珊 & 关红军．（2023）．改良正念减压疗法对大学生社交焦虑、自我接纳的影响研究．中国公共卫生管理，39（06），812-814，818．https：//doi：10.19568/j.cnki.23-1318.2023.06.0014．

罗淦．（2024）．基于正念冥想的大学生学业心理压力的弹性团体干预策略研究．科学咨询，（21），84-87．

中华人民共和国教育部．（2018）．《高等学校学生心理健康教育指导纲要》印发．http：//edu.cnr.cn/list/20180718/t20180718_524304800.shtml.

彭聃龄. (2010). 普通心理学. 北京师范大学出版社.

彭亭亭 & 郝志红. (2020). 希望对大学生专业心理求助态度的影响：自尊和污名的链式中介效应. 中国临床心理学杂志, 28(06), 1270-1273. doi：10.16128/j. cnki.1005-3611.2020.06.039.

蒲清平 & 徐爽. (2011). 感恩心理及行为的认知机制. 学术论坛, 34(06), 164-167. doi：10.16524/j.45-1002.2011.06.016.

沈彦斐, 解子秋 & 刘晓玲. (2022). 正念训练对手机依赖者注意偏向的干预效果. 中国健康心理学杂志, 30(11), 1611-1618. doi：10.13342/j.cnki.cjhp.2022. 11.003.

王财玉 & 雷雳. (2018). 大学生自然联结现状及对抑郁情绪的影响. 黑龙江高教研究, (02), 89-93.

王财玉, 姬少华 & 陈霞. (2020). 自然联结与大学生人生意义体验的关系：自然欣赏的中介作用. 信阳师范学院学报(哲学社会科学版), 40(05), 45-48, 65.

王财玉, 罗润锋 & 姬少华. (2022). 自然联结与社交网站使用中的妒忌：生命意义感与向上社会比较的中介作用. 中国临床心理学杂志, 30(03), 619-624. doi：10.16128/j.cnki.1005-3611.2022.03.024.

王财玉 & 王春枝. (2018). 大学生自然联结和自尊与抑郁情绪的关系. 中国心理卫生杂志, 32(09), 792-794.

温忠麟, 张雷, 侯杰泰 & 刘红云. (2004). 中介效应检验程序及其应用. 心理学报, (05), 614-620.

吴明隆. (2003). SPSS 统计应用实务：问卷分析与应用统计. 科学出版社.

习近平. (2017). 决胜全面建成小康社会 夺取新时代中国特色社会主义伟大胜利——在中国共产党第十九次全国代表大会上的报告. 人民日报, 第 1 版.

许蓉. (2020). 大学生正念水平、应对效能与压力知觉的关系及干预研究(硕士学位论文, 苏州大学). https://link.cnki.net/doi/10.27351/d.cnki.gszhu. 2020.004229.

杨烁. (2022). 正念对性格优势的影响：机制探索与干预研究(硕士学位论文, 华东师范大学). https://link.cnki.net/doi/10.27149/d.cnki.ghdsu.2022.

002902.

杨盈, 耿柳娜, 相鹏, 张晶 & 朱丽芳. (2017). 自然关联性：概念、测量、功能及干预. 心理科学进展, 25(08), 1360-1374. https://doi.org/10.3724/SP.J. 1042. 2017.01360.

余思, 张春阳 & 徐慰. (2022). 特质正念与大学生焦虑和攻击性的纵向关系：心理弹性的中介和留守经历的调节. 心理发展与教育, 38(05), 711-719. https://doi:10.16187/j.cnki.issn1001-4918.2022.05.12.

张蓉. (2010). 性格优点与医学生心理健康的关系研究(硕士学位论文, 浙江大学).

钟佳涵, 李波 & 刘素贞. (2015). 团体正念认知训练对大学生焦虑水平的影响. 中国健康心理学杂志, 23(07), 1067-1071. doi:10.13342/j.cnki.cjhp.2015.07. 031.

钟晓钰, 李铭尧 & 李凌艳. (2021). 问卷调查中被试不认真作答的控制与识别. 心理科学进展, 29(02), 225-237.

周文君. (2013). 自然关联性与环境行为关系的研究(硕士学位论文, 南京大学).

左春荣, 欧阳儒阳, 李相南 & 李志勇. (2019). 高校贫困生感戴与心理健康的关系：压力知觉的中介作用. 哈尔滨学院学报, 40(09), 141-144.

AFTERWORD

As an exploratory study, this book aims at laying a preliminary research foundation for the development of positive psychological qualities among students at the primary, secondary, and tertiary levels. At the current stage, the localization and revision of the Nature Relatedness Scale have been completed among Chinese university students. Additionally, the study has explored the mechanism through which Nature Relatedness influences Character Strengths among university students in China and Malaysia. Building upon these findings, future plans include conducting Nature-Based Mindfulness Intervention among university students. After verifying its effectiveness, the intervention will be extended to primary and secondary school students. Ultimately, a longitudinal study will be carried out to identify the critical period for the development of Nature Relatedness in children, with the goal of constructing a cross-grade natural education intervention system. This book serves as a starting point, and it is hoped that through implementing a five-year research plan, an evidence-based and developmentally appropriate nature education intervention system spanning all educational levels can be established, thereby providing scientific evidence and practical guidance for promoting adolescent mental health and positive personality development.

The completion of this book has been made possible by the generous support and invaluable contributions of many respected mentors and colleagues. First and foremost, I would like to express my heartfelt gratitude to Associate Professor Shafrin of Universiti Sains Malaysia, whose profound expertise in positive psychology and rigorous academic approach provided professional guidance throughout the research process. Her outstanding Character Strengths have also been a great source of inspiration to me. I am deeply thankful to Professor Nisbet of Trent University, Canada, for her guidance throughout the translation and back-translation of the Nature Relatedness Scale. I also wish to thank Dean Rahimi, Dr. Syed, Dr. Fazzuan, and fellow colleagues of the School of Educational Studies at Universiti Sains Malaysia; Professor Ma Xiting from the Positive Psychology Experience Center and Dean Li Junliang from Feng Ru Honors College of Beihang University; Lecturer Li Xiangnan from Shaoxing University, and colleagues from Huainan Normal University, for their professional support during the data collection and analysis stages. Special thanks go to Associate Professor Yang Ying of Tianjin University, my senior research partner, who introduced me to the field of Nature Relatedness and continuously offered intellectual guidance throughout the research process. I am also grateful to Professor Duan Wenjie of East China University of Science and Technology for his valuable suggestions on the measurement and mechanisms of Character Strengths, which provided critical insights for the cross-cultural aspects of this study.

The publication of this book has been generously supported by the Academic Monograph Publication Fund of Huainan Normal University, to which I express my heartfelt gratitude. Additional support was received from the following projects: the Ministry of Education's Humanities and Social Sciences Research Project (Research on College Counselors) "A study on the influence mechanism and intervention of positive psychological qualities among impoverished college students" (24JDSZ3201), the Key Project of Philosophy and Social Science Research in Anhui Provincial Universities (2023AH051513), the General Project of Educational Science Research in Anhui Province (JK23117); and the General Project of Teaching Reform Research in Anhui Province (2022jyxm1444). The funding from these projects has been used to support data collection, academic exchange activities, publication of research findings, and related research expenditures. I would like to express my sincere appreciation to all the funding agencies for their generous support. In addition, this book has benefited greatly from the work of many scholars both in China and abroad, to whom I extend my deepest respect and gratitude.

Finally, I am especially thankful to my family for their unwavering understanding and support. My husband and children, who form my strongest support team "Bao Tong Qian," have been my greatest source of strength on this academic journey. I dedicate this book to all those who have cared about and supported this study.

Chunrong, Zuo

February, 2025